Film's Ghosts

Stephen Barber

Film's Ghosts

**The Transmutations of 1960s Japan
and Tatsumi Hijikata's Butoh**

DIAPHANES

Contents

ACKNOWLEDGEMENTS

I am deeply grateful to the foundations and funding bodies who supported my work on this book project: the Daiwa Anglo-Japanese Foundation, the Japan Foundation, the Japan Foundation Endowment Committee, the Saison Foundation, the British Academy and the Leverhulme Trust. I'm especially grateful to Susan Meehan at the Daiwa Anglo-Japanese Foundation.

I began work on this book project while living in Tokyo in 1997–98, meeting or interviewing many of Hijikata's collaborators and his widow, Akiko Motofuji (who died in 2003), before abandoning the project because of the difficulties or impossibilities in accessing many of Hijikata's films. Instead, I eventually wrote a book briefly summarising Hijikata's work (*Hijikata: Revolt of the Body*, Chicago: University of Chicago Press, Solar series, 2010). Twenty years after that initial attempt to write about Hijikata's films, the situation had entirely changed, in large part through the work of the Hijikata Archive at Tokyo's Keio University, so I decided to complete the project, and returned to Tokyo in 2017–18 to conduct new research and interviews (some of them with figures I had previously met in 1997–98), and also to visit the Documentation Center of the Osaka Expo '70.

I am deeply grateful also to the staff at the Hijikata Archive – Takashi Morishita, Yu Homma and Hayato Kosuge, who is now the Director of Keio University's Research Centre in Liberal Arts – for their generosity, support and invaluable expertise. It was only through the intervention of Yu Homma that I was able to undertake research at the Expo '70 Documentation Center, and to meet its current curator, Masashi Tatsukawa, and the now-retired curator from the 1970s, Toshihiku Okaue. I am also grateful to the curator of the Kazuo Ohno Archive at the University of Bologna, Elena Cervellati.

When I began my research, all of the artists who had worked most closely in the medium of film with Hijikata remained alive:

Eikoh Hosoe, Donald Richie, Takahiko Iimura and Hiroshi Nakamura. In 2019, all are still alive, with the exception of Donald Richie, who died in Tokyo in 2013, and to whose memory this book is dedicated.

In 1997–98, I met with Hijikata's widow Akiko Motofuji many times, along with her daughters, Gala and Bella, usually at the Asbestos Studio. In Tokyo, I also interviewed or discussed Hijikata's work with many of his surviving friends and collaborators: Nario Goda, Eikoh Hosoe, Takahiko Iimura, Arata Isozaki, Ko Murobushi (whom I also met several times in London in subsequent years, before his death in 2015), Hiroshi Nakamura, Kazuo Ohno (who died in 2010), Yoshito Ohno, Hironobu Oikawa, Donald Richie, Min Tanaka, Kuniichi Uno and Tadanori Yokoo. I also discussed Tokyo's urban cultures with Edward Seidensticker (who died in 2007).

In 2017–18 in Tokyo, I again met with Eikoh Hosoe, Hiroshi Nakamura and Kuniichi Uno, and also with Masao Adachi and Tatsuo Ikeda.

In 1999 in London, I spoke with Ian Buruma about Hijikata's work; in 2001, I discussed Hijikata's films via email with Chris Marker (who died in 2012); in 2006, I met with William Klein in London to discuss his experience of photographing Hijikata in 1961; and in 2016, in Arezzo, Italy, I discussed the architecture and film-projection environments of the Expo '70 pavilions with Dante Bini, who designed domes for the Fuji Group pavilion and experienced the Midori pavilion.

Many researchers of Hijikata's work (or its wider context across art and performance) generously shared their knowledge, ideas and insights with me: Romina Achatz, Bruce Baird, Dominique Baron-Bonarjee, Katja Centonze, Peter Eckersall, Carol Fischer Sorgenfrei, Vangeline France, Richard Gough, Rosa van Hensbergen, Mark Holborn, Tatsuro Ishii, Marilyn Ivy, Namiko Kunimoto, Samantha Marenzi, William Marotti, Nanako Nakajima, Sawako Nakayasu, Keiko Okamura, Maria Pia D'Orazi, Elena Polzer, Cody Poulton, Julian Ross, Marie-Gabrielle Rotie, Yoshiko Shimada, Shinichi Takeshige, Tadashi

Uchino, Kimiko Watanabe, Nicole Vivien Watson, Duncan White and Yukihiko Yoshida. I'm especially grateful to Katja and to Gilly for their great kindness. I'm also appreciative of my many dialogues in Berlin with the artist Richard Hawkins, whose research-based project *Hijikata Twist* was exhibited at Tate Liverpool and art spaces in the USA in 2014–15.

I had many invaluable discussions about Hijikata's work, Tokyo in the years 1959–70, and Expo '70, with David Peace and Akiko Miyake in Tokyo in 2017–18.

Finally, I would like to thank my colleagues at the Kingston School of Art, at Kingston University, London, especially Irene González-López and Toyoko Ito.

In this book, Japanese names are given with the family name after the first name.

Conjuring Hijikata's Ghosts in Film:
HUMAN SACRIFICE and WARGAMES

I remember … : In the snowfallen Tokyo winter month of February 1998, I took a night walk with the writer and filmmaker Donald Richie, then seventy-three years of age, through the eastern alleyways of the city's Shinjuku district, beneath the amassed presence of history and the immense building-top image-screens. Richie had arrived in Tokyo at the very beginning of 1947, and, apart from a few intervals, he had already spent over half a century deeply immersed in the city. By the time I emerged from a pedestrian underpass beneath the innumerable railway tracks and platforms at the northern end of Shinjuku station, to meet Richie by its East Plaza exit, I could see him already standing alert and motionless in his slate-grey overcoat, evidently impatient to begin that walk, though we were both early for the encounter.

As Richie outlined our Shinjuku itinerary for the next hours, raring to go and looking directly upwards, I watched iridescent moving-image fragments from the vast projection screens overhead envelop his face's skin, those fragments' fast-cut ricochets repeatedly engulfing that worn carapace in momentary bursts and vectors of glaring colour – ultramarine, scarlet, iris, vermilion – so that his face's skin held the successive projections of manic J-Pop idols' contortions and *sumo* wrestlers' beer commercials. His face was deeply furrowed and crisscrossed by age, and those insistent projections engrained themselves even into the furrows, as though Tokyo's virulent projections were now inhabiting that face. I fixed my eyes on the image-sequences from the plaza's surrounding towers as they incised their way ever deeper into those furrows, while casting wider animated colour-pulses across Richie's offered-up facial skin, then suddenly darkened and vanished, as the sequences lapsed for a moment, in malfunction or in anticipation of being re-launched. In Tokyo's illuminated plazas, the overhead projections' immediate images perversely incorporate themselves as deep-seated memories, corrosively infiltrating and abrading the bodies below them, honing in especially on the face, eyes and mouth, instantly enlivening and resuscitating even the most disintegrated skin surfaces before inversing their work to render that skin into a detrital and abandoned screen.

That plaza and the adjacent Shinjuku avenues had been a primary site of Tokyo's momentous riots of the final years of the 1960s. I naively asked Richie if he had taken part, but he had not, was doubtful he could have participated, as a foreigner, even if he had felt compelled to, though the writer Jean Genet was there to participate in one riot, taunting the police, and the filmmaker Nagisa Oshima had filmed this plaza of riots and experimental performances, directly in front of us, for his film of that era, DIARY OF A SHINJUKU THIEF, and another prominent filmmaker of that moment, Toshio Matsumoto, had also filmed this plaza, along with Shinjuku's sex-subterraneas, for another film, FUNERAL PARADE OF ROSES. Richie dismissed that era of riots with an outstretched hand rendered convulsive by acetylene jolts of malfunctioned neon: 'If you want to know about all that, just ask Adachi… When he gets back from Beirut, or when he gets out of prison.' Richie now gestured towards the alleyways of the Kabuki-cho district which led to the Golden Gai compound of minuscule bars, telling me: 'But I'll take you through this hell on earth.'

The cacophony of Shinjuku's plazas and avenues, still aberrantly inflected by their status as locations for Tokyo's noise-seething riots three decades earlier, faded out immediately as we left them behind, and the snowfall silenced our steps. Soon – with only a few words' prompting, and a moment after we entered Kabuki-cho's alleys – Richie was vocally evoking bodies he had known across his five decades in Tokyo, as though his life now depended on that invocation, each of those bodies attached to a particular location in this city, or in another city: Yasunari Kawabata, with whom he had walked through the firestormed wastelands of the Asakusa district in 1947 as they searched for landmarks that had been incinerated, a fragile body, then Yukio Mishima, whom Richie first met in New York City in 1951, assigned to show the young writer around the city, but had then met again in Tokyo, their walks taking them through districts in which Mishima always feared to be recognised, a body gradually in transformation, honed in the gyms they often visited together. Through Mishima, Richie met and befriended a then unknown, now legendary but always provocative dancer – 'you'll know him by his reputation', Richie laughed – from the north of Japan, four years younger than Richie but possessing the body of an ailing, exhausted dancer when Richie had last seen him alive, in 1985 (he had also seen him dead, in January of the following year, 1986, lying in his flower-surrounded coffin, a framed photograph of the vividly living dancer positioned so as to look down obliquely at the eyes-closed face of the dead dancer), and, reversing in time, an incessantly moving, lithe and shaven-headed corporeal entity when they first met, in 1959, and soon decided to make films together: Tatsumi Hijikata, an astonishing but tumultuous body.

Richie stopped speaking abruptly as we reached Shinjuku's Koma Hall, its enormous auditorium used both for performances and film shows, and gazed up at its facade lovingly, murmuring that it had been there for nearly as long as he had lived in Tokyo, but he feared it would disappear soon in the district's ongoing transmutations (and it was demolished, a decade or so after our walk). That Shinjuku walk, along with Richie's memories, was punctuated by sudden silences every time we passed another of the district's surviving, last-gasp cinemas (or the sites of now razed cinemas to which Richie remained attached), occasionally taking tickets from the vending machines outside and entering the almost vacant, dilapidated auditoria for a moment to watch fragments of the yakuza or sex films being projected and to survey the scattered audiences – Richie whispered to me that in his own Tokyo district, Ueno, he had sometimes made his assignations with exiled Iranian young men at the back of the auditoria of the pornography cinemas located alongside the lotus-covered Ueno Pond, the malfunctioning projectors' cacophony accentuating the many sex acts' gasps, though those uprooted young men had since mostly been deported or had melted away into the city's facades – before we left those auditoria and returned to the alleyways, and Richie resumed the incantation of his ghosts of Tokyo, since everyone he conjured – Kawabata, Mishima, Terayama, Hijikata – was now dead.

During the following years, I heard many people who had known or collaborated with Tatsumi Hijikata assume his voice, and speak an adroit or inept approximation of its distinctive accent of the Akita region of Japan's north, usually laughing in alarm as they curtailed the experiment. Richie was the first person I heard take on that voice, as he evoked their first meeting and vocal exchanges, as though Richie were one of the blind, wizened mediums who locate and expectorate the lost voices of the dead, for relatives offering small fees, alongside the infernal sulphurous streams and ochre-tinted lake of Mount Osore, notoriously the entrance to hell, on an axehead-shaped peninsula in the Aomori region of northern Japan. Then, Richie began to speak of the two films he had made with Hijikata, one very soon after their first meeting, HUMAN SACRIFICE, in 1959, and another, WARGAMES, in 1962.

Now, after three or four hours, we were at the heart of the Golden Gai compound of bars, the adjacent alleyways sharpened down to one-person-wide pathways between the mainly decrepit two-storey buildings, each with its illuminated or inscribed sign. Richie had offered to take me to the bar, signposted 'La Jetée' in silver letters, of his acquaintance, the filmmaker Chris Marker, whose 1982 Tokyo-focused film SUNLESS recorded Marker's own obsessions with the conjuration and vanishing of memory, above all his memories of the future and its cities. Tokyo pre-eminently disgorges time as though as the material for an inexhaustible experiment, to be petrified or rendered catastrophic or annulled in its linearity, so that time oscillates between attachments to future-directed reconfigurations and to now lost, obsolete corporeal gestures, leaving behind memories that simultaneously inhabit the megalopolis's facades and also irradiate the image-imprinted bodies inhabiting that city.

The barkeeper sighed in resignation at Richie's appearance within the intimate, otherwise empty space of La Jetée, and she simultaneously beckoned him inside and waved him away, since Richie no longer drank alcohol, though in the years he had known Tatsumi Hijikata, as a friend and collaborator, they had certainly drunk. It was still the very beginning of the night in that bar, whose usual clientele would arrive far later on. Chris Marker himself was absent, back in Paris, and the barkeeper, now laughing, told a cryptic story about a lost or stolen cat at the origins of Marker's temporary renunciation of Tokyo. Richie drank a Pepsi-Cola on that night of the reanimation of film's ghosts, vocally remembering Hijikata – his skin, their experience of wars, their Tokyos, their films together, his death – until it became time to go, and Richie promised me more walks, then we exited the Golden Gai compound and returned to the Shinjuku station's East Plaza exit, and I watched Richie traverse the ticket barrier and enter the passageways that, even late at night, were saturated with moving bodies, his aged decelerated speed mismatched with those bodies' pervasive velocity. I knew that, sooner or later in the future, I would be remembering him, too, as one of Tokyo's innumerable memory-ensnared ghosts.

Hijikata's work began with an obsession with crime. As Jean Genet had done, he intended to create an amalgam of art and crime. Crime in art is deathless and cannot be expunged in the way that a social crime is soluble to time or to being pardoned; it possesses instead a rigorous spectrality that enduringly creeps up behind the hypocrisies of corporate contemporary art in all of its forms, while driving arts of corporeal interrogation, negation and activism forward. As such, Hijikata's art possesses a vital but uneasy presence, in Japan and across the world.

Hijikata is known internationally for having instigated a dance art: 'Ankoku Butoh', the 'Dance of Utter Darkness', working intensively to develop it across the 1960s, when it possessed an incessant involvement and co-existence with film. That dance art, concerned with the transmutation of the human anatomy and the multiplicitous entity of death, proliferated in inspiration and influence beyond Japan from the moment of Hijikata's own death in 1986 (and even before), across Europe, and North and South America, in part through its traces in film and in part via the work of choreographers and artists who had witnessed or directly participated in Hijikata's work, and had subsequently decided to leave Japan, permanently or temporarily; across time, those figures who had directly worked with Hijikata themselves died (such as Ko Murobushi, in 2015, and Yukio Waguri, in 2017), shifting that source of primary inspiration increasingly to Hijikata's films.

But instigating a dance art was only an element of Hijikata's work, with its furious eras of momentous, unstoppable, multi-directional invention, pre-eminently at the end of the 1960s. Above all, Hijikata actively collaborated across art forms, from choreography to film to visual art to photography to writing to architecture and to interventions in urban space, instigating an experimental obliteration of borderlines between art forms that renders him, in many ways, the seminal figure in Japan's art from the end of the 1950s on, and more deeply as the decades elapsed, into the contemporary moment; his influence is so profound in Japan that it is often refused or renounced, either so that art can enter its dissolution in corporatised forms, or because that influence is so engulfing that, in order to breathe, contemporary artists must contradict it.

Hijikata's pivotal work, from one end to the other of the 1960s, took place within and alongside an immense urban transformation. Tokyo remained a destroyed city when Hijikata first travelled there from his home region of Akita, in Japan's north, and it maintained that aura, throughout his work there, of a city prone to destruction (it had been largely razed by an earthquake in 1923, before being firebombed by US forces in 1945): an aura which other cities, in Europe – such as Berlin, Wrocław or Chisinau – also still transmit in the contemporary moment. The 1960s was a decade of turmoil, riots and violence in Tokyo, notably in the Shinjuku district, flaring especially at that decade's beginning and end, and focused against the enduring influence and presence of the US government and military authorities, following Japan's postwar occupation of 1945–52; that turmoil was mediated in urban space through the revolutionary desires of its young students and citizens. The city, already reconstructed after its destruction, was extensively rebuilt again in the 1960s, partly for the spatial demands of the 1964 Olympic Games, expanded and interlaced by overhead highway systems and vast zones of multi-storey business towers, and embedded with a network of urban surveillance and prohibition; its upheavals were always simultaneously corporeal as well as urban ones. For much of the 1960s, Hijikata's work, with its contrary approach to urban matters, was largely disregarded or unseen by public audiences, developed in a small studio space in the Tokyo district of Meguro and performed only intermittently in public venues, for audiences of several hundred spectators or less, or in local street environments. But at the end of the 1960s, with the Osaka Expo 1970 World's Fair event, which materialised itself in the form of an immense experimental city of pavilions located on the edge of the city of Osaka, Hijikata's work – in the form of his filmed body's art, alongside a single live performance – was abruptly exposed to audiences of millions, who gathered to experience that work immersively conjured by multiple projectors in a technologically unprecedented pavilion, as part of what was the greatest ever global human amassing (with over sixty-four million visitors) in one site. After that extraordinary urban exposure, Hijikata gradually withdrew from public view into near invisibility, in his Asbestos Studio in Meguro, inviting occasional visitors into that studio for provocative encounters, and working on scrapbooks and writings, but leaving behind the exposed multiple physical trails of his art, pre-eminently those still gripped by film's ghosts.

Richie observed and occasionally collaborated in Hijikata's work, from Hijikata's first performances as an independent artist in 1959 (prior to that, he had worked in choreographers' companies, and appeared in entertainment spectacles), through his withdrawal from direct corporeal involvement across the early 1970s, until his final insular works of the mid-1980s. At every moment of that quarter-century, but most keenly in its first decade, Richie viewed Hijikata against, at the aberrant periphery, or within – but simultaneously positioned askew to – the acute transmutation of Tokyo and its surroundings, with Hijikata's body and Tokyo's urban upheaval illuminating one another in their volatile intersection. To seize that intersection, Richie began by filming Hijikata, and later by writing about his work, in his English-language art columns for the metropolitan *Japan Times* newspaper (alerting international audiences, to Hijikata's work for the first time), then, beyond the 1960s, when the immediacy of that writing had exhausted itself in Hijikata's disappearance, by remembering and voicing Hijikata at the sites through which Richie had accompanied him. Sometimes, in the on-site vocalisation of Hijikata, Richie's eroding memory suddenly misfired, and another figure or voice (from an apparent infinity of them) insurged into the frame for an instant – that of Mishima, or of Shuji Terayama or others – so that Hijikata's figure formed a momentarily awry constellation with other histories, other corporealities. But in Hijikata's capture on film, by contrast, that misfiring takes another form, directly into the spectator's eye.

Between Hijikata's largely unseen first film with Richie, HUMAN SACRIFICE, in 1959, and the film of his work projected to many millions at the Midori pavilion of the Osaka Expo in 1970, Hijikata's films span an immense terrain of experimentations and preoccupations, notably with the mutating urban environment of Tokyo, which he experienced in its unprecedented turmoil of art and riots, across that decade. He collaborated with the celebrated photographer and filmmaker Eikoh Hosoe, especially on an extended project over the second half of the 1960s, *Kamaitachi* (*The Sickle-Weasel*), which oscillates between moving-image and photographic dynamics, inhabiting peripheral sites of Tokyo and darkened panoramas of the Akita region in its re-imagining of the status of the large-format photography book as a medium able to incorporate obsessions with the human body. At the end of the 1960s, Hijikata participated as a performer in grotesque horror films funded by Japan's film studios, such as Horrors of Malformed Men, in which he took the role of a deranged figure who intends to conduct a reinvention of the human anatomy from monstrous, cast-aside elements; Hijikata's work also collided obliquely in that same era with the work of filmmakers such as Masao Adachi and Koji Wakamatsu, who were moving from society-refusing pornography in Japan to concerns with violent global revolution. Hijikata's pivotal 1960s performances, such as *Tatsumi Hijikata and the Japanese People: Revolt of the Body* and The Masseur, were solely filmed by experimental filmmakers and artists, such as Hiroshi Nakamura and Takahiko Iimura, who were concerned with imprinting physical fragments, cuts, blurs and impacts onto 8mm celluloid, rather than with constructing linear performance documentation in film. Hijikata's films traverse multiple experimentations and also illuminate the ways in which even mainstream, studio-funded film in 1960s Japan often took outlandish forms.

Hijikata's work, above all his Ankoku Butoh project, is traced most revealingly in film. Film (rather than memory, or text) is the uniquely sensitised medium for dance and its corporeal dimensions, and became so even from the first moments of celluloid filmmaking and film projection in 1895, with works such as the filmings of dances – especially the Serpentine Dance, which was vastly popular in that era – by the Skladanowsky Brothers in Berlin, the Lumière Brothers in Lyon and Paris, and William Dickson in New Jersey. Film originally existed to render dance, as one of its seminal, originating motives, in part because dance, with its concentrated movement and tension, formed an equivalent to film's capacity for only momentary captures of movement, over two or three seconds, expanded subsequently via looping techniques to create the sustained ocular experience of dance. At the same time, film always constitutes a duplicitous power, which will seek to transmutate corporeal movement into the domain of film's own dynamics and its own preoccupations; it operates with an insidious treachery, of the kind that Hijikata admired in Genet's work.

The filmmakers and artists who collaborated with Hijikata were without exception experimenters: with fragments of bodies, with the interval between the still image and the moving image, with the desire for social outrage, with the instigation of revolution, or with film's destructions and resuscitations of the human body. They all worked within and against an urban environment that proved exceptionally conducive, at that moment in Tokyo, to the realization of those experiments, until the decade's end – marked by the immense governmental and corporate event of the Osaka Expo, to which Japan's experimental artists were invited to participate, but at the risk of their work's annulling – finally exhausted that furore.

Hijikata's naming of his work as the dance of utter darkness intimates a primary tension with film's operation via illumination and light. Film's spatial environment, in cinematic projection, demands an act of sudden darkening, together with the engulfing of spectators into darkness, in order to be initiated, and darkness's oscillation with light is integral to the eye's apprehension of moving images; at the same time, filmmaking also originated as a medium of light, as in the first films from the mid-1890s of dance performers filmed at noon, in open-air environments or on rooftops, in order to capture and register the dancing body against maximal sunlight. In its self-immersal into darkness, Hijikata's corporeal work presents a contradiction to film which all of his films emanate. That refusal, with its potential overpowering and manipulation of film, and of its technologies and instruments, is embodied in the accounts – by witnesses from the end of the 1960s such as Hosoe, Richie and Hijikata's widow, Akiko Motofuji – of Hijikata's own projections of the films of his work within his darkened Asbestos Studio, dancing while holding the studio's heavy celluloid film projector in his arms, so that the film sequences veered wildly around the walls and ceiling of the small space, and became layered over, or infiltrated themselves into, the dazzled faces of his audience, as an act to subjugate and negate film, especially in its status as a medium to document and represent dance.

Hijikata's emphasis on 'utter darkness' also constitutes a wider historical and cultural refusal and contradiction. Throughout Japan's East Asian invasions and conflicts from the early 1930s on, through the ensuing Pacific War, and even into Tokyo's postwar occupation era urban culture of vying street gangs and of those gangs' black-market operations, the invocation of salutary illumination and brightness remained constant. Light, as with film, operates via duplicity and beguilement. The historian John Dower emphasises that 'the word and the images and connotations associated with [brightness] – light, radiance, the rising and shining sun, clarity of purpose, purity of motive – had been ubiquitous during the war years. In July 1941, on the fourth anniversary of the outbreak of war with China, for example, the government exhorted its people to carry on under numerous slogans including "The Hundred Million Fighting, Bright and Strong". Slogan after slogan sought to instill bright attitudes and confidence on both the battlefield and the home front – and also to project Japan as the radiant hope of all Asia ("Light of Asia" was one of the propaganda names the Japanese used in South-east Asia). When the boss of the Ozu gang opened the "Light from Shinjuku" market, he was moving from wartime to peacetime sloganeering without even breaking stride.'[1]

Darkness possesses innumerable lineages and conceptions, including those of refusal and spatial territorialisation, in Europe's as well as in Japan's cultures; Hijikata's obstinate emphasis on darkness and on subterranean hiddenness, during an era of what he perceived as the human body's gradual dissolution and loss, isolated his 1960s project even in relation to the fragile territories of Japan's avant-gardes. Hijikata distanced himself from those avant-gardes too, preferring to cast his dance of utter darkness as a more primordial entity of corporeal exploration, in extremity. As Miryam Sas notes, Hijikata rejected Japan's avant-gardes and underground cultures of that era whenever they strived for an elevated popular profile: '... Hijikata disparaged even the so-called underground theater of his day for being too public, too much in the light, bowing to the necessities of popularity and commercial success. For him, darkness, and by extension the underground arts, should be something private, covert.'[2] Hijikata's preoccupation with darkness necessarily positioned film too as a light-defined entity to be viewed with deep suspicion, as an agent of representation, but also contrarily as a medium which, through film's own capacity for contrary twists and dark aberrations, and its direct sensory collision with the human eye and body, could activate his experiments.

Moving images and their projection to public audiences began in an obsession with visualising dance, through Eadweard Muybridge's sequences of dancers projected from glass discs onto the screen of his self-designed Zoopraxographical Hall, at the Chicago World's Columbian Exposition in 1893; in many ways, film was created to render and project corporeality via its manifestation in gestures of dance. But by the end of the 1950s, with Hijikata's collaborations with Richie on the films HUMAN SACRIFICE and WARGAMES, film now pre-eminently transmitted warfare, along with the street-located fierce confrontations of activist bodies and riot police that film would seize throughout the 1960s in cities worldwide. That wrenching of film's intent, from the terrain of dance to that of military action or training, accorded it a fluid capacity to oscillate between or amalgamate those two domains, as in such films as Claire Denis's BEAU TRAVAIL, 1998, choreographed by the Ankoku Butoh-inspired dancer Bernardo Montet, with its sequences of a group of Foreign Legionnaires dancing their military training, through violent embraces and stares and assaults, on barren plateaus above the Djibouti ocean.

The war in Japan itself was often filmed in terrifying, outlandish sequences, especially in its cities, such as the nocturnal footage from the first months of 1945 of the aerial firebombing of Tokyo, Osaka and other cities, shot from ground level by cinematographers in which warfare descends vertically from the sky, in velocity-propelled incandescent pulses of fire that register on film as intense white against the surrounding utter darkness, immediately consuming buildings and bodies around the filmmakers, who appear to have been filming in conditions of extreme danger. Many of Hijikata's collaborators, such as the artist Hiroshi Nakamura – who filmed Hijikata's 1968 performance *Tatsumi Hijikata and the Japanese People: Revolt of the Body*, and who was a child in 1945 in the bombed city of Hamamatsu – experienced the abrupt overnight vanishing of their cities. Film footage of urban devastation and depopulation was incorporated into cinema newsreels projected to Japan's wartime population of women, the elderly and children, to intimate the catastrophes to come if the US forces reached Japan's main islands, and to emphasise the necessity for last-ditch, last-breath resistance. The US army's cinematographers also extensively filmed their advance, island by island, towards Japan. In his film LEVEL FIVE, 1997, focused on the Battle of Okinawa, Chris Marker incorporated US military footage shot in 1944 of the terrified Japanese population of the Pacific Ocean island of Saipan (part of Japan's territory since the end of the First World War), many of them poised on cliff-edge precipices and ready to leap, but first attentively studying the film cameras recording their imminent deaths.

Hijikata's 1960 film-collaboration with Eikoh Hosoe, NAVEL AND A-BOMB, explicitly evokes the war that ended fifteen years earlier. By contrast, in Hijikata's collaborations with Richie, in 1959 and 1962, on either side of that work with Hosoe, that explicitness is absent; but warfare and the imminence of death still permeate and engulfs the two films' corporeal figures and their environments. Both Richie and Hijikata were physically configured by warfare. By the age of eighteen, in 1942, Richie had left his hometown of Lima in Ohio for long hitchhiking journeys, before entering the US Maritime Service (rather than the US Navy) as a merchant seaman; he became a purser and medical officer, travelling incessantly through the war years via China, Algeria, Italy and other countries, on ships always vulnerable to torpedo attacks. As well as shaping his body through exacting exercise and training, warfare for him also possessed its miraculous and liberatory dimension, as a medium of escape from what he saw as the stultifying social culture of the US and his own likely grim future as a small-town shoe-shop clerk or other menial role; in defiance of war's genocides, massacres and immense suffering, he perceived it also as vitally opening for him new creative and sexual ground, explored in urban locations he would otherwise never have experienced. After the war's end, he enrolled in the US Civil Service's programme of appointments in Occupied Japan, initially as a typist, soon switching to journalism, and arrived in Tokyo on 1 January 1947.

Hijikata, four years younger than Richie, lived through the war years in the isolated region of Akita. His war history is less officially imprinted than that of Richie's itineraries and appointments. His widow, Akiko Motofuji, then 70 years old, recounted narratives of Hijikata's war years to me in 1998, twelve years after his death and five years before her own. Sitting in an upstairs room of the Asbestos Studio, usually along with one or other of her children, Gala and Bella – the two daughters of Tatsumi Hijikata – who followed their mother's words attentively, she often appeared an intentionally duplicitous, contradictory narrator with a lithe and unverifiable sense of truth. In that sense, she was an adept conduit for Hijikata's own living words, also lithe and contrary. She recalled Hijikata's evocations of the scarring of his back by fire while he was working at a munitions factory in Akita City, which was bombed, at night, at the war's very end, along with the many other physical assaults he endured in those wartime years of his youth (he was pushed down school-stairs during a fight, injuring one leg, which healed as shorter than the other, making it impossible for him in later years to accomplish conventional dance gestures). Several of his older brothers were conscripted, and after valedictory drinking sessions which left their faces flushed red had left Akita for Japan's zones of warfare, returning in the form of ashes enclosed in small wooden boxes. If Hijikata had been any older, he would have been conscripted before the war's end and very likely killed. One of his artist friends of the 1960s, born in the same year as Hijikata, Tatsuo Ikeda, was hastily conscripted and entered training as a *kamikaze* pilot at the age of 16, before the war's abrupt end left him still unused; he outlived Hijikata by over three decades, remaining alive and celebrated with retrospective exhibitions at the age of 90 in 2018.

Akiko Motofuji had her own narratives of the era of warfare and especially the nights of Tokyo's firebombing, during one of which she had raced through the night streets in panic and confusion, hand in hand with her closest female friend, until a blast of fire incinerated her friend alongside her, that combustion so total that her friend vanished without trace while she herself remained unharmed, her hand now holding a void, not even ashes. Hijikata hesitated to leave Akita for Tokyo after the war's end, despite his desire, even wounded and inapt for dance, to become a dancer; when he did finally leave for Tokyo, he endured years of destitution and desperation, supporting himself as a dockworker and through petty crime. Finally, he began to show up at the Asbestos Studio, the dance studio run by Akiko Motofuji with her first husband, a celebrated expressionist-dance choreographer, Nobutoshi Tsuda, and established for her on land owned by her father, an asbestos magnate, using profits from his asbestos production. By 1959, Tsuda had been displaced, and the Asbestos Studio became Hijikata's own base for his experiments in choreography which at that time he called 'Dance Experience', and by 1961 he also began to name 'Ankoku Butoh'.

Richie remained in Japan permanently, until his death in Tokyo in 2013, apart from several years in which he returned to the US for studies at Columbia University, and a period around the end of the 1960s in which he worked as the curator of film at the Museum of Modern Art in New York. The period of the US occupation of Japan expired after seven years in 1952, and the original military-associated impetus for Richie's employment in Japan elapsed, though the US military presence there remained strong, especially through naval bases such as Yokosuka and air bases such as Tachikawa in the Tokyo region, as well as the wide-scale, long-term appropriation of Okinawa for vast US bases; especially during the 1960s, with the use of the US's Japan bases to supply the war in Vietnam, that military presence was violently contested by activists, students, unions and other entities in Japan, together with the US–Japan Security Treaty, signed in the US in January 1960, that was perceived by its opponents as subjugating Japan to US military and economic imperatives. In the interval between Hijikata's collaborations with Richie on HUMAN SACRIFICE and WARGAMES, immense urban riots took place in Tokyo in the spring of 1960 and the parliament building was stormed, resulting in the death of a female activist, Michiko Kanba, in the same month, June 1960, that the treaty – to be renewed ten years later, in 1970 – was finally passed in Japan's parliament. During those 1960 protests, Tokyo's central districts became spaces of uproar, with dense crowds of protestors amassing in its streets, emitting sonic turmoil. Neither Hijikata nor Richie took part directly in those protests, but both of their film collaborations, with their aura of unleashed disintegration, are inflected and infiltrated by that ongoing urban upheaval, which would only intensify across that decade as the treaty's renewal approached.

By the end of the 1950s, when he met Hijikata for the first time, Richie had entirely extricated himself from his initial role in Japan as an agent of its conquest and subsequent reformulation as an obsequious ally of the US, and was creating an identity and notoriety for himself as an experimental artist, writer and filmmaker, entirely unique in his capacity to collaborate effortlessly with Tokyo's experimental artists (no other American or European figure worked so intimately with Japan's artists as he did in the 1960s), and also in his disregard for boundaries between the media he worked across: among them music, film, writing, photography, and urban observation. Richie's work was fired by an incessant urban curiosity that took him to investigate every district and periphery of Tokyo. At the end of the 1950s, at the time of the filming of HUMAN SACRIFICE, he was also a supporter and advisor for young experimental filmmakers working in Tokyo's university film-club scene, such as Masao Adachi, who became notorious a decade later for his films of revolutionary provocation and his close affiliation with Japan's Red Army Faction terrorist group.

Many of Richie's other collaborations in Tokyo emerged through the direct intervention of Yukio Mishima. In 1951, when he was asked to show Mishima around New York City, he took the visitor to the gay bars that Mishima wanted to see; he and Mishima renewed that contact when Richie returned to Tokyo after his time at Columbia University, and remained close, in a combative intimacy, until Mishima's death in 1970, two months after the closure of the Osaka Expo, which also marked an ending to Japan's teeming experimental art cultures of the previous decade. Richie stopped making films himself at the end of the 1960s, shifted ground and generated a new profile for himself as an eminent scholar and promoter of Japan's film culture, especially the work of Kurosawa and Ozu, while also working on fiction until the end of his life, with his final novella, *Hell on Earth*, interrogating the US's detention camps in the aftermath of the wars in Iraq. He also wrote journals, collected and published in 2004, of his innumerable observations and encounters in Tokyo, conserving some of their sexually focused elements – such as his account of 1990s encounters with young Iranian men in Ueno Park and the adjacent pornography cinemas – for posthumous publication as a volume to be titled *Vita Sexualis*, documenting his sex life from his arrival in Tokyo in 1947 onwards.

In the Summer of 1959, through Yukio Mishima, Richie met Hijikata for the first time, along with the writer and translator of Sade, Tatsuhiko Shibusawa, at a special performance at the Asbestos Studio of Hijikata's first independent work *Forbidden Colours* (*Kinjiki*) – ostensibly inspired by Mishima's novel of that title, but more directly resonating with the novels of Jean Genet – which had already created a furore at its initial public performance. Mishima was meeting Hijikata for the first time too, and they would also have their own intense collaborative rapport over the following decade, underlined by Mishima's many texts promoting Hijikata's performances. Richie told me that, intrigued by the aura of outrage which had attracted him in Mishima's invitation to attend the performance, he turned off a short alleyway with a factory chimney at its end, and entered the coolness of the decrepit, darkened wooden studio that was lost among Tokyo's innumerable backstreets, escaping the city's humid heat and traffic pollution. He had then received a revelation – one of the most vital, seminal illuminations over his six decades in Tokyo – as well as an urgent friendship. He and Hijikata, with their dual insatiable curiosities and relentless demands, their corporeal obsessions and their open desires for innovation, quickly became close friends, and decided to collaborate together across joint public events, but firstly, immediately, through a film.

Tokyo and its surroundings form the site for the two films that mark the origin in 1959 and the ending in 1962 of the intensive collaborative friendship between Richie and Hijikata; after 1962, they would not film together again, but they continued to meet frequently, at the Asbestos Studio, in south-western Tokyo, or in the northern district of Otsuka, where Richie lived during that era in a small wooden house. They also took many nocturnal walks through the north-eastern districts of Ueno and Yanaka, the location of an immense cemetery in which Richie shot his final film, CYBELE, in 1968, over the course of one day, with the performance-art group Zero Jigen, which then possessed the reputation of the most outrageous and uncompromised of Japan's performance groups. Across the 1960s, Richie alerted and guided English-language audiences to Hijikata's Ankoku Butoh project, especially in his role as arts editor of the *Japan Times*, thereby serving an allied status to Yukio Mishima in their joint media-instilled capacity to consolidate the often scarce audiences for Hijikata's work. Hijikata intended those audiences to be international, and generated bi-lingual promotional material.

The ascendant media and promotional cultures of Tokyo around the end of the 1950s formed only one element in the great upheaval that the city was undergoing, as the last firebombed wastelands of the inner city vanished and a new, engulfing technological megalopolis replaced them, with constellations of transportation and consumer axes growing along the western edge of the inner city (Shibuya, Shinjuku, Ikebukuro) and serving as arrival points for the vast commuting populations of the western suburbs who could then join the city's loop railway or subway lines to reach their destinations. The suburbs proliferated, conjoining with adjacent cities (Yokohama, Kawasaki) along the sea coast and stretching out towards western mountain boundaries.

Those transportation axes often incorporated breathing-space plazas, such as the one located at the Shinjuku East Plaza exit where I met with Richie for our first Tokyo walk and which, at the far end of the 1960s, had formed a primary, unintended site for the flaring of activist protests and performance-art. Immense screens surmounted those plazas' surrounding buildings, initially inscribed textually in night-illuminated neon letterings but later transmitting moving-image and digital sequences. Those screens announced the immediacy or 'actuality' of their own urban-technological status, as well as habituating spectators' eyes to the insignias of corporate power. The historian William Marotti emphasises the way in which corporeality in Tokyo in that era experienced simultaneous concentrations of activities, as in those urban axes which multi-functioned as department stores, train stations, arts venues, and drinking and entertainment complexes: 'By the late 1950s everyday life in urban Japan was being transformed at all levels, especially within the urban spaces reconfigured by a host of new and interdependent working, living, and consuming practices.'³ Time and the human body transmutated together in sensorial compressions and conjunctions.

The urban apparition of Tokyo that appeared as a volatile entity at the end of the 1950s, unprecedented in its generation of intricate apertures for the manoeuvrings and surgings of corporeality, formed a kind of 'experimental metropolis', as the promoters of Expo '70, a decade later, would extol their own body-saturated, shortlived megalopolis on the northern edge of Osaka. The 1959 city of Tokyo in which Hijikata and Richie made their first film together was layered over multiple past-cities of ghosts, scorched and seismic terrains, and still held many spectral, overlooked sites. Alongside its sustaining sensory concentrations, Tokyo remained always ready to fall abruptly into the abyss, or to endure cataclysmic striation, as with the street-riot events of the Spring of 1960 which annexed a simultaneous mark of negation over the city's new architectures. That city was already being recast in anticipation of the 1964 Olympic Games, with the development of its immense networks of inner-city highways and new subway routes whose construction left behind their own urban erasures, as districts endured demolition to clear space for those networks. A great deal hinged for the institutional organisers of the Olympic Games on finally restituting Japan's postwar international reputation and on enhancing Japan's new technological and corporate ascendancy, thereby justifying Tokyo's extreme urban upheaval in advance of those Games, just as a great deal hinged for the perpetrators of Tokyo's 1960 anti-governmental riots on envisioning an unsubjugated and peace-committed Japan, thereby validating their urban insurgency and fierce confrontations with riot police.

Miryam Sas – in evoking Tokyo's urban dynamics at the time of the collaborations between Richie and Hijikata – emphasises the city's ascendant security-guard and surveillance culture, along with the incessant car collisions that took place at the junctions of those newly built highways, in conditions of dire air contamination and within a dense chemical smog that frequently darkened the city during daylight hours at the end of the 1950s. Those new ocular dynamics, crashes and contaminations accelerated across Tokyo's urban space into the early 1960s: 'Rapid alterations to the urban setting (the construction of skyscrapers in Shinjuku and new underground spaces), disturbing new levels of pollution, along with changes in media (such as the rise of television and the media of "actuality" and the decline of the studio system in cinema) all contributed to an intensified focus on environment, apparatus, and mediation that clearly demanded a new approach to artistic practice.'[4] Sas identifies the configuration of that new arts practice – conceived as a direct response to a haywire urban environment of compressed media data-projection and technologised corporeal contamination – as 'intermedial', necessitating 'reconceived relationships among art, technology, and environment'.[5]

As the location for the two films of Hijikata and Richie, that new manifestation of Tokyo is wrenched away to the side – towards the city's eastern peripheries, with their marine landscapes and edges – or is visible only at an askew tangent. HUMAN SACRIFICE was shot in the grounds of a factory-building that was neglected or abandoned, and had originally been constructed on reclaimed land in Tokyo's Shinagawa district, on the edge of Tokyo Bay. WARGAMES was filmed even further from Tokyo's centre, on the deserted Kujukurihama black-sand beach coast to the east of the city. Many other Tokyo-based experimental filmmakers and performers were attracted to those zonal edgescapes: Takahiko Iiimura, who would film

Hijikata's performances in 1963 and 1965, made his first film, JUNK, 1962, at the edge of Tokyo Bay, filming fragments of disintegrated environments of carcasses and detrita at the waterside, then projecting the resulting film in an art-gallery environment rather than a cinema. And Eikoh Hosoe's sole filmic collaboration with Hijikata, NAVEL AND A-BOMB, 1960, was also filmed on a beach environment, to the south of the Kujukurihama beach. The beach at Kamakura also especially attracted Tokyo's artists. Richie saw such locations as being intimate to Tokyo (easily reachable, for the short durations of filming he envisaged) and resonant of the city and of its ongoing turmoil, but at the same time forming pressed-out or expelled sites, so that they emanated an alien wasteland aura.

Film, corporeality and urban space always generate a distinctive amalgam, especially whenever approaches to filmmaking attempt unprecedented experiments, whenever corporeality – as filmmaking's focus – is placed under immense pressure or is rendered aberrant and intransigent (as in Hijikata's Ankoku Butoh project), and whenever urban spaces or their edges transmit a profound tension as the result of ongoing transmutation or violent unrest at their heart. The city under interrogation – with its memories of conflict, and its woundings and capacities for abrupt violence – may appear distant or absent, but it is being probed still more intently for all of its vanishings or evasions. In HUMAN SACRIFICE and WARGAMES, Hijikata and Richie conjure filmic means to make performance actions illuminate the embedded fractures, darkening contaminations and subterranean unrest of the newly conceived, newly rebuilt Tokyo.

In the autumn months of 1959, Richie shot the first moving-image record of Hijikata's choreography and body, in his film HUMAN SACRIFICE, made in close creative collaboration with Hijikata. The film possesses the momentous aura of that first seizing of Hijikata's project, but at the same time it is immersed in such distinctive, outlandish preoccupations with corporeal-

Ill. 1 – HUMAN SACRIFICE, 1959, filmed by Donald Richie – Hijikata's dance of protruded buttocks.

ity and urban space that its sense of holding an unprecedented filmic status is undercut. Along with Hosoe's film NAVEL AND A-BOMB, Richie's two films are those which manifest Hijikata's active involvement and evident desire for his work to be filmed; following his collaborations with Richie, Hijikata's approach to the moving-image capture of his dance became far more ambivalent, torn or indifferent. But Richie's own approach to filming Hijikata's work as a corporeal spectacle – still in its raw state of formulation at the moment of HUMAN SACRIFICE, and still two years before that work's naming as 'Ankoku Butoh' – in itself possesses ambivalence through his presentation of Hijikata's work as virulent and dangerous, ready to torment and fatally eradicate any corporeality or gesture unaligned with its experimental imperatives. Through that act of killing, its perpetrators themselves are transformed into a social entity of power, propelled from experimental art into the exercise of collective subjugation. Richie's films often hold an isolated figure who is unaligned to the point of risking provocation, perversely determined never to cohere with any collectivity, and thereby embodying Richie's perception of his own position in Japan.

Richie had been making 8mm and 16mm films since the age of 17 in 1941, and HUMAN SACRIFICE was already his twentieth film; in 1959, he worked on two other films, THE DOUBLE, about a man hunting himself through a house in Tokyo, and SEI-CHU-DO, exploring the movements of young *sumo* wrestlers in close-up. His films were often unprojected to public audiences in that era, shown only to friends at Richie's house or at university film clubs, but were occasionally shown at prominent venues such as the Sogetsu Art Center, then newly designed by the influential architect Kenzo Tange (who would design major buildings for the Tokyo Olympics and Osaka Expo, and go on to determine Tokyo's startling civic and corporate architecture through to the 1990s) and opened in 1958 as an experimental cross-media space overseen by the filmmaker Hiroshi Teshigahara, with its auditorium also used for concerts, performances and other art events.

Richie was inspired in his work on HUMAN SACRIFICE by short films made by French poets and writers, notably Jean Genet's UN CHANT D'AMOUR, 1950, which envisions a prisoner's hallucinations of homo-erotic sexual contact through the apertures between cells in a prison environment, as well as the films of Jean Cocteau, which also take place in hallucinated, death-inflected environments. Another inspiration for Richie's work was the film FIREWORKS, 1947, by the young American experimental filmmaker Kenneth Anger (whose work also inspired Genet and Cocteau), which investigates the same processes of corporeal subjugation and dissection as Richie's film; in Anger's FIREWORKS, it is his own body which is infiltrated and maimed via film. Those films pivotal to Richie's own approach were not shown in Tokyo until the mid-1960s (Richie had seen them in the USA and on his extensive travels in Europe); alongside his incorporation of elements from them into his own films, he vocally evoked them to artists and filmmakers in Japan prior to their opportunity to view the films themselves.

The performance recorded by Richie for Human Sacrifice was created solely to be filmed, shot as an outdoor-space action performed by Hijikata and the group of dancers who were then beginning to amass around him at the Asbestos Studio, following the outrage generated earlier that year by his performance of *Forbidden Colours*. As well as planning new performances, Hijikata was also writing intensively at that vital moment of the delineation of his dance project; most explicitly through his text *To Prison*, published in 1961, he used the form of provocative, Genet-inspired manifestoes in which he aligned his emergent dance with criminality and homosexuality, against the society of commodification and productivity (Hijikata viewed his dance contrarily as being aimless) that was then consolidating itself in Japan.

As though impelled by the darkness of Hijikata's work, Richie mistakenly shot the entirety of Human Sacrifice with his film camera at the wrong light-setting, blackening the urban space in which the film was shot and obscuring the bodies into shadows; the film's first spectators' eyes had to search through that engulfing darkness to locate traces of bodies or to follow the film's narrative of a figure's torture and killing. As well as projecting the film for Hijikata and his dancers at the Asbestos Studio, Richie also showed it at the auditorium of the Sogetsu Art Center; he then gave the film's sole print to Hijikata as a gift, and it was projected occasionally at the Asbestos Studio by Hijikata himself until his death in 1986 and then as part of biyearly film programmes arranged by his widow, Akiko Motofuji. Nearly fifty years after the film was made, Richie decided to digitally correct its deep darkness at a film laboratory; it became one of his last creative acts, on 28 February 2008, since he fell ill later that year on his return to Tokyo from the Venice Film Festival, and was unable to work in any sustained way over the final five years of his life, remaining mostly silent.

Since the film's origins were totally unknown in 2008, and Richie had never written about them, I asked him to write an account of his work with Hijikata on HUMAN SACRIFICE, and he replied to me on the day following his visit to the film laboratory: 'Hijikata had already seen my 8mm films before we met and wanted to make a film with me... During 1959 we often met to discuss what kind of film this would be. We both wanted some kind of ritual-like entertainment and I suggested that the argument be about segregation of some kind. An individual would be eventually punished by society. He liked the idea and began to imagine the choreography. Both the story and the dance itself would reflect our theme. The individual would know only one way to dance, the simple Japanese *matsuri* dance; society, however, the rest of the dancers, would move in the full complicated vocabulary of Butoh movement. We decided to call it Gisei (HUMAN SACRIFICE), a title which indicated the degree of shock it promised. To emphasise our theme we used for the individual a non-Butoh person, a non-dancer, a young truck-driver friend of mine named Hatakeyama. We then assembled the props we would need for the lynching and the choreography evolved around the slender anecdote that we had agreed upon... On the following day (a Sunday) we piled into a borrowed truck and went to an abandoned factory that one of the dancers had discovered. From ten in the morning until five in the afternoon we practiced and filmed, the story evolving from the dances themselves. Just as the last of the dancers filed out, leaving the body behind, the sun set and the light failed. We used a Bolex 8mm camera with Fuji film stock and almost everything was underexposed (I was my own cameraman as well as editor) making for a very dark print. Hijikata liked this, saying that it caught the *ankoku* flavour of the choreography... It was from the first to have had sound and I had wanted to add blasphemy to transgression and use the 'Hallelujah' chorus from Handel's *Messiah* as music. This I was able to experience only once, when the film was shown at the Sogetsu Art Space in 1959 and we played a recording with it.'[6]

The film is heavily scratched, especially in its first minutes, and the entire film's black-and-white footage remains extremely grainy, that accentuation of its status as scarred celluloid marked especially in Richie's many sequences of filming facial plains. Richie also marks his own presence in the film: its first shot pans vertically upwards from the dirt and weeds of the factory grounds to the filmmaker's name and the film's title hand-inscribed on newspaper pages, arranged on the ground and weighted down with rusty sticks and wire, before continuing that pan upwards to establish the film's urban location in the dilapidated yard. At the film's closure, that pan is reversed, beginning from the factory building's roof and descending back across the dirt ground.

Throughout the film, Richie's primary emphasis is to film faces, from the side and face-on, often with repeated close-ups, in a discordant rhythm of facial interrogation, focusing especially on the face of Hijikata – wearing a white beret, unfastened leather boots and black trunks underneath a loose, chequered coat – as well as that of Akiko Motofuji, alongside the other dancers. While those dancers are undertaking their act of torture and killing, their faces emanate a sombre determination, intercut with outbursts of hilarity. That facial and figurative approach is also applied to the 'non-dancer' who will be sacrificed, with sequences of close-ups in which the camera moves relentlessly closer to the face, in a style evocative of Genet's UN CHANT D'AMOUR as well as Anger's FIREWORKS.

Hijikata's group of dancers enter the factory yard in a procession and configure themselves into a revolving circle, each dancing differently, but all making wild and extravagant, obscenity-evoking movements; Hijikata's own emphasis in his dance is on protruding his buttocks. The bare-chested figure who is to be sacrificed dances with the others in a way that is immediately distinct, confined to repeated maladroit movements of his arms that evoke festival dances. At first, he appears a figure of ascendant power and attraction in the group, potentially overturning the other figures' elated volatility; that attraction is filmed by Richie as sequences of gazes, as the eyes of the bare-chested figure scan the bodies of the female dancers, and his gaze is returned with increasing anger by those dancers. His gazing and fixed gestures initially lead only to his suspension from participation in the group; he is ejected from the dancers' circle by Hijikata and made to stand in disgrace by the factory's front wall. But after he races back to the dancers' circle, participating again with evident delight, the dancers exact retribution on him for his crime of performing a banal, popular dance that infiltrates and may annul their own wild dance of experimentation. Hijikata and several other dancers knock him to the ground, then hold him down and subject him to a succession of tortures and humiliations.

To his horror, the prone figure is repeatedly straddled by the dancers; Hijikata himself does not participate directly in the act of sacrifice, only constraining him by holding down one of his arms. Akiko Motofuji either urinates on him (urine is seen only momentarily, as liquid trickling over the constricted figure's chest) or rapes him, laughing as she extricates herself; subsequently, a male dancer drops excrement onto his chest, then a female dancer vomits over him. Those initial tortures drive the dancers into exultation, and that furore in itself materialises a previously unseen cleaver in the hand of Akiko Motofuji, who then castrates the screaming figure, to the delight of the other dancers; his light-coloured trousers are now saturated in blood. His figure is elevated overhead in a ceremonial movement by the dancers, then returned to the ground for his moment of death, eyes wide open before his head falls to one side, arms spread-eagled. The dancers begin a slow dispersal from their site of killing, each face carrying oblivious resignation or bewilderment, as they leave the yard; the sacrificed body is shown in a final sequence of four static shots, increasingly lost in darkness in the abandoned space, once the dancers have vanished.

Richie's particular approach to filming, with its intricate corporeal and facial interrogations emphasised above the coherent identification of space, renders the film difficult to follow, and the linear direction of its sequences becomes apparent only with repeated viewings. The film transmits its multiple immediacies through the evident sense that its shooting has been undertaken within a curtailed duration, through the wildness of the dancers' gestures, and in the nonchalance of the act of killing. In his editing of the film, Richie's focus is on honing the interplay of gazes between the sacrificed figure and the adversaries whose lethal domain he has somehow fallen into. The action is distinctively located in an urban world of cruelty and slaughter, conjured out of nowhere for the film as a dangerously prohibitive and punitive terrain, but simultaneously one that also generates exhilaration and exultation, via dance's intervention. As a collaboration exploring and rending anatomical boundaries, HUMAN SACRIFICE is manoeuvred into an extraordinary sensory amalgam by Richie's filmic obsessions together with Hijikata's unrestrained readiness – at that instant of his dance-project's coalescing – to give the film raw and frantic corporeal animation.

Two months after our walk through Shinjuku, Richie proposed a further walk, to the location in Tokyo of the filming of HUMAN SACRIFICE, which I had seen projected by Akiko Motofuji and her daughter Gala, from its only print, on a screen at the Asbestos Studio, a few weeks earlier. Richie told me that we could try to find the site of the abandoned factory, that it was such a forgotten, peripheral area of the city that the factory's yard could conceivably still be there, though it was now almost forty years since the Sunday in 1959 when he had filmed Hijikata for the first time. We would start out from his two-room apartment on the eighth storey of a building in Ueno district, overlooking the lotus-covered Shinobazu Pond with its temple on an island reached by causeways from three directions; he had moved there only a year or so earlier, leaving his nearby wooden house by the Yanaka cemetery. I took the elevator and entered the first room packed with shelves of books, with a space cleared for Richie's writing desk and computer; the second room's contents were far sparser, with a rolled futon against one wall, since

Richie slept in that room. The apartment had no bathroom; Richie would walk to the public baths through the illuminated streets of prostitution behind his building. At that moment, the women in the streets were mostly Russian, and Richie told me he had spoken last night to a teenager from Nizhny Novgorod, who had recounted to him in English her life in that holy city prior to her sudden sex-traffic transportation to Tokyo, leading Richie to imagine the journeys to Gorky (as Nizhny Novgorod had been known, until 1990) of his favourite filmmaker, Andrei Tarkovsky, whose film IVAN'S CHILDHOOD was made in the year of Richie's final collaboration with Hijikata.

We stood on the balcony reached from the apartment's second room, and Richie pointed out the networks of causeways and pathways that crossed and surrounded the Shinobazu Pond. Until recently, the young Iranian men he had told me about on our last walk – left stranded and homeless in their hundreds in Tokyo by a visa scam, surviving by selling telephone cards or themselves in Ueno Park – had spent their evenings smoking and passing time along those causeways. Now they had vanished, replaced on those causeways by cardboard-box houses inhabited by destitute young men from Japan's north, from the island of Hokkaido and from Akita, part of the isolated Tohoku region, which Hijikata left behind to travel to Tokyo, arriving in 1952 at the Ueno railway station. The city Richie and I were overlooking from his balcony had entered a time of severe economic hardship, at least for its vulnerable figures, as it had when Hijikata first arrived in Tokyo and devoted himself to petty crime and dock labour, prior to Japan's spectacular economic resurgence, marked by the 1964 Olympics and the 1970 Expo.

Standing on the balcony, Richie told me that whenever he walked those causeways late at night, with the sound of crows cawing around him, the pungent smell of the destitute young men's bodies reminded him of the smell of bodies in the era in which he himself first arrived in the city, in 1947. I asked him how Hijikata's body had smelled, and he replied that it was an irresistible, compacted tang of sweat, semen, excrement, together with something that evoked death to him. The artist Nam June Paik had known Hijikata in the same era as Richie had filmed HUMAN SACRIFICE and WARGAMES, and also evoked the smell of death emanating from Hijikata's body: 'Hijikata smelled of the Tohoku farming village – desolate, poor, earth-bound and death-struck.'[7] Richie went on to speak of Hijikata's skin – lithe from the dancer's muscles below, striated and scarred on his back, and far darker than the skin he usually encountered in Tokyo, especially when set directly alongside the pallid skin of Akiko Motofuji, as documented in photographs made by Eikoh Hosoe at the beginning of the 1960s. I asked Richie if he had considered positioning Hijikata as the 'HUMAN SACRIFICE' of his film, rather than his truck-driver friend, and Richie laughed at the idea of Hijikata castrated and assassinated by his own group of Ankoku Butoh dancers, even before his work had really begun. Reading Genet had made Hijikata love treachery and betrayal, so that insurrection by his dancers would have appealed to him. But Hijikata would not have wanted to lose his beautiful, dark-skinned penis, Richie concluded, and in that era he had only wanted to dance aberration rather than festival-style dances, remembering Hijikata's factory-yard experimental dance of furiously protruded buttocks.

We took the Yamanote train line from Ueno southwards to Tamachi station, which Richie estimated was the closest station to the location of his film's factory yard. One station exit headed into a dense terrain of office towers seething with bodies, while the other headed into an under-populated wasteland of grass-grown demolition sites and abandoned warehouses. Soon, we were crossing the deserted Shibaura district's bridges over desolate canals, industrial barges passing beneath us through the reeking, oil-polluted water, and Richie laughed that it certainly wasn't Venice, not even Amsterdam. Overhead, two elevated transportation lines on immense concrete struts transited that space on the edge of Tokyo Bay: the monorail, built for visitors to the Tokyo Olympics, heading south to Haneda airport, and the newly opened Yurikamome line veering abruptly eastwards to the Odaiba artificial island in Tokyo Bay, newly redesignated as the city's unique seaside resort, its hotels dominated by a vast corporate media-centre of metal spars and globes designed by Kenzo Tange. In the early 1960s, Hijikata's architect friend Arata Isozaki, who trained with Kenzo Tange, had envisioned never-realised tower-cities to be built upwards from the seismic ocean floor of Tokyo Bay. The accumulation over decades of that Bay's reclaimed-land edges – designed to generate extra space for the seams-bursting megalopolis – possessed multiple strata of time, some long obsolete, others just about to coalesce: ghosts of once-future cities and ghost bodies, in intimacy with new cities and new bodies. Once we reached the water's edge, between two empty brick-built maritime warehouses, Richie told me that we must be close to the film's location.

Now Richie spoke of his memory of Hijikata's elation, curses and laughter as he, his dancers and Richie, all crammed into an old truck, had left the Asbestos Studio alleyway on that Sunday morning in 1959 and entered the Meguro traffic haze on their journey to that film location, which Richie had only ever seen on that day. In his arms, Richie had held his Bolex film-camera and the vat of blood to be used for the human sacrifice's castration, still unsure how he was going to approach the day's filming. By nightfall, he would have shot the first-ever film of Ankoku Butoh, even before that dance was named.

But as we walked southwards between the bayside's warehouses, towards the boundary between Tokyo and Kawasaki, scanning the innumerable disused factory installations and gutted buildings for the one with the distinctive elongated windows and adjacent yard that had been the location of Richie's film, I could see him grow exhausted. We had no map and now had no idea where we were. As in the Shinjuku plaza, glaring overhead illumination suddenly seared and infiltrated Richie's deeply lined face, on and off, this time projected from the immense red orbs surmounting metal towers that guided ships into the nearby port quays, along with melancholy sirens. Darkness had fallen, and the factory yard that had been the site of Hijikata's first filming could not be found. Urban memory itself was tangibly disintegrating – still faster than the corporeal entities memory holds – at Tokyo's peripheries, and the past is lost, in this multiply erased city, with its negated or resurgent ghosts, above all those of film. Over the next two decades, that part-abandoned urban terrain we had traversed was gradually transformed into salubrious districts of new apartment complexes, promoted as fashionable marine-side living environments with dedicated rapid-transport infrastructures. 'Let's give up,' Richie told me. 'We're never going to find it. But next month we'll try again.' We entered a dock workers' ancient beer-hall to rest at the empty trestles before the long walk back to Tamachi station.

Three years on from their work together on HUMAN SACRIFICE, in the summer of 1962 Hijikata and Richie decided to collaborate on a new film, WARGAMES. This time, the film would be shot by Richie with a 16mm camera, giving a far clearer image than HUMAN SACRIFICE, and once again in black-and-white celluloid. By that moment, Hijikata had begun to name his project of dance experimentation 'Ankoku Butoh', alongside its pre-existing name, 'Dance Experience'. Richie's initial idea had been to shoot a film of confrontations between gangs of young boys on the immense Kujukurihama black-sand beach, close to Tokyo on the Chiba coastline. As with their previous collaboration, Hijikata and Richie developed the film over the course of several months, in Asbestos Studio drinking-meetings, formulating and rejecting ideas, with Hijikata demonstrating his ideas via gestures of dance. In Richie's memory, Hijikata showed a determined commitment to participate in the film, in distinction from his subsequent deep ambivalence towards film. Hijikata was convinced it would be impossible for Richie to direct the unruly boys (all the sons of families making their living by fishing), but that he himself could do it effortlessly, by enticing or beguiling or terrifying them.

Ill. 2 – Donald Richie, Tokyo, 1962.

As with their work on HUMAN SACRIFICE, it would be a short filming trip; Richie and Hijikata left Tokyo in the morning, travelled by train to the nearest station, then walked with Richie's film camera and tripod to the beach; once there, Hijikata rounded up a group of boys (Richie remembered that it took him no time at all to recruit them) in the nearest fishing village, Osato, for the next day's shooting, and bought a white goat, which he would kill. He and Richie spent the night drinking Johnnie Walker Black-Label whiskey (Hijikata's favourite) at the village inn, then collected the goat and started shooting with the boys very early the next morning. By midday, the calm weather had changed and a violent typhoon began to blow in from the east, with wild waves, necessitating an acceleration in the shooting before the winds made it unworkable or dangerous to continue to film. The final curtailed sequences were shot as the typhoon engulfed the beach. Finally, after the boys had left, Richie filmed the typhoon itself, which was already diminishing as he and Hijikata walked back to the train station to arrive back in Tokyo that night. Richie had shot the film without sound, and he spent far longer assembling a soundtrack than he had on the shooting; he composed and recorded a short ritualistic sequence of percussion and wind instruments which he then deployed repeatedly to punctuate the film's action, then synchonised the film's sequences to noises of storms and breaking waves at a Tokyo sound laboratory.

Only the fourteen boys, in their swimming-trunks, appear in the film. Hijikata is absent, but also incessantly present, in the boys' responses to his direction, especially during the sequence in which they burst into hilarity, provoked by Hijikata dancing with his navel protruding forward, so that the boys all look at one another's navels and at their own. Throughout the film's shooting, Hijikata remained just outside Richie's camera-framing, performing in invisibility. Richie's main preoccupation in filming the action was to avoid incorporating Hijikata's figure, always to exclude him from sight, in anti-filmic edge-space.

Watching the film after the 2011 Fukushima calamity, Richie's shooting of the Kujukurihama beach and its massive typhoon-driven waves irresistibly evokes the sequences shot from far overhead (by news-agency or weather-agency cinematographers in helicopters) of the east-facing beaches to the north of Kujukurihama as they were crossed by *tsunami* waves unleashed by the Tohoku-coast earthquake, driven on beyond the beach landscapes to inundate and destroy coastal towns and drown their populations. WARGAMES, entirely shot on the Kujukurihama beach, evokes a volatile, fissured environment of imminent as well as future catastrophes, ghosted by film also with past catastrophes, and ready to be transposed and expanded to Japan's cities. Richie's film, in its miniaturised location, forms a magnifying lens between spatial proliferations of future and past cruelties and calamities. The film's sequences of action were conceived by Richie and Hijikata at their fishing-village inn after their initial Tokyo discussions – but were also improvised in Hijikata's direction of the boys, and abbreviated and accentuated by the imminent typhoon's closure of their filming. Those sequences focus upon the human dynamics of conflict, slaughter and isolation, evoking a sensation of despondency and an aura of cruelty, along with an unprecedented openness to erasure, which, for Richie, still distinctively permeated Tokyo, as it had on his arrival in the city fifteen years earlier. The historian John Dower characterised that urban sensation as being 'surreal' – intimating its immediate, aberrant transmissibility from the urban into experimental art and film – in his evocation of the post-war Japanese urban moment, following the erasures of Hiroshima and Nagasaki: 'There was a widespread sense of having experienced a forbidding, surreal new dimension of existence which no other people could hope to comprehend. Such consciousness of nuclear destruction became an integral even if not always evident part of all subsequent attempts to come to terms with the war's meaning. It reinforced a pervasive sense of powerlessness and lent an eerie kind of specialness to what might otherwise have felt like a pointless defeat.'[8]

At the opening of WARGAMES, Richie foregrounds shots of the typhoon and its noise to position the spectator's approach to the film: from the first moment, the watching eye is already set in calamity. Hijikata determined all of the corporeal dimensions of the film: it begins with sequences of the fourteen boys, aged between around seven and twelve years, running left to right in elation along the ocean's edge. The shots are brought to a sudden halt when one boy freezes in his run at the left side of the film frame: that boy embodies the malfunctioned figure of separation and dissidence in the boys' group, as with the bare-chested dancer in HUMAN SACRIFICE, but this boy will not be sacrificed. Instead, as he approaches the gang of boys who have also now halted, he finds them surrounding a white goat, held around its throat by a string leash gripped by one boy. Where the goat has materialised from is a mystery. At first, the boys stroke the goat in their delight at its apparition, but soon the boy holding it begins to jerk the leash, and jolt its horns, making the goat's head contort. Seeing the danger, as the goat's leash is passed from hand to hand and the maltreatment intensifies, the separated boy reprimands the goat's tormenters, who appears outraged at that revolt against their power. The separated boy appears able to draw a faction of the boys around himself, but the tormenters then punish them, pushing them in the chest, backwards to the sand, and a struggle fires up between the boys who want to extricate the goat (perhaps to torment it themselves) and its tormenters.

Abruptly, and unseen, the goat's neck is broken in the wargame (Hijikata was assigned that act, since Richie himself could not perform it), and the struggle ends: the boys now gaze at the goat as it lies on its side at the ocean's edge, then its head falls towards Richie's camera lens. The boys form a line within the ocean itself to observe the goat's death. Increasingly now, Richie films close-ups of the boys' faces, as he had for the dancers of HUMAN SACRIFICE, occasionally so close that only indistinct fragments of faces are visible. The storm is generated directly by the boys' killing of the goat, and several of them now turn in unease to face the ocean, whose waves immerse the goat. The boys' faces appear sombre as they realize the gravity of their wargames' residue in the goat's dead body, and they devise an expiation, lifting the animal's body above their heads in a procession moving in the reverse direction, left to right, to their elated runs. They construct a burial mound of hand-pounded sand above the goat, and assemble around it for a moment, but suddenly convulse into laughter, their sombreness immediately annulled, through Hijikata's presence around them, compelling them to laugh with his navel dance. Only the separated boy will not laugh, having refused to participate in the burial, sitting away at a distance, taking the watching status of a witness. Now one boy incites the others to resume their elated run, and they race away, Richie's camera switching position from its habitual orientation directly towards the ocean in order to follow their course along the ocean's edge until they vanish in the typhoon mists. The storm's waves unearth the goat, gradually cracking apart the mound so that one leg and then its head are

Ill. 3 – WARGAMES, 1962, filmed by Donald Richie – the beach children laughing at Hijikata's navel dance.

revealed, and the film's final shot is of the broken mound and the seated, watching boy, against the ocean.

WARGAMES is a film of conflict, performance and death, driven by hallucination. When the boys disperse, it appears they are being compelled to locate and dispute a new site and focus of killing, oscillating between the contemporary moment and lost or future cruelties. War is a hallucinated entity that slips beyond all national imperatives, and finally concerns only the transmutations of the body, solitary or grouped, and overseen and manoeuvred invisibly by Hijikata in WARGAMES. Richie had visited the Kujukurihama beach once before, in the 1950s, and its strange amalgam of desolation and liberation (close to his experience of Tokyo itself) haunted him. In his journals, he recounts a dream, recorded on 5 January 1960, which appears as a prequel to the shooting of WARGAMES two years later, or else an element within its intricate corporeal architecture: 'I dream of an experience I had thought forgotten. I am again on the beach at Chiba, and it is the day of the dead, before dawn. I cannot sleep, and wander out onto the beach, looking upward at the summer stars. At my feet is a boy curled up in a hole in the sand and sound asleep. I look further and find the beach is full of sleeping boys, all children. Like animals in their burrows, two and three to a hole, they are curled sleeping. Then I remember that today is the day the dead return. The children are waiting for the dawn, when their dead come from the sea.'[9]

In the spring of 1998, a month or so after our misfired walk to locate the shooting-site of HUMAN SACRIFICE, Richie proposed another walk, this time along the Kujukurihama beach where he had shot WARGAMES, thirty-six years earlier. He had never returned to Kujukurihama since, and told me he wanted to see the beach again, but I sensed too the walk would be a kind of expiation for the HUMAN SACRIFICE walk (which we never tried a second time, despite Richie's suggestion of another attempt, at that walk's abandonment). I met him again in Ueno, in the early morning, this time outside his apartment building, since he was eager to start; instead of his slate-grey overcoat, he was now wearing a light-blue jacket over a black shirt and red tie, and carrying no map, trusting that our journey would be guided to its location through unerring filmic time and space.

From Tokyo, we changed trains at Chiba station and took the decrepit one-carriage Kujukurihama train that ran only a few times each day, carrying passengers to the sparse fishing communities along the beach. 'It must be the same train I took with Hijikata,' Richie told me, pointing to the ancient carriage's baggage area which held two black goats. As we entered the marine landscape, white light flooded the carriage, and Richie was smiling and emanating happiness, in that momentary intermission from Tokyo, as though that light and absence had annulled the intervening decades since his last journey to Kujukurihama. He consulted with the train's conductor and several of the passengers, and we left the train at Naruto station, then began the long walk over the marine flatlands, between thorn-trees blown into horizontal contortions by the Pacific typhoons. It reminded me of the walk to the Dungeness beach on the south coast of England where the filmmaker Derek Jarman had lived, alongside the Dungeness nuclear power station; no nuclear power plants were visible from Kujukurihama, but to the north, Japan's first-built nuclear plant was located, the UK-designed Tokai power-station (still under construction at the time of WARGAMES' filming), and further north still, the Fukushima Daiichi nuclear power plant.

Soon, we were standing on the Kujukurihama black-sand beach, extending far to the north and south, and disappearing into mists at either end. The fishing village where Hijikata had assembled the boys now appeared derelict, eroded to a few wooden shacks, and Richie told me he imagined the fifteen boys in his film, now in their forties, had relocated to Tokyo long ago to escape the hard life of the beach's fishermen, now running *pachinko* parlours in Asakusa, day-labouring in San'ya district, or else sleeping in cardboard-box houses in the Ueno park. 'Maybe I've met them again there,' Richie laughed. The beach was deserted, apart from the sudden roaring transits of miniature roofless jeeps driven at speed by young figures in rubber wetsuits, replacing the transits of the conflict-seared boys of Richie's film. He was able to pinpoint the shooting location exactly through the presence of a large offshore black rock, seen in the film at its end as fourteen of the fifteen boys race away from their site of killing and vanish.

We walked along the ocean's edge where the boys' elated runs take place in the film. The sea appeared calm, in incandescent midday light that illuminated Richie's smiling face, highlighting the deep fissures in his skin as the digital image-screens of Shinjuku had done on our walk there. I stripped to my swimming-trunks and took a long swim in the cold ocean, while Richie gazed around. I had only seen WARGAMES projected once, at a screening of Richie's films at the Image Forum cinema in Tokyo in the previous autumn. Richie himself had only seen it rarely in recent decades, but he told me that he still dreamed frequently of that beach, and of Hijikata's body as he danced to incite the boys' joyful oblivion about their act of killing; those dreams were the probable source of his happiness to be standing there again. I had no towel and had to simply stand shivering and let the drops of ocean-water gradually dry, though Richie, still radiating pleasure, showed no impatience. As I was drying, I asked him if he could make another film there, from those dreams, but he shook his head: 'That moment was very special, in the 1960s. You could do anything. But that freedom burned out by the end of that decade. Between me and Hijikata, it burned out too.' He told me that throughout the day of shooting WARGAMES, he feared that his 16mm film camera would jam from the salt air or be ripped from his arms by the typhoon gusts. He remembered the way in which he and Hijikata had needed to accelerate the filming as the typhoon struck, but Hijikata had been determined and calm, dancing and incanting stories to beguile the boys between every shot. For Richie, at every moment, Hijikata had transmitted acute, extreme life, along with his obsessions with death. I got dressed again – soon, it would be time to walk back to Naruto station, on the narrow untarmaced road through the marine thorns, but for another moment we stood together on the Kujukurihama beach, engulfed in light and in Richie's memory.

Unlike the filming of HUMAN SACRIFICE, Richie had once written about the filming of WARGAMES, shortly after Hijikata's death in 1986, in his book *Different People*: 'We had been drinking in a small country inn by the sea. It was late summer... I was making a film and he had come along to help – no choreography, just a group of children, some fifteen little boys, to be controlled. The plot involved their killing a goat by accident, while playing at war, then holding a funeral for it. They were then meant to forget all about it, to return to being little boys. One of them, however, stays to watch the sea unearth the corpse. The film was called WARGAMES.' He wrote of how Hijikata – 'so death-filled' – had danced and pointed at his navel, then at those of the boys: 'Soon all the little boys were laughing and pointing at each other, mouths open, eyes half-shut in mirth, and Hijikata still just outside camera range was dancing about, shorts slipping, the spirit of the festival, his navel like a large, comic eye … I see him now, hopping on one foot, then on the other, arms at antic angles.'[10]

All of the films inhabited by Hijikata's body, as experiments with his envisioning of dance and with the status of corporeality, eventually became *his* films, even when he remained invisible, as in WARGAMES, still permeating the film in his directing absence. In many ways, WARGAMES slipped from Richie's grip as its ostensible 'director', through Hijikata's act of thievery in infiltrating it with the overruling aura of his dance. Richie was not alone in losing his film to Hijikata's adept gestures. All of the films of his work, made by filmmakers with their own priorities, became Hijikata's films once his presence within them had overturned every pre-existent priority or agenda, reducing their directors to spectral intermediaries. Often, Hijikata did not actively want those films to be made (though he appears to have been deeply attached to his participation in HUMAN SACRIFICE and WARGAMES), or was indifferent or ambivalent towards them. Even when he was unnamed in those films – as with WARGAMES, which omitted Hijikata's role as co-director on its credits when Richie screened it at 1960s film festivals – they attached themselves to him as primary traces of his work and its experimentation, especially across its first decade.

Once we were almost back in Tokyo, I asked Richie why he had not credited Hijikata's work on WARGAMES, noting that his film-credit absence mirrored his body's intentional exclusion beyond the film frame. Richie told me he had only added the credits rapidly before the film's first festival screening, and anyway hoped it could be seen as his own film. When he eventually prepared WARGAMES for release as a DVD with several other films, in 2003, he spoke on the commentary about Hijikata's pivotal work on that collaboration. On the train, I had wondered if Hijikata's work had been *too* pivotal for Richie's own fierce sense of creative solitude and autonomy. He never gifted a print of the film to Hijikata as he did with the sole print of HUMAN

SACRIFICE, and he and Hijikata worked on no further films, though they remained friends.

Alongside the silent filmic contestation of WARGAMES (Hijikata never reproached Richie for not crediting him, and appeared indifferent to the matter), the film also resonates with multiple corporeal contestations: that of the boys struggling proprietarily over the goat, that of the separated boy's faction set against the killing faction, that of the typhoon's intervention supplanting Richie's filming time, and that between Hijikata's body and Richie's body, or the bodies of the other figures who accompanied Hijikata in that era. In his journals, Richie records a visit he made in 1994 to the opening reception in Yokohama of the museum exhibition *Scream Against the Sky: Japanese Art After 1945* – in which Richie's collaborative work of 1959–62 with Hijikata constituted that of the sole non-Japanese participant in the entire exhibition – and seeing a prominently displayed cast in gold-covered papier-mâché of Hijikata's penis (an exact replica of that used in Hijikata's 1968 performance *Tatsumi Hijikata and the Japanese People: Revolt of the Body*, in which he had danced naked apart from that phallus). Richie wrote: 'I turn to his widow, Ms. Motofuji, a large, commanding and self-possessed woman, and ask her if that is really a cast of Hijikata's cock. [She replies:] "Now, you would be just as good a judge of that as myself".'[11] Akiko Motofuji was widely perceived, by young artists in Tokyo in the late 1950s such as Eikoh Hosoe, as an exceptional dancer and choreographer in her own right – the sole filmic trace of that ascendant work surviving in Richie's HUMAN SACRIFICE – before the expanding reputation of Hijikata's Ankoku Butoh project, based at her Asbestos Studio, cast aside the profile of her own choreography.

In both HUMAN SACRIFICE and WARGAMES, Richie generates an accentuated rendering of Hijikata's body, and of its anatomical, urban-located upheavals, via film, even when that body remains superficially absent, as in their second film together. Ankoku Butoh's origination forms a uniquely interconnected entity of film and dance, along with Hijikata's written manifestoes of provocation that propelled it further into notoriety in Japan's art and dance culture of the early 1960s. Film irresistibly activates corporeality, coalescing dance's fragments but also illuminating dance's shatterings; film incorporates darkness, together with darkness's multiple dimensions in Hijikata's dance, but also possesses the connection to brilliant light that propels dance's sequences into human vision. Richie's films with Hijikata possess an immediacy that emerged from the temporal risk of their imminent annulling – by nightfall in HUMAN SACRIFICE's shooting, by the typhoon's arrival in WARGAMES' shooting – as well as from the volatility which film's encounter with dance ignites.

In Hijikata's collaborations with Richie, film also works to map Hijikata's specific corporeal history against the history of that era's (and contemporary) corporeal Japan, which is anatomised and revealed by film – even against the grain, even against the (separate) intentions of Hijikata and Richie – through the relentless emphasis which those films give to corporeal transmutation, in its urban and marine frameworks. The bodies in those films are in intimate contact with the particular configuration of Japan at that moment of its preoccupations with renewed and reactivated conflicts, with contamination from its industrial (and especially chemical-industrial) proliferations, and with the survival of memory in an encompassing era of memory's obliteration. And above all, those films initiate the positioning of Hijikata's body against the urban space of Tokyo and its edge-lands, configuring that city through the disparate but film-conjoined perceptions of Richie, as an alien resident of Tokyo, and Hijikata, as a constant interrogator of that city. The two collaborations between Hijikata and Richie trace Hijikata's corporeal history against that of Tokyo's warfare-striated history and urban-topographical history at the two exact instants of their filming, forming the first manifestation of the sustained filmic exploration of urban corporeality, via Hijikata's body, that would develop across the 1960s before reaching its most contested form in Hijikata's presence at the 'experimental metropolis' of the 1970 Osaka Expo. That decade-long filmic tracing of Hijikata's urban corporeality also remains a resonant one for all contemporary envisionings of Tokyo's current endangered memory, its renewed dangers of contamination and erasure, and its engrained strata of conflict and slaughter.

Hijikata's films, from his collaboration with Richie in 1959 onwards, form awry, fragmented and shattered apertures into the entities of corporeality and urban space, operating through film's integral non-linearity and its guiding sense of aberration. As such, those films comprise intimate counterparts to dance's own gestures. The long-time unseenness and near-forgottenness of Hijikata's filmic collaborations with Richie – resolved only through Richie's last-gasp concern in the 2000s with resuscitating those films, through his digital transfer of HUMAN SACRIFICE and his DVD edition of WARGAMES – remain enduring elements of the films' existence, in their evoking of the obscure, invisible or lost bodies of Ankoku Butoh, especially Hijikata's own body. Those films conjured by Hijikata and Richie are now all the more illuminating and darkly irradiating for their contemporary spectators – in their capacity corporeally to position Hijikata's work against the great transmutations of 1960s urban Japan – through film's essential awryness, fragmentation and shatteredness.

Notes

1   John Dower, *Embracing Defeat: Japan in the Aftermath of World War II*, London: Penguin, 1999, pages 174–75.

2   Miryam Sas, *Experimental Arts in Postwar Japan: Moments of Encounter, Engagement, and Imagined Return*, Cambridge MA/London: Harvard University Press, 2011, page 56.

3   William Marotti, *Money, Trains and Guillotines: Art and Revolution in 1960s Japan*, Durham NC/London: Duke University Press, 2013, page 132.

4   Miryam Sas, 'Intermedia, 1955–1970', in Doryun Chong (ed.), *Tokyo 1955-70: A New Avant-Garde*, New York NY: New York Museum of Modern Art, 2012, page 141.

5   Ibid, page 139.

6   Donald Richie, letter to the author, 29 February 2008.

7   Nam June Paik, 'To Catch Up or Not to Catch Up with the West: Hijikata and Hi Red Center', in Alexandra Monroe (ed.), *Japanese Art After 1945: Scream Against the Sky*, New York NY: Abrams, 1994, page 77.

8   Dower, (see note 1), page 493.

9   Donald Richie and Leza Lowitz (ed.), *The Japan Journals: 1947–2004*, Berkeley CA: Stone Bridge Press, 2004, page 120.

10 Donald Richie, *Different People*, Tokyo: Kodansha, pages 98–101.

11 Richie and Lowitz (ed.), (see note 9), page 315.

PART TWO

Motion Photography: *Kamaitachi*

At the instant when a sequence of still images – of the human body, of city environments – is driven into movement, its spectator experiences an extraordinary ocular and sensory propulsion in which perceptions of corporeality and urban space are often conjoined. The first experimenters with enacting that transition for spectators from the still image to the moving image – Eadweard Muybridge, with his glass-disc public projections in San Francisco from the beginning of the 1880s, and the Skladanowsky Brothers and Lumière Brothers, with their celluloid projections in Berlin and Paris from 1895 – intentionally emphasised it and made it a pivotal moment of their projections, so that those spectators who had seen that transition before now anticipated it, and those who had not seen it before underwent its unprecedented shock. But that activating moment can also be overturned, within the desire to experiment in the sensitised interzone between moving images and still images, and spectators who expect to experience a film may instead be confronted with artworks that – drawing on film's propulsive motion and dynamic deploying of space – reverse backwards across moving-image time, returning to a form of still-image photography that retains vital motion: motion photography. That reversal may be variably motivated by preoccupations with technological innovation, exhibition environments, finance, or the aesthetic capacities of the large-scale book; in every instance, it demands that the spectator, imbued with film, and especially with films of dance, now undertakes a sharp adjustment or contortion of the eye. Such a reversal, or adept manoeuvre, into motion photography can take the spectator into unforeseen or outlandish terrains.

In 1965, Hijikata, together with the young filmmaker/photographer Eikoh Hosoe, decided to return to the outlandish terrain of Japan's north, where they had both been born, for part of a project entitled *Kamaitachi* (*The Sickle-Weasel*), whose Japanese title is also used for its English-language book publication. The *kamaitachi* is an invisible demonic intruder into the cultivated fields of northern Japan, incessantly invoked in fear in the era of the childhoods of Hijikata and Hosoe, but already vanished and obsolete by the 1960s (and all the more fearsome and mythical for its vanishing). The *kamaitachi* has the attribute of a weasel in that it will never take the same path twice, and its teeth are as sharp as the sickles used in harvesting, lacerating the farmers' legs during the moments when small storms or tornadoes whip up in the isolated, often frozen fields of the north. In order to do its work of wounding, the *kamaitachi* must enter the peasants' lands, approach their houses and even steal the farmers' children. It is too invisible and too unseizably fast to be rendered in film's frames-per-second linearity, but photography's erratic mix of light and darkness, alongside its malleable ability to operate across the future, past and present, and with its own image-based devilry, has the capacity to manifest it. The *kamaitachi* is then caught in the image, and is vulnerable too to being trapped, even transported to the city.

Hosoe had already made a 16mm black-and-white film with Hijikata, and he initially began to envision *Kamaitachi* as a film, but without the resources needed to make a film, and for other reasons, he instead undertook a lengthy photographic collaboration with Hijikata to generate a large-format book that was intended to *look* filmic, with strange and awry but closely interconnected sequences of action, and an expanded, borderless form of printing of its images on the pages, darkly accentuated and intended to engulf the spectator's eye. *Kamaitachi* presents a corporeal journey that begins in the urban space of Tokyo and returns there, to its peripheral areas, for its final sequences, but inbetween it travels to the north, to an isolated, inland region of rice cultivation in Akita prefecture. There, Hijikata's figure, incorporating that of the *kamaitachi*, runs headlong through the panoramic expanses of rice fields and wastelands, carrying a child he has stolen from the farmers' families. He also performs for them, enticing and ensnaring them, but through that intimacy (and his trapping in the lithe photographic image), he loses his invisibility and becomes vulnerable to being snared himself.

Hosoe's distinctive medium – that of the large-scale photography book that wants (or at an early stage, desired) to be a film – is distinct in time from the 1890s experiments across the boundaries of photography and moving images, but still strongly resonates with those experiments; in its immediate moment, that medium collides with the work of the filmmaker/photographer William Klein, especially his Tokyo sequential urban street photography (which included sequences of Hijikata's work) of 1961, and also with Chris Marker's film composed almost entirely of filmed still images, LA JETÉE, from 1962. *Kamaitachi* also connects intimately with the work of other photographers – especially Daido Moriyama, who had been Hosoe's assistant in 1961–64, during the era of his photographing of Yukio Mishima – who were beginning to travel to the north, to Aomori and Hokkaido as well as Akita, and would continue to do so through the 1970s, determined to explore and reconfigure the 'wild' north as a negation of the (post-1970 Osaka Expo) riot-free, pacified megalopolises of Tokyo and Osaka.

Hijikata's film with Hosoe, NAVEL AND A-BOMB, was shot in the summer of 1960, two years before WARGAMES, on the Ohara beach to the south of Kujukurihama, on the same eastern coast of the Chiba peninsula. In July of 1998, I travelled to the film's beach location, this time alone, though I had invited Richie, but he complained of the near 40-degree humid heat and proposed instead a cool nocturnal walk through San'ya, adding with a Genet-like adroitness that he had always felt ambivalent towards Hosoe's film, perversely convinced it had thieved elements from WARGAMES, though he was well aware it had preceded his second film with Hijikata, and that the similarities between the two films were generated by the enduring tenacity of Hijikata's corporeal obsession, and by his own. Richie had

Ill. 4 – Navel and A-Bomb, 1960, filmed by Eikoh Hosoe.

attended the first projection of Hosoe's film in October 1960, at the Yurakucho Video Hall, as part of a 'Jazz Film Workshop' event, and had even prepared English-language sub-titles for the film.

The Ohara beach was much closer to a town than Richie's Kujukurihama location, though Ohara town itself is now merged with adjacent towns and has vanished (at least in name), along with the Osato village whose fishing families' shacks of 1962 had eroded to a few windsurfers' shelters by the time Richie and I had travelled there, two or three months earlier. The shooting location on the beach – as with Wargames, identifiable by distinctive offshore rocks – was empty, perhaps due to the extreme heat, though as I descended the cliff path, I was warned by locals, shielding themselves with umbrellas from the fierce sun, that swimming there was always dangerous and rarely attempted. The sun was shimmering against the peaks of the strong waves, as it does in Navel and A-Bomb, so I swam anyway, soon exhausted by the waves and drying instantly in the heat, spreadeagled back on the black sand.

The black sand at Ohara beach configures naturally into the shape of gatherings of small mounds or near-pyramids, resembling the goat's burial mound built by the boys of WARGAMES. I walked to the edge of the beach and ran my hands over the smooth sand of the five mounds that had appeared at the ocean's edge. In many ways, WARGAMES forms a more sombre, streamlined variant of NAVEL AND A-BOMB, with its rigorous retraction from visibility of Hijikata's body (present in Hosoe's film, intermittently naked, and at one point performing the navel dance which, unfilmed by Richie, propels the WARGAMES boys into hilarity), heightening that sense of severity. Richie also excludes the presence of poetry, which bursts out in Hosoe's film in surreal sequences invoking atomic disaster. Both films contain their gangs of young boys, the nine of them naked in Hosoe's film (while Richie keeps his filmed boys in their swimming-trunks), and crawling together across the sand in the film's final part, filmed by Hosoe from the cliff top overhead, before amassing into a heap. One boy's navel is sealed with a taped 'X' of negation, which Hijikata emerges from the ocean to steal, leading the boy to weep in denudation at its loss. Hosoe's film also has its animal presence: four goats, carried into the ocean by four fishermen, then two goats, carried along the ocean's edge by Hijikata and his young collaborator Yoshito Ohno (who had appeared with him in the *Forbidden Colours* performances in the previous year), along with a cow that screens away the bodies of Hijikata and Ohno, and a chicken whose decapitated dance of scrabbled claws at the ocean's edge incites a clawed dance of Hijikata's fingers across his oiled torso, generating a raw language of gestures inscribed in the oil. The four fishermen from the Ohara town perform their rear-facing dance, choreographed by Hijikata, demonstrating a precision that is absent from WARGAMES, with its urgent, abbreviated shooting.

The correspondences between NAVEL AND A-BOMB and WARGAMES show just how much the preoccupations of Hijikata's film with Richie belonged to Hijikata, especially his obsession with the navel as an instrument of loss and negation, as an aperture into death, as well as a means to manoeuvre the axis of the body into a hilarious state of contortion. It appears to have been Hijikata who brought the presence (and deaths) of animals into both films, and Hijikata's collective choreography of the boys in both films is distinctively his own, while Richie's concern to isolate one figure away from the others, for that separated figure's killing in HUMAN SACRIFICE and its role as a witness to killing in WARGAMES, transmits his own preoccupation. NAVEL AND A-BOMB also lacks the compulsive filming of faces and especially facial plains which Richie deploys in his two films with Hijikata. Hosoe gave his film a soundtrack of jazz, explosions and cacophony, while Richie composed his own ritualistic music and attempted to simulate the typhoon that had disrupted his filming.

Although Richie never knew Hosoe well, meeting him only through the intermediation of their mutual friends Hijikata and Mishima, he contributed to the film's public profile; Hosoe was far more determined than Richie to generate an international profile for his film. As well as his preparing of sub-titles for NAVEL AND A-BOMB when it began to be projected in international film festivals in the 1960s, Richie also eventually wrote an essay about it in 2000 for the catalogue of a retrospective exhibition of Hosoe's work, emphasising the film's aura of experiment and negation, and situating it in Japan's film-cultural history: 'Around 1960 a decade of extraordinary artistic activity began in Japan ... Among other manifestations was the sudden emergence of the experimental film, a genre hitherto little known in Japan ... The production methods [of NAVEL AND A-BOMB] were very much of their time. Hosoe had written a script, now lost, and he himself helped photograph and edit the film. Fellow cinematographer [Meiki Higashikata] was an out-of-work college classmate and Hosoe used a handheld Bolex.' Richie remained fascinated by the moment in the film in which the taped 'X' is ripped by Hijikata from the weeping boy's navel: 'The navel, symbol and scar of life itself, is marked by an X. In Japan as elsewhere an X can mean exclusion or

Ill. 5 – NAVEL AND A-BOMB, 1960, filmed by Eikoh Hosoe – Hijikata steal-ing the child's navel by the ocean.

deletion ... In the Hosoe film, however, it is the Xs themselves which are eradicated.'[1] In an interview in 1998, Hosoe told me: 'All the film reflects is my sheer hatred of the atomic bomb, and my attempt to come to terms with the complexity of Hijikata's body ... Whenever a negation is erased, especially for children, some kind of liberation is possible. Everything is torn open. But that can lead to yet more disaster.'

In many ways, NAVEL AND A-BOMB eludes Richie's idea of it constituting one of Japan's first experimental films, alongside his own work and that of Takahiko Iimura (whom Richie saw as a young upstart) and others. NAVEL AND A-BOMB is such a strange, non-linear film of aberrant fragments that it appears resistant to incorporation into an experimental-film geneal-ogy. Many previous works across Japan's film history – such as Teinosuke Kinugasa's A PAGE OF MADNESS, 1926, projected in Tokyo then lost for decades but rediscovered and repro-jected, in 1971 – also demonstrate an experimentation which moves beyond film and photography, exploring and annulling boundaries and definitions of corporeality and madness. But

Richie's citing of 1960 as the year precipitating a unique decade of exploratory film and of activism-generated involvement with moving-image culture serves to pinpoint the distinctiveness of that tumultuous decade, which exactly coincided with Hijikata's own vital experiments with film.

Hosoe was an intensely curious young artist even before his involvements with Hijikata and Mishima, eager to be involved in all elements of Tokyo's arts cultures from the early 1950s onwards. He had first visited Akiko Motofuji's Asbestos Studio in Meguro in 1955 and began to photograph her in that same year; he knew her as a close friend long before Hijikata began to appear at the Asbestos Studio and eventually transformed it into the base for his own Ankoku Butoh work. Although born in Japan's north, Hosoe grew up in the north-eastern Tokyo districts in which the final images of *Kamaitachi* were photographed; his father was a shrine caretaker, at the Yotsugi-Shirahige shrine in the Katsushika district, as well as an amateur photographer. Hosoe was evacuated for one year during the firebombing of Tokyo and returned, four weeks after the war's end, at the age of twelve, to find most of the city razed, though his family house had survived. He became determined to learn fluent English, and in 1949–50 he frequented the US military bases close to Tokyo and the adjacent towns, such as Yokosuka, which US naval personnel visited for entertainment; many of his first photographs were taken on the bases and in the surrounding urban environments. He became a close friend and supporter of Hijikata during the period when Hijikata's attempt to develop an innovative corporeal art medium with criminal potential was still fragile, and Hosoe created two brochures of his photographs in July 1960 and September 1961 designed to expand the profile of Hijikata's project (still known as 'Dance Experience' rather than 'Ankoku Butoh' at that moment), both titled *Eikoh Hosoe's Portfolio Dedicated to Tatsumi Hijikata*.

It was through his friendship with Akiko Motofuji that Hosoe was able to assemble the participants and animals for NAVEL AND A-BOMB; Motofuji had worked as a teacher at a dance studio in Ohara, and had connections there. As a result, the film appears less spare and sparse than WARGAMES, whose participants had to be conjured up in a few minutes by Hijikata on his and Richie's arrival at Kujukurihama. But Hosoe's film was undertaken with similar brevity, over two days, and as with Richie's film, with no money. The cliff-enclosed beach at Ohara, with its strong sunlight, generated an illuminated aura for NAVEL AND A-BOMB, distinct from the mist-effaced, typhoon-darkened environment of WARGAMES.

While Richie's two films with Hijikata transmit relentless, abbreviated narrative incidents of separation and killing, Hosoe's collaboration with Hijikata intimates more of the oblique and fragmentary corporeal clashes of Hijikata's emergent dance project. For Hosoe this was intentional: he had no interest in narrative cinema and (as he told me in 1998) saw no precedents for his film in film itself, only in art and dance. He interposed jarring sequences into the actions unfolding on his beach location: archival footage of an atomic bomb explosion and a recreation with black fluid of another atomic explosion, as well as sequences of poetry. The film is initiated in conflict, with disembodied arms contesting an apple poised on one of the black-sand mounds of Ohara beach; one combatant's arm appears badly scarred, its flesh scraped. That apple's contestation precipitates a nuclear explosion, and the apple will reappear in the film's final shot, now abandoned in the water at the ocean's edge. In filming the decapitated chicken (again, killed by Hijikata) in its sightless transits into and out of the ocean, Hosoe focuses on the spasmodic gestures of its claws, transferred to the human body through Hijikata's convulsive scratches into the oil on his torso: final, terminal gestures, for a dance form that is only beginning to animate itself.

Once the film is over, it leaves behind only a sensory residue of dislocated images, so that it can be perceived in new ways at each projection. Its aura is that of a film in combustion, burning up the autonomous filmic world it has created, in its disengagement from forming a coherent document or record of

Hijikata's emergent Ankoku Butoh project. It mediates instead a detrital ocular afterburn, constellated with fragments of irresoluble conflict and oscillating abruptly in magnitude from the minuscule last disjointed clawings of its headless chicken to the immense atomic power that (along with firebombing accelerants) had decimated Japan's cities. The film's beach location intensifies and compacts the sensory transmission of those non-narrational fragments of corporeality and conflict. Hosoe told me in 1998 that without the spatial concentration of the beach his film's bodies would appear redundant and diffused; it was rare for him to confront Hijikata's body so full-on, since he usually preferred to photograph him from one side or askew, but using film propelled him into that direct contact.

The photographic historian Mark Holborn notes that Hosoe's obsession with marine and beach landscapes ended abruptly in 1961, the year after the filming of NAVEL AND A-BOMB. He had already returned several times with Hijikata to the beaches on the Chiba coast to develop ideas for future filmic or photographic projects. But on seeing the German-born British photographer Bill Brandt's new book *Perspectives of Nudes*, published that year in the UK by Bodley Head, with its photographs of corporeal elements positioned against marine or cliff landscapes, Hosoe abandoned his work: 'The site of many of Brandt's nudes was a beach. Hosoe knew he could not continue his series.'[2] Later that same year, Hosoe began his portrait collaboration with Yukio Mishima, *Ordeal by Roses*, and his next work with Hijikata, in 1965, with *Kamaitachi*, would focus on their conjoined preoccupations with Tokyo and with Japan's north.

Hosoe filmed Hijikata's work only once, at that first moment, in 1960, but then photographed it relentlessly; his final photographs of Hijikata were taken after his death, in January 1986, with Hijikata in his open coffin at the Asbestos Studio (Hijikata was also filmed anonymously by one of those attending the funeral ceremonies, in bleached footage, with those moving-image sequences capturing the ultimately strange stillness of Hijikata's arrested body, the motion present in the images solely accorded to friends – Tatsuhiko Shibusawa, then Kazuo Ohno – approaching his coffin to touch his face, and the movements of the surrounding crowd veering through the space in their apparent bewilderment). Hosoe adamantly never wanted to document Hijikata's work, only to respond to it in his own corporeal and ocular way; even so, Ankoku Butoh became perceived and understood in great part directly through Hosoe's photographic and filmic sequences of it (he also photographed Hijikata's collaborators, especially Kazuo Ohno). Ankoku Butoh can be seen as an art medium primarily and most valuably of film and photography, rather than as a medium of dance: deeply connected to film and photography, more allied to those two experimental media than to the often standardised and stultified vocabularies of dance, and with its pivotal inspiration for contemporary artists emerging predominantly from filmic and photographic traces of the work of Hijikata and his 1960s collaborators in Tokyo, especially now that he and many of those collaborators are dead. Writing of Hosoe's work, Miryam Sas notes: 'One approach to *butō* that is opened by this work but remains for fuller study: in what ways is *butō* itself as much imbricated in the paradigms of film and photography as in dance?'[3] To go further: Ankoku Butoh is not a dance medium at all, except in its rapport with dance's deaths, but instead an amalgam of its own anatomical acts, the urban (or beyond-urban) space of its performance, and its incorporation in film and photography, especially the moment of ignition when film transmutates into photography, or when photography transmutates into film. In *Kamaitachi*, Hosoe and Hijikata explored that moment of ignition, in which one medium vanishes and another emerges.

That volatile instant of oscillation between moving images and photography already possessed a long history in the 1960s, and was a particular focus of experimentation in the period immediately preceding the years 1965–68, in which Hosoe and

Hijikata created *Kamaitachi* as a work that apparently reversed backwards into photography from their filmic collaboration of 1960, but actually interrogated new, unforeseen ground, especially in its envisioning of the journey and interval between Tokyo's urban space and the 'wild', urban-exceeding space of Japan's north.

At a certain point in Eadweard Muybridge's public moving-image projection lectures, held in the US and Europe between 1880 and 1893, he would move between showing still photographic images to his audiences and, through the sudden activation of his self-designed projector, the Zoopraxiscope, project moving images in the form of his circular glass discs. Invariably, his audiences were astonished. Muybridge's first projections were of horses in motion, but as the 1880s went on, and especially after his years obsessively photographing brief sequences of human and animal actions with multiple cameras, at his open-air laboratory in Philadelphia and at the Philadelphia zoo he amassed innumerable other sequences: dances (including dances of naked figures), animal and bird movement, awry and contorted movements of human figures suffering from polio and other impairments (which inspired Hijikata as well as artists such as Francis Bacon), as well as the cities in which he worked, San Francisco above all.

In 1891, Muybridge extensively toured cities in Central Europe such as Berlin and Vienna, always privileging the instant in his projection events when, in darkness, he transformed the still photographic image into the moving image. He stood directly alongside his screen to accentuate that moment and to receive the adulation it precipitated. In 1893, he designed his own moving-image auditorium, the Zoopraxographical Hall, for construction in the Midway Plaisance area of the Chicago World's Columbian Exposition; for the first time, the audience entering his auditorium knew they would witness moving-image projections, and that the photographic image had been superseded and appeared obsolete. But perversely, on his return to his hometown of Kingston-upon-Thames in England after his Chicago projections (unaccountably, Muybridge told his relatives that he was returning from Japan, rather than from the US), Muybridge reverted to photography for public presentations of his work, abandoning the use of the Zoopraxiscope moving-image projector and returning to photographic slide projection. Muybridge had also been one of the initiators of the light-manipulation of skies and clouds during photographic development processes; he often added an intense darkening to the skies he photographed, beginning with his San Francisco skies of the 1870s; Hosoe, inspired by Muybridge's work, frequently darkened his Akita skies (and in a later project, his Tokyo skies) almost to near-black opacity, above Hijikata's rice field headlong runs, in the pages of *Kamaitachi*.

Muybridge projected his images from glass discs; the first public celluloid-based moving-image projections were undertaken by two Berlin conjurors, Max and Emil Skladanowksy, in the ballroom of the Central Hotel in Berlin in December 1895. The Skladanowskys made their own films, of dances and of the urban industrial space of northern Berlin. As with Muybridge, the Skladanowskys accentuated the moment at the outset of their spectacles when they would freeze their twin-lens Bioskop projector's momentum so that it appeared they had only still images to show their audience, before unleashing the movement of their films, projected in repetition in loops. That conjuration appeared all the more outlandish since the Skladanowskys always projected their moving-image sequences unseen, from behind their screen, which had to be doused in water immediately before the projection; the audience in the ballroom never saw the filmmakers until the end of the projection, when a final film, APOTHEOSIS, was shown of their two filmed figures emerging from either side of the screen as cinematic divinities to receive their applause, instantly overlayered with their live, corporeal figures making that same transit. Press accounts of the Skladanowskys' projections emphasised how the audience perceived their films as spectral, and as holding ghost bodies of dancers, so that when the filmmakers' own bodies manifested themselves at the projection's end, film's ghosts became tangible bodies, but still more spectral. By 1897 the Skladanowskys had vanished from film, inept magicians overtaken by adroit competitors; one brother, Max, reversed backwards from filmic innovation into photographic time, switching from filmmaking to the already obsolete medium of the flick-book.

Along with Hosoe's photographs of Hijikata's 1960s work, those by William Klein, taken in 1961 at the Asbestos Studio and across urban locations around Tokyo, resonate intimately with that era of Hijikata's work that is otherwise transmitted via moving images, through Richie's films as well as Hosoe's Navel and A-Bomb. Klein also oscillated between film and photography; in 1957, he had made Broadway by Light, filming the eruptions of neon hoardings in New York. He saw himself at that moment as an urban image-hoarder, intentionally inept and maladroit, scouring the raw streets of New York to seize images as immediately and confrontationally as he could, across photography and film. His large-format New York photography book *Life is Good & Good for You in New York: Trance Witness Revels* was published in an edition in Japan in 1957 and deeply impressed Hosoe and other Tokyo artists; Klein then extended his urban interrogation via askew corporeal photographic sequences to other cities, including Rome and Moscow, via Tokyo, where he spent several months in 1961. As with Hosoe's *Kamaitachi*, Klein's four photographic city-books are simultaneously films, their sequences condensed and bursting at the books' seams.

Klein visited the Asbestos Studio, and photographed Hijikata, along with Kazuo Ohno, in a sequence of over 200 images, now stored at his archive in Paris. Several of the photographs were incorporated into his *Tokyo* city-book, published in 1964. Klein told me in 2006 that Hijikata (and Ohno) spoke incessantly to him of Genet's work: 'They were crazy, crazy enthusiasts.' The small studio constrained Klein's expansive spatial imperatives, and he soon insisted they leave it and go out into the streets (though he emphasised that Hijikata was also eager to do so); Klein photographed Hijikata over the course of that day – evidently as intense, in its way, as the film-shooting days of that era of Richie and Hosoe with Hijikata – in the alleyways of Meguro, then eastwards into central Tokyo, on the Ginza avenue and in the alleyways of the Shimbashi district, where Hijikata and Ohno performed an image-condensed variant of Genet's novel *Our Lady of the Flowers* solely for Klein's camera, startling passers-by, with Hijikata in a whole-head black mask and black shorts, and Ohno in a flowered hat and dress. For Klein, his experience of photographing the corporeal insurgency emanating from Hijikata's figure, across that day's accelerated transits through Tokyo's urban space, possessed a hallucinatory intensity: 'Yes, it could have been a film,' he told me. 'A chase, a ghost story, a funeral.' Unfamiliar with Tokyo, he had been curious to see if they would all be arrested, but with New York nonchalance, he didn't care.

Chris Marker travelled frequently to Tokyo from Paris in that era, with the initial intention of filming the Olympic Games of 1964 and the great urban transmutation preceding it. His films and photography (dark-skied, as with Muybridge's work) also impressed Hosoe in the years before his work on *Kamaitachi*. As a book editor in Paris, with his influential series Petite Planète, Marker had first published Klein's New York city-book in 1956 after it was declined by US photography publishers. Klein recalled visiting Marker's office in Paris to arrange the publication with him: 'There were spaceships hanging everywhere from threads; he wore futurist pistols in his belt. And he looked like a Martian.'[4] In 1962 in Paris, over one weekend, Marker made his film LA JETÉE, in which a survivor of Paris's near-future apocalyptic warfare is transported back through time by his tormentors to the undestroyed Paris, where he meets a woman and walks with her through the deserted museums and parks of that pre-spectral city; Klein appears briefly in the film as one of several figures from the future who have the ability to reactivate Paris. The entire film is made of sequences of still images, apart from one momentary moving-image fragment in

Ill. 6 – Hijikata, Tokyo, 1965, photographed by Eikoh Hosoe.

which the woman's eyes are filmed opening on her awakening, as astonishing as the instant between photographic projection and moving-image projection. In the final sequence, the man is killed by his tormentors on the pier at Paris's Orly airport, under immense, black-clouded skies. Thirty years after the film's making, a photography book was published in 1992 that assembled the still images of LA JETÉE. Of all of Hijikata's films that he had seen, Marker most admired Richie's WARGAMES, though he only ever saw it once (projected for him by Richie himself, at his house in Tokyo in 1964): he far preferred the subtraction of Hijikata's body, and the resulting sense of a haunting void, to the over-explicitness of seeing Hijikata dance on film. From Hosoe's work, Marker particularly recalled a photograph he had once seen of Hijikata in the dawn streets of Shinjuku, close to the location of Marker's own bar, also called La Jeteé, which I had visited with Richie; Hosoe recalled that, after a night of drinking in 1965, shortly before they left for the north and the *Kamaitachi* project, Hijikata had persuaded a milk-delivery boy to loan him his bicycle for a moment, and Hijikata then precariously circled the tram tracks, barefooted and almost asleep, passers-by staring, his figure photographed by Hosoe against the sign-imprinted facades of buildings on the far side of the avenue.

Hosoe underwent a seminal upheaval in his work's approach between the filming of NAVEL AND A-BOMB in 1960 and the photographing of *Kamaitachi* in 1965–68. He was commissioned in 1961 by Yukio Mishima, who had admired his work with Hijikata, to create a sequence of portraits of him. Mishima was by then already celebrated, his work's reputation in international ascendancy but also often viewed with outrage in Japan. Between November 1961 and the spring of 1962, Hosoe (assisted by Daido Moriyama) undertook his project *Ordeal by Roses* with Mishima's full complicity. They began in the garden of Mishima's baroque house in Tokyo, with Mishima's body encircled and confined by the coils of his garden hose; Hosoe recalled: 'He didn't blink until I had exposed two rolls of film.'[5] Later in the series, Mishima's body was encircled by ropes. They pursued their work at the Asbestos Studio; Hijikata and Akiko Motofuji appear in several images. Hosoe's approach to Mishima's body has none of the sheer propulsion he would soon generate for Hijikata's figure in *Kamaitachi*; his images of Mishima decelerate into multi-layered obsessive anatomisations of sexual flesh, filmic in their hallucinatory aura. The sessions were technically demanding for Hosoe: he projected slides of paintings by Giorgione and other works over Mishima's body, often using several slide projectors simultaneously, and also amassed multiple superimpositions into single, condensed images. He created numerous apertures in his images: accentuated eyes, orifices within eyes. The first, large-format edition of *Ordeal by Roses* appeared in 1963 (at that time Hosoe gave it the English-language title *Killed by Roses*); a new edition, designed by the artist Tadanori Yokoo (who also designed posters for Hijikata's performances) was in preparation at the moment of Mishima's spectacular death in November 1970, and Hosoe deferred its appearance until Mishima's widow assured him that Mishima had anticipated the new edition with such pleasure that Hosoe was compelled to release it in January 1971.

I visited Hosoe's studio in the Tokyo district of Yotsuya in the days following my visit to Ohara beach. Hosoe's studio was crammed with the residues of his work, and books by other photographers; many of his own large-scale photography books had been issued in limited, expensive editions and he had long ago given his copies of them away to friends. After we had spoken about his work with Hijikata on NAVEL AND A-BOMB, which he remembered vividly, Hosoe had thoroughly entered a propulsive momentum of dialogue and wanted to go on: 'Ask me more questions ... Ask me anything ...'. And so we talked about *Kamaitachi* too, and the strange interval that exists between filmmaking and photography.

After NAVEL AND A-BOMB, Hosoe had wanted to continue to make films, but his marine-located projects had been abandoned, and Mishima had wanted only photographic portraits that could be manipulated, via Hosoe's lens and darkroom overlayerings, into the terrain of his obsessions, to the maximum, unadulterated degree. Hosoe reflected on the extent to which his initial planning of *Kamaitachi* had envisaged it as a potentially filmic project. Experimental filmmaking was uniquely possible in 1960s Tokyo, through the collaborative imagination and generosity of friends (as Richie's films demonstrate: he ceased making films in 1968, when, in an era of increasing activist turmoil and state power pressure, that generosity was consumed). But Hijikata himself had shown no interest in *Kamaitachi* taking the form of a film; by 1965, the initial enthusiasm for film that entered his filmic work with Richie and Hosoe, with its intensive durations, had gone. *Kamaitachi* was envisaged from its origins as a long-term project, involving several journeys to Akita prefecture. Finance and exhibition were also issues: films such as HUMAN SACRIFICE and NAVEL AND A-BOMB were projected only a handful of times in that era in Tokyo, at venues such as the Sogetsu Art Center, and otherwise efforts needed to be made to present them at the rare experimental film festivals that had begun to take place in Europe, such as that instigated by Jacques Ledoux (who appears as the time-traveller's principal tormenter in Marker's LA JETÉE), in the Belgian resort-town of Knokke-le-Zoute. By contrast, a photographic project could be published in a large format (as with Klein's city-books) that resonated with filmic projection and exhibited in Tokyo's art galleries, which were often housed in department stores at railway-station junctions.

In Hosoe's memory, the preoccupations of *Kamaitachi* could have been transformed into the space and movement of film, in 1965, but he had had in mind no specific films (neither experimental films nor studio films) that could have helped to coalesce those preoccupations, which he remembered as emerging equally and directly from his and Hijikata's experience of their childhoods in the north. If *Kamaitachi* had been a film, it would have been one without precedents, sources or parallels. Hosoe had only one photographic assistant, and no resources for a film crew. But his assistant's record of Hosoe's photographing of *Kamaitachi* shows how dynamic and exacting that photographic act had been; in several photographs, Hosoe is seen leaping at speed behind Hijikata in the Akita rice fields, leaping still higher than Hijikata, in the same moment as he photographs. The ghost film of *Kamaitachi* had manifested itself only momentarily in 1965 dialogues with Hijikata, such as the one which ended with Hijikata's dawn milk-delivery bicycle ride, before transmutating into its realization in a hybrid form of photography in which film's sequences and preoccupations remained impaled.

Hosoe had especially wanted to instil corporeality into his images, extending from the body of Hijikata to the cityscapes of the peripheral areas of Tokyo which he photographed for *Kamaitachi*'s first and last sequences, and to the Akita rural landscapes, with their black earth and waterlogged rice fields. He told me that he had extended that preoccupation more fully, into a large-scale project that followed *Kamaitachi*, without

Hijikata: *Simmon: A Private Landscape* (which I had not seen at the time of our 1998 meeting, since Hosoe abandoned it in the early 1970s, and it was only published, retaining its status of abandonment, in 2012), with its askew blurrings and overlaps between the figure of the young transvestite Simmon Yotsuya and the city wastelands he inhabits around the eastern rivers of Tokyo. And then again much later, with Hosoe's long stays in Barcelona to photograph Antoni Gaudi's architecture, so corporeal in itself that it needed no intersecting human figure, for his 1977–84 project *The Cosmos of Gaudi*.

At the moments of *Kamaitachi*'s photographing, in Tokyo and on three journeys to Akita between 1965 and 1968, Hosoe was convinced that the corporeality of the project's urban location and rural landscape would both imminently disappear, and that the near-vanishing itself generated the compulsive momentum and aberrant spectrality of his images. But, in a further aberration, those locations persisted, and in 2019, the vertical rice-drying racks upon which Hijikata's *kamaitachi* positions himself in the village of Tashiro to search for victims, remain intact, just as Tokyo's Togenuki Jizo temple in Sugamo, where Hijikata's magnified eye is studied, and the wooden houses and temples of Katsushika district (where Hosoe spent the Tokyo years of his childhood) endure, at least in part. That anticipated vanishing is an ongoing, perpetual and resilient one; in 2016, when the Kamaitachi Museum was established on the site of the project's photographing (located in a merchant's house whose interior, a *kamaitachi* hide out, appears in several of the photographs), a contemporary farmer, interviewed for the film documentary accompanying that opening, insists that it will all finally vanish soon, everything around him will disappear.

On 26 November 1965, Hijikata and Hosoe took a train between Akita (where they had visited Hijikata's birthplace) and Yuzawa stations, then a taxi via the Nanamagari Pass, through a mountainous area, to the then remote village of Tashiro in the south-east of Akita prefecture. Hosoe, holding a strip he had shown me from the photographic negatives of *Kamaitachi*, told me that he and Hijikata – equally adept at securing the participation of strangers – announced to the village's farmers that they were from a film or television company (though all they had with them were Hosoe's photographic cameras), and so the peasants and their families would need to do as Hosoe and Hijikata asked. Finally, Hosoe's immediate memory was that of the exhilaration of working with Hijikata, who would always impede their work through the tenacious insistence of his re-imagining of its next moment.

After speaking with Hosoe, I went to a photographic archive in Tokyo's Ebisu district and held an extremely rare, pristine copy of the original edition of *Kamaitachi* (Hosoe himself only owned two well-worn copies). After turning the pages, my fingers had turned blue from the book's ink, and the massive book still emitted a strong, nearly tangible smell of that blue ink and of the darkened ink inside used to render Hosoe's photographs (later, the decayed film of Hijikata's Expo '70 film would emit an even stronger smell). I was holding a seminal artefact of Hijikata's corporeality.

The book, published by the prominent Tokyo experimental-arts publisher Gendaishichosha in November 1969, is enclosed in a hard white card slipcase with details in English on one side, in blue and black typescript: 'photography Eikoh Hosoe/dance Tatsumi Hijikata/preface Shuzo Takiguchi/poem Toyoichiro Miyoshi/design Ikko Tanaka'; on the other side, the book's title, also in English, is given in capital letters: 'KAMAITACHI', in dark-blue characters surrounded by two light-blue patches covering the title elements 'KAM' and 'AITACHI'. The book's spine gives the title, along with 'photography: Eikoh Hosoe' and 'dance: Tatsumi Hijikata' in Japanese. To lift and manipulate the heavy book demands manoeuvres and contortions: in some ways, an intricate dance of reading. Its vertically elongated format needs to be switched to a horizontal axis whenever an image inside is oriented to the horizontal. All of the photographic pages require the opening, towards the right, of fold-outs in order to view them, as in a reconfigured, lateral opening and closing of an eye. The pages enclosing those fold-outs' complex arrangement are printed in bright blue ink. The first fold-out contains the title information, and the second and third hold the essay of the surrealist poet Shuzo Takiguchi, first in Japanese and then in his own idiosyncratic English translation of his text. Every photograph in *Kamaitachi* (mostly one photograph to each page, though a few pages hold several interconnected photographs) extends to the pages' far edges, and each page is enclosed in an elongated folded form, opened via the blue-coated reverse of the photograph; each photograph's folded form is attached to the following page with a narrow vertical flap, blue on the front and black on the back (though for the material at the front of the book – the title page and then Takiguchi's text in Japanese and English – the vertical flap is blue on the front but white on the back). Each photograph is folded vertically along its centre, and in its extension by its spectator's hand forms an elongated screen, as though for film projection; whenever more than one image appears on a page, to comprise several sequential images, the page takes on the form of a split-screen projection. Most images are horizontally oriented, but a few – including *Kamaitachi*'s first and last images – are vertically oriented (but still printed horizontally in the book), requiring a special contortion of the eye or body, or an arduous repositioning of the book, in order to view them. All of the photographs (or each page with several photographs) are numbered, 1–34, in black, at the top end of their page's flap.

Kamaitachi's 5th photographic page shows Hijikata's abduction of what Hosoe, in his acknowledgement notes at the book's end, calls a 'fashion model', Asako Sai, into the Asbestos Studio's entrance, alongside a hand-painted sign attached to the wall and inscribed with the words '650 Experience/Dance Experience'; the Studio appears as a shabby, low-lying, concrete-facaded building in its mid-1960s variant. The 1st to 6th photographs are all located in Tokyo; then the book makes its journey to the north, until the 24th image; it returns to Tokyo with the 25th image, with Hijikata now in the company of what Hosoe, in his acknowledgements, calls the 'bride' and the 'elderly ladies', though it will finally return again to the north. The book's cover, across its front and back, shows one of the final images (number 33, the second to last photograph), with Hijikata's figure poised, leaning forwards, in a flooded rice field.

Hosoe was concerned to mark the exact locations of his photographs, as though their corporeality could only be projected through that precise delineation of topography. In his acknowledgements, he locates Hijikata's body at temples and streets in Tokyo's Sugamo and Meguro districts for the first sequences of the book, and at houses in peripheral areas of north-eastern Tokyo for its final sequences: in Nishi-Kameari, Katsushika-ku for the 'bride' sequence and Horikiri, Katsushika-ku for the 'elderly ladies' sequence.

Shuzo Takiguchi had been the most prominent of Japan's surrealists, publishing his journal *Yama mayu* (*Mountain silkworm*) in the 1920s; he travelled to Paris and met André Breton, who appears to have been largely baffled and supercilious in his response to Japan's surrealists. As Japan's militarism escalated in the 1930s, Takiguchi's work had been in acute tension with it. He supported Hijikata's Ankoku Butoh project throughout its emergence, perceiving it not as dance but as a surrealist art experiment. His essay for *Kamaitachi* examines the book's interlocked dimensions of film and photography through his preoccupation with the medium of the camera ('the divine machine'), which is always doubled and duplicitous, creating a void around the body it records that also resonates with the void that surrounds the *kamaitachi*. Takiguchi writes with irony of Hijikata's conflictual experience of having his work infiltrated and seized by Hosoe's camera: 'If ever an unexpected and happy chance visited the dancer, it was the camera's paradoxical existence which made it possible to possess a great void, in spite of the intention of possessing a protrusion ... Thus, the paradoxical vacuum secretly destined to the camera, may have been the divine machine to our dancer.' Takiguchi conceives of that trapped subjugation to the camera as a form of sacrifice on

Hijikata's part, in a way that extends Richie's first filmic incorporation of Hijikata's body into film as a sacrificial act alongside the act of killing: 'When one is to be photographed for his own portrait, one will be stripped of his own shadow, being forced to offer himself as a sacrifice.'

Takiguchi identifies Hijikata's *kamaitachi* figure as being determined to beguile the village's children as a 'sudden kidnapper from heaven', but whose ambitions in child-thieving and attempts at laceration are overturned by the children's own wily strategies: 'It is the dancer that gets wounded.' The children's own beguilement of Hijikata has a future sexual dimension: 'Anyway sooner or later they will know the orgasm of life and death.' Takiguchi provides the sole information in *Kamaitachi* that probes the lost history and memory of the demonic weasel that he, Hijikata and Hosoe had all frequently heard about in their childhoods; the sudden whirlwinds in the peasants' fields that left their limbs lacerated have now become obsolete and extinguished woundings, consigned to oblivion, so that Hosoe and Hijikata are materialising ghosts in their images (and the *kamaitachi* itself forms a volatile entity, taking the multiple form of the invisible weasel with sickle teeth, the physical laceration it inflicts, as well as the void around it). Once the *kamaitachi*'s history and memory are dissolved, into raw corporeal movement and contrary spectrality, it no longer belongs to the domain of the rural north, but can inhabit Tokyo and be rendered vulnerable to its crushing and trapping by the megalopolis's own beguilements. Takiguchi emphasises that *Kamaitachi* is integrally a collaboration, between Hijikata and Hosoe, rather than solely Hosoe's own work: 'Such an extraordinary document, however, can be only realized in the encounter with an unprecedented dancer, Tatsumi Hijikata; to speak in a tragic metaphor, the man who can change himself, for a moment, into a bird, but what a bird!'[6]

After Takiguchi's text, the spectator of *Kamaitachi* sees Hijikata's figure for the first time, dressed in shorts, a loose shirt and *geta* sandals, eyeing a child in a pushchair for potential abduction in a Meguro-district alleyway. The elderly woman pushing the child eyes Hijikata back with glaring suspicion. That image initiates *Kamaitachi*'s obsession with the stealing and wounding of bodies, along with the probing but exposed aperture of the eye which had also been a preoccupation of Hosoe's photographic collaboration with Mishima. In the second image, Hijikata's eye is now being scrutinised with a magnifying glass, by an aged fortune-teller at a stall in the grounds of the Togenuki temple. *Kamaitachi*'s action shifts into the journey to Tashiro village, and the villagers carry Hijikata alongside the rice-drying racks on a litter, one woman holding an umbrella on a pole over his head, prefiguring the opening sequence of his solo dance performance *Tatsumi Hijikata and the Japanese People: Revolt of the Body*, in 1968 (filmed by the artist Hiroshi Nakamura, in the year of *Kamaitachi*'s completion), in a ritual that, for Hijikata, evoked the excessive rituals performed around the body of the Roman emperor, Heliogabalus. Hijikata's *kamaitachi* performs for the villagers, seated on a mat, propelling them into hilarity as Hijikata had done with the boys of WARGAMES; in a further image, he performs solely for the village's children. The *kamaitachi* perches on the rice-drying racks, ocularly pinpointing children to steal. A female child is married to him in a children's ceremonial procession. In the book's later sequences, located in Tokyo, the *kamaitachi*'s bride has become grotesque, elderly and obese, and appears to have subjugated the *kamaitachi*, who is now exhausted and older too (at the end of the project's three-year duration); soon he is in the company of still older women. The book then abruptly insurges back to the *kamaitachi*'s initial infiltration of the village in the north. He runs at elated speed across the rice fields, holding in his arms a small child whose mouth is open in a great 'O' of horror or ecstasy, at night or under manually darkened clouds. But in the final image of the original edition of *Kamaitachi*, Hijikata's figure has been crushed and immobilised in a framework of bamboo and cloth, perhaps a buckled cart or carriage, suspended and trapped, in limbo. In its final sequences, *Kamaitachi*'s narrative – always perverse, fragmentary and elusive, as Hosoe intended – collapses into disintegration, mystery and opacity, especially with the *kamaitachi*'s return to his Tokyo locations. A black, blank page in the book accentuates that return, and a gap in time.

Kamaitachi's images mostly follow the chronological sequence of their photographing, over the three journeys Hosoe and Hijikata made to Tashiro village, and to other areas of Akita prefecture, between 1965 and 1968. But occasionally an image that disjoints that chronology appears, interposing itself against time. Most of Hosoe's skies are darkened through printing; in one image, the sky and earth are darkened into the form of a narrowed aperture, or ocular iris, within which Hijikata's figure is seen running through a field, and in another image, Hijikata is lying naked on his front on the black earth, within the illumination of glaring moonlight set against an entirely black and vast sky within which the contours of surrounding hills are just discernible. Contrarily, as ever, Hosoe also incorporated a single image with a whitened, bleached-out sky.

Once the immense book is set aside, or returned to the photographic archive, it leaves behind a sense of the aberrant corporeality, expanse and fragmented sequential movement of *Kamaitachi*'s original edition, as well as a muscular spectatorial residue in the manipulation demanded by the book. Its ocular remnant, in defiance of Hosoe's abandonment of the project at its onset as a filmic one, is an experience of shattered moving images. Alongside the book's image sequences, unfolded as the eye moves through it, *Kamaitachi* possesses a further, experimental sequence: from film, to photography, to Hijikata's corporeal figure performing the *kamaitachi*'s acts in Tokyo and in Akita – and back – each element simultaneously interlinked and compacted with the others, but each also autonomously insurgent and propelling the eye askew.

Kamaitachi's original edition from 1969 explored the intersection between photography and film, in the intricate sequential form of its large-format panoramic mappings of corporeality, rural landscape and urban space, with intimations of near-filmic flashbacks in the *kamaitachi*'s physical, memorial or near-death hallucinatory propulsion back to Akita from Tokyo in the book's final sequences. Forty years on, in 2009, the Kyoto-based publisher Seigensha and the US photography publisher Aperture Foundation issued a new 'trade' edition of *Kamaitachi* (four years earlier, both companies had also published a limited-edition facsimile of *Kamaitachi*'s first edition), both identical in form apart from the translation in the US edition of the textual material accompanying Hosoe's photographs, including a new essay by the scholar Donald Keene.

The 2009 edition of *Kamaitachi*, prepared with Hosoe's cooperation, expands the number of photographs incorporated into the book, drawing from the many hundreds of images Hosoe took in Tokyo and on the three journeys he and Hijikata made to Akita prefecture. A further eight photographs are included, totalling 48 to the previous 40, and all photographs now occupy one page, or extend across two pages, as opposed to the deploying of several photographs on some pages of the 1969 edition. Rather than involving a folding-out and manoeuvring of the original edition's 34 pages, thereby generating arrangements of multiple filmic screens through those ocular and manual imperatives, the new edition's images are immediately visible, with unused pages coloured in the blue that appeared in the 1969 edition. As well as adding photographs, the new edition sometimes replaces the original images with variants from a sequence photographed at a particular location or with the same constellations of bodies, or with different images altogether, and also reverses the sequencing of particular photographs, so that, for example, the first and second images – of Hijikata eyeing the child in its pushchair, and of the fortune-teller's magnifying glass examining Hijikata's eye – are reversed, and the book begins with a new emphasis on probing vision and the lens.

The ending of the book is also transformed: the resonant image of Hijikata's *kamaitachi* terminally constrained in a framework of bamboo and cloth is excised, rendering it a ghost image for eyes habituated to the 1969 edition, and is replaced with the image of Hijikata running across the Akita rice field with the open-mouthed child in his arms, so that the trapped closure of Hijikata's body is overturned into its open acceleration across the pitted earth. That new ending evokes film's capacity to endure variant endings (often in response to spectators' and financiers' misgivings). Among the newly incorporated photographs is one of Hijikata's *kamaitachi*, arms outstretched and one hand holding a vertically positioned sickle, photographed by Hosoe from ground-level, with the rice-drying racks appearing as an elongated, awry screen behind Hijikata's figure. In a new image from the *kamaitachi*'s transportation to Tokyo, Hijikata now strums a *samisen*, head tilted back as though he were ecstatically playing an electric guitar, with one of the 'elderly ladies' kneeling alongside him, the interior space around his bare-chested figure voided, though irresistibly darkened by Hosoe at its upper level, as though it were a sky; in a further image (now forming the final Tokyo-located element of the 2009 edition, which afterwards returns for its final sequence to Akita), the *kamaitachi* appears to have been accidentally killed by the old women, one of whom holds his body in one arm as she presses a hand to her face in mortification, while three other woman survey the mysterious death of the *kamaitachi* with a gravity that appears ready to transmutate into hilarity at any instant, as with the boys of Richie's WARGAMES. Hijikata's dead, outstretched hand is marked with white paint, and a short length of piping is held between the toes of one foot.

The book's reconfiguration entails a disassembly of its original sensory architecture and an ocular displacement, so that the spectator's eye in movement follows the guiding dynamics of an entirely different set of sequences, now less fragmentary and opaque, more streamlined in its evocation of the *kamaitachi*'s woundings and fall, with its post-death coda in which he is miraculously returned to the exhilaration of his child-thieving and lacerations. To overturn the original book itself forms a kind of performative cutting or wounding, and in his afterword to the new edition, Hosoe proposes that, alongside Hijikata's *kamaitachi* performance, his own actions as the project's photographer (as with his jumps while photographing) also constituted a performance: 'In our performances, we became, just for a moment, two *kamaitachi*.'[7] That assuming by Hosoe of the photographer's performative status as being allied or equal to that of the *kamaitachi* – able to wound at will, to beguile wide-eyed figures (such as the villagers whom Hosoe convinced that he and Hijikata were from a film or television company) and to abruptly vanish from location to location, through his photographer's power as the carrier of the 'divine machine' which Takiguchi evokes – also extends to the entity of the book itself, which is ultimately malleable in its openness to woundings, supplantings and to the imposition of voids. If that book had become a film, as Hosoe had tentatively envisaged at its origin, it could equally have been cut and re-cut in its editing, transmuting from variant to variant and back again, from a raw template through to a director's 'redux' version, as with Coppola's film Apocalypse Now.

In many ways, the 2009 edition of *Kamaitachi* supplants the original edition, now so invisible as to be almost unlocatable, as with the *kamaitachi*'s obsolete body in Takiguchi's emphasis on the near-total disappearance of that demonic creature's aura, once so feared by Hijikata and Hosoe as rural children in the 1930s and 1940s, but irreparably lost by the 1960s. Without that new, accessible edition, *Kamaitachi* – as one of Hijikata's most pivotal 1960s projects, vital to his corporeal experimentation and its intricate oscillations between moving images, still images and performance – would itself be near lost, as with Richie's films with Hijikata before their digitisation or transfer to DVD-media. At the same time, the original edition of *Kamaitachi*, with its tactile dimensions and its closer intimacy to Hosoe's re-envisioning of Hijikata's body and of what he viewed as the corporeal topographies of Tokyo and Akita, possesses its own distinctive aura: almost unhandleable, its contents saturated to the page-edge with wild adrenaline, and able still to taint its spectator's skin. That riotous book of Hijikata's body appears ready to overhaul time, able at will to annul that future edition. Although Hijikata may appear to be the more vulnerable of the 'two *kamaitachi*' that Hosoe evokes – his figure wounded back by the children whom he attempts to beguile and steal away in the Akita fields before being seized or mortally injured by the elderly women who appear to subjugate or to own him on his return in Tokyo, with that exposed figure of Hijikata's performance also trapped and appropriated by the instrument of Hosoe's camera, which is able to conjure an engulfing darkness around it – his overruling corporeality will finally determine the future of the book: *Kamaitachi*.

In the years after their collaborative work on *Kamaitachi*, Hosoe still frequently photographed Hijikata, especially at the Asbestos Studio, but never again for a project of the depth and immensity of *Kamaitachi*. But in the years 1970–71 – those of the death of Hosoe's friend Mishima, the Osaka Expo and the collapse of the accumulated intensity of Japan's 1960s experimental art culture – Hosoe worked on a new project which in many ways takes *Kamaitachi* forward, again exploring the corporeal intersections between performance and urban landscape (now located exclusively in Tokyo, primarily on its eastern wastelands and at its river edges), and the interconnections between still images and moving images. When Hosoe had evoked that project – *Simmon: A Private Landscape* – to me in 1998, it was as a semi-forgotten and abandoned work which had resulted for him in an impasse. In the end, the body of his protagonist had suddenly vanished, and Hosoe was left wandering the now emptied-out urban wastelands of Tokyo for years in solitude with his camera, searching for the corporeality he wanted to instil into his cityscapes, as the project disintegrated. For Hosoe, that project approached the same preoccupations as *Kamaitachi* – 'the unfathomed strangeness and impenetrability of humans'[8] – but with a more remote and capricious collaborator than Hijikata.

Simmon Yotsuya acquired his two names from his attachments to the voice of Nina Simone and the area of Tokyo (also the location of Hosoe's studio) adjacent to Shinjuku. In *Simmon: A Private Landscape*, he appears in full view in the city as a heavily made-up, lipsticked, suspended figure of acute provocation, sometimes manifesting himself in dense crowds, but more often in isolation (performing solely for Hosoe's camera), in the abandoned lands beside bleak rivers. Hosoe had met him in 1967 when he was working as an actor, usually playing female roles, in the Jokyo Gekijo company of the theatre director Juro Kara, which often performed in the grounds of the Hanazono shrine in Shinjuku, close to the Golden Gai area where Marker had his bar. Yotsuya appeared in Oshima's 1969 film DIARY OF A SHINJUKU THIEF. At the time of the photographing of *Simmon: A Private Landscape*, Yotsuya was 26 years old, while Hijikata began his work on *Kamaitachi* at 37 and ended it at 40 years old. Yotsuya became a friend of Hijikata in around 1965 after beginning to attend his performances, and in 1967 he encountered the translator Tatsuhiko Shibusawa, who had first alerted Hijikata to the work of Genet and Artaud that proved crucial to the aberrant corporeality of Ankoku Butoh; Yotsuya's friendship with Shibusawa was also inspirational for his own future work.

Across the years 1970–71, Hosoe and Yotsuya took innumerable photography walks around the arcades and amusement parks of the Asakusa district, and to its Senso-ji temple; Hosoe photographed Yotsuya's figure as a negligible entity below the then decrepit facade of the Asahi brewery (where prostitutes had once gathered) that loomed on the far side of the Sumida river to Asakusa, but also on the intervening bridge, his exultant lipsticked face now dominating almost the entire image, with the river's barges and adjacent highway-overpasses now the negligible elements behind him. Simmon's figure is a provocation in movement; whenever other figures appear in the photographs of him, they almost invariably gaze at him with outrage and appear about to insult or assault him, or else view him with hilarity.

Hosoe and Yotsuya went deeper into the areas to the eastern side of the Sumida river, to Mukojima and the Hatonomachi red-light area, then further east to the Katsushika district, in which Hosoe had lived as a child and where he had photographed the final Tokyo sequences of *Kamaitachi* with Hijikata. They walked further still, to the edgelands and river-dissected wastelands at the city's eastern periphery. In several of the sequences' images, which often appear as lost filmic urban fragments, with Simmon's body blurred across the city, he appears consumed with dejection, in other images illuminated, his face in a fixed, lip-sticked smile. Hosoe photographed Yotsuya under a supremely blackened sky in scrubland alongside the wide Arakawa river, and they sought out other rivers and drainage canals in the eastern Tokyo area, with their surrounding flood-plain wastelands, since Hosoe wanted to position Yotsuya's corporeality within ultimately desolate locations. In one image, Simmon is seen burrowing into a hole within an earth embankment.

That Simmon figure vanishes abruptly; in the last image in which he appears, he is sprawled, apparently dead (as with Hijikata's *kamaitachi* with the 'elderly ladies'), in an overgrown river-edge wasteland, pylons marking the far distance. After Yotsuya had left the project in 1971, Hosoe persisted with it for four more years, until around 1975, its corporeal dimensions now entirely transferred to the Tokyo cityscapes through which he walked, again from Asakusa to the districts, wastelands and void zones to the far side of the Sumida river. From those cityscapes, any distinguishing trace of Tokyo itself often appears lost, and all that sustain the images are pylons and electricity-generating plants, empty highways, and bleak facades such as that from 1973 of the Tobu Bowl Nishiarai bowling-alley (an image eventually excluded from the published book); the images are at their most strangely filmic when all movement appears cancelled out from them, as though a long-neglected film has decelerated into extreme decomposition. The final, undated image of the book is of many kites flying in the darkened sky over an industrial river landscape.

Hosoe exhibited several of the project's photographs in 1972 at an exhibition at the Kinokuniya Gallery in Shinjuku, but then suspended plans to publish it for forty years, and the images disappeared into a void until 2012, when he finally decided to incorporate them into a book, with the project's original title still intact (the book also remains intact in its abandoned form, since Hosoe took no further photographs in Tokyo's new wastelands to 'conclude' it). By that time, Simmon Yotsuya had long ago abandoned performance, and had become renowned as a maker and exhibitor of mechanical, grotesque and spectral dolls; Shibusawa had introduced him to the German artist Hans Bellmer's contorted dolls, which also fascinated Hijikata and appear in his early-1970s choreography in the figures of 'Bellemers'. In his afterword to the book, Hosoe commented on how he now perceived that four-decade blackout in the time of his images: 'Due perhaps to the fact that compiling photographs in a book after a period as long as four decades is for myself a rare experience, when re-examining how these works are reflected in my eyes and heart today, I feel remorseful for leaving them untouched all those years.'[9]

A film on celluloid traversing its projector's gate, if caught and arrested through any malfunction of time, and stilled at a particular image, will be pinioned for its spectators to examine that frame, as intently as they wish, before the device's bulb intended to illuminate it will instead finally overheat and combust it, and the image will melt into darkness and oblivion. Spectators of *Simmon: A Private Landscape* knew only the very few images that Hosoe had exhibited in Tokyo in 1972 (alongside a small scattering of others, published in catalogues of his work during the decades when the project remained abandoned), as though those images formed the pinioned, stilled frames from a film whose narrative rationale had otherwise gone haywire, or had been consigned to oblivion. With that project, the expanse of the four decades that passed after Yotsuya's withdrawal from it, before Hosoe's corporeal restitution of it following his belated, remorseful decision finally to publish the book, provided a uniquely extended opportunity to scrutinise those isolated images, finally so eroded in time that they slipped through the domains of photography and film, and entered the wasteland terrain of the fragment.

Hosoe's photographing of Tokyo as an urban entity, in collaboration with Hijikata and then Yotsuya between 1965 and 1971, imbued his images with distinctive corporeal and filmic auras, together with a volatility that emerged from those two figures' capacity to inflict outrages or woundings upon the city, but also unaccountably to vanish from it. In the subsequent decades, Hosoe's travels took him again to Japan's north, this time accompanied by Hijikata's determining absence. In a project with Hijikata's closest Ankoku Butoh collaborator, Kazuo Ohno, Hosoe returned to the north in 1994, still further north, this time to the island of Hokkaido, to photograph landscape panoramas of Ohno dancing in the Kushiro National Park wetlands on the island's remote eastern side, the images resonating with *Kamaitachi* in their scale but now cast in elegiac form, without the raw velocity of Hijikata's corporeality.

Ohno had been born in Hokkaido's marine city of Hakodate in 1906, and was 88 years old at the time of that project with Hosoe. He had previously been filmed dancing through wastelands and abandoned sites in Hokkaido, far closer to *Kamaitachi*'s era, as part of a series of three long experimental works by the filmmaker Chiaki Nagano – PORTRAIT OF MR O, 1969, MANDALA OF MR O, 1971 and MR O's BOOK OF THE DEAD, 1973 – which reflected his preoccupation of that era with dance as a medium of dirt and squalor. Ohno's performances in the three films often take the form of gradual traversals via elliptical dance gestures of corroded landscapes and sites in which human inhabitation appears to have been negated, including now ruined former military installations, sometimes in marine locations or on the edges of cities, especially those of Yokohama. In defiance of its engulfing darkness, *Kamaitachi* appears in many ways a publicly face-on and confronting work, as for example through Hijikata's intimate performances facing the Tashiro villagers and children, and through the project's readiness for publication as an immense book shortly after its completion; Ohno's three films with Nagano, by contrast, form secretive and intentionally elusive artefacts, filmed almost covertly (Ohno told me in 1998 that he had sometimes neglected to tell his family before abruptly departing for journeys to Hokkaido and other location sites over the four-year duration of the project), barely known and rarely projected or seen.

Although the older of the two by over two decades, Ohno outlived Hijikata by over two decades, and danced almost to the last years of his life, even in frailty and increasing immobility; in 1999 he was filmed dancing alongside the figure of the filmmaker Michelangelo Antonioni, after being awarded the Antonioni Prize at a Venice theatre. Across Ohno's final four years, before his death in 2010 at the age of 103, the young artist Michiko Yokogawa regularly visited his house in Yokohama to make sequences of drawings of Ohno's face, published as a catalogue in 2015. In an accompanying text, she emphasises her abiding sense of hesitancy and the repetition that defined the project. In its final sequences, Ohno is immobilised in bed, seemingly disturbed by dreams, and has passed almost beyond spoken language, his mouth opening wide in silent cries and facial convulsions. The gestural hesitancy of Yokogawa's drawings imparts a sense of awry movement to the images, while their repetition evokes experimental film loops. Ohno's face is disintegrating as it is seized in the drawings, which form near-filmic motion sequences focused upon the apertures of the mouth and eyes; Yokogawa omits her drawings made immediately after Ohno's death.

Hijikata returned to Japan's north in 1969, also to the eastern side of Hokkaido island, with a large film crew, in order for his work to be filmed for projection at the following year's Osaka Expo. In the 1960s and early 1970s, Japan's north, and especially Hokkaido, formed an alien entity, opposed in extremity to Japan's more southerly megalopolises and shortlived utopian environments such as the Expocity. As well as for its status as an unknown terrain for exploration – pristine but contrarily also subject to intensive despoliation, especially at the industrial edges of its principal cities, such as Aomori and Sapporo – the north also attracted Tokyo's filmmakers and photographers for its aura as a tainted-Eden site in which to escape that era's transmutations in Tokyo. Its opposed demonic infernality and paradisiacal emanations (often accentuated by childhood memories, as for Hijikata and Hosoe) is underlined in Shuji Terayama's filmic sequences shot at Mount Osore, on the Shimokita peninsula that forms the northern tip of Aomori prefecture (close to where Terayama was born), for his film Pastoral Hide and Seek, 1973; Terayama's filming of the reeking caldera lake and the vividly coloured sulphur-streamed volcanic wastelands at Mount Osore's base – a site of the dead's transits, especially those of unborn children, marked by dolls and toys, as well as an entrance to hell, in Japanese culture – resonates with the photography by artists such as Daido Moriyama of the acute pollution in that era of Aomori and of adjacent, smoke-darkened cities of the north.

Moriyama began his obsessive travels to the north at the beginning of the 1970s, and photographed his iconic image of a stray dog, its head and eyes turned to the camera, in Aomori prefecture's Misawa city in 1971; his own work veered sharply from that of Hosoe after he ceased his work as his assistant in 1964, though the final, bleakly body-emptied sequences of Hosoe's *Simmon: A Private Landscape,* from 1972–75, interconnect with Moriyama's work of that era. Moriyama's sequences of photographs taken from the frozen decks of winter ferries crossing the Tsugaru Strait between Aomori and Hokkaido, over a tumultuous sea and through wild snowfall, seize the outlandishness and corporeal demands of that journey to the north (Hokkaido ferries disastrously capsized on numerous occasions, especially during 1950s typhoons, and a railway tunnel was opened under the Tsugaru Strait only in 1988). His Hokkaido and Aomori urban photographs are constellated with trains, trams, dirt-track streets, city-edge wastelands, snow, zones of blackness, eroded cinema facades, smoke pollution, and mountains looming over the cities and their inhabitants, who often appear bewildered or who descend to the ground in alcohol stupors to replicate the position of the stray dog whose menacing and imploring gaze Moriyama recorded. The photographic celluloid of those images is correspondingly contaminated, scarred, darkened and damaged. Moriyama travelled repeatedly to the north in the early 1970s, often hitchhiking with few possessions other than his cameras; he also made a long stay in Hokkaido, later that decade, at a time of crisis in his work.

Before (and after) his journeys to the north, Moriyama concentrated his work in Tokyo, as well as in the streets and alleyways around the Yokosuka and Yakota US bases in the Tokyo region, following Hosoe's own inhabitation of US bases in 1949–50. Moriyama also photographed cityscapes in Osaka in 1970, the year of the Osaka Expo, in overwhelmingly darkened images that form extreme contrasts with films and photographs of the adjacent Expo-city pavilions' virulent colours. As with Hosoe, Moriyama accorded performative dimensions to his own mobile acts of photography: 'When I take photographs, my body inevitably enters a trancelike state. Briskly weaving my way through the avenues, every cell in my body became as sensitive as radar, responsive to the life of the streets.'[10] Amalgamated together in their hundreds, in immense volumes that resonate with the scale of the original edition of *Kamaitachi* – though devoid of that project's coalescing corporeality – Moriyama's images of urban Hokkaido comprise insistent interrogations, as though forming the malfunctioned moving-image detrita amassed from countless lost films.

In 2016, the Kamaitachi Museum was opened in the exact location of the book that Hijikata and Hosoe had begun there in 1965. As the museum's building, the large merchant's house that appeared in several *Kamaitachi* photographs held ghosts both of images and of Hijikata's body. In the documentary film made to mark the opening, Hosoe is first taken by taxi to the Asbestos Studio's current form (the building renovated by Akiko Motofuji following Hijikata's death, with a domed facade and a great eye-shaped window at its summit), evidently not having been there for many years, and also to a temple in Meguro where he had photographed one of the *Kamaitachi* images (absent from the 2009 edition), showing Hijikata's capacity to beguile and captivate groups of children. Hosoe then travels north and arrives at the museum's opening, immediately casts aside his walking-stick and dances adeptly in the building's courtyard, where welcoming musicians are playing; he is also seen alongside the rice-drying racks that still form prominent elongated screens in the nearby fields. The documentary shows the child, then aged one and with its mouth forming an 'O' as it is carried in Hijikata's arms in his headlong acceleration across rice fields, now transformed into a 52-year-old woman with short black hair, who weeps with emotion when encountering Hosoe at the Museum's opening ceremony. Other figures from *Kamaitachi* are also identified in the film, including several of the children who watched Hijikata's mat-seated performance for them, and an adult villager who glimpsed that image's performance warily and whose figure is seen in its background.

In 2018, after an interval of twenty years, I visited Hosoe at his studio in Tokyo's Yotsuya district, this time along with the dance historian Katja Centonze. We speak first, mostly in English, about Hosoe's keen awareness of his now failing memory and his fear of losing it altogether; he tells us that he remembers best what happened farthest back in time, and also through the exertion demanded in speaking in English. He especially wants to speak about his memories of returning to the near-vanished city of Tokyo soon after the war's end, and of climbing an embankment close to his family's home, looking over it, and seeing the incinerated Tokyo in ashes. But like many children of that era in Japan's cities who later became artists or architects, and had collaborated with Hijikata or had been his friends – Arata Isozaki, Juro Kara, Hiroshi Nakamura, among others – the urban destruction also conjured a sense of liberation, with the apparent definitive erasure of Japan's militarism. A negation had been torn open, as with the 'X' of NAVEL AND A-BOMB. Hosoe tells us of his many journeys of the postwar years outside Tokyo with his father, accompanying school-excursion parties which his father photographed, later gifting his son cameras and delegating that excursion-photography to him; Hosoe soon learned to photograph at speed, moving around the children's figures, on those assignments. He was never attached to his photographic or filmic cameras, discarding them at will, and only conceived of attachments to the startling or propulsive movements of bodies he could seize with them.

Once he has spoken of his childhood, Hosoe speaks of Hijikata, and *Kamaitachi*. He opens the pages of one of his two battered copies of the original *Kamaitachi* edition on the table between us, and looks intently at image after image, needing expanses of time to absorb and focus his memory back into those images' moments, with long intervals devoted to each image, as though examining film stills now so decelerated that they could be perceived only in the form of near-autonomous fragments. He tells us he has to work to activate his memory, which, he says, laughing, now operates best in sudden bursts, when something especially stirs it. He gazes first at the image in which Hijikata is careering along a tarmac path, a shoddy urban apartment block in the background, a wasteland of rocks and black earth in the foreground, the image sliced at an upper margin by sunlight, light above, darkness below, as though holding an interzone in the *kamaitachi*'s journey from Tokyo to Akita, or back. Hosoe tells us that the flag Hijikata grips is a special battleship flag, which he had instructed him to wrap around his chest, above his bare legs, so that its bursts of undulating red-and-white strips appear expelled directly from his body. He examines other images. Then he looks, again intently and across memory's veering time, finally and after more than half a century, at the book's image (one of its last) of Hijikata's child-carrying elated run across the earth-pitted rice field, Tashiro village in the distance and a succession of hillsides, outlined in white light, directly behind it. He takes his time and looks still more intently. In that interval, it strikes me that Hosoe's gaze, in extremis, could annul contemporary image sequences, such as that of the museum-opening's documentary, and resuscitate instead the originating part-filmic preoccupations of the *Kamaitachi* project, generating a manifestation of memory that possesses tangible form, in part from the sheer effort required to ignite it, along with the dense corporeality of memory, in order to align the photographic images of *Kamaitachi* with the filmic sequences of NAVEL AND A-BOMB, as conjoined explorations of Hijikata's body, alternately poised against the topographies of Tokyo, with its temples and alleyways, and against the marine or rural locations to which that body, to elude the city or to discover aberrant refractions and emanations of it, or memories or wounds, has travelled.

Then Hosoe's intent gaze ends, he looks up, laughing, and tells us that the image's child is not a girl-child at all. It's instead a boy… And as we leave the studio, at the visit's end, Hosoe takes out his smartphone and photographs Katja and me; the image instantly misfires.

Notes

1   Donald Richie, 'Navels and A-Bombs: Some Notes on Eikoh Hosoe's Experimental Film', in *Eikoh Hosoe: 1950–2000: Photographs*, Tokyo: Kyodo, 2000, page 304.

2   Mark Holborn, *Beyond Japan*, London: Jonathan Cape, 1991, page 54.

3   Miryam Sas, *Experimental Arts in Postwar Japan: Moments of Encounter, Engagement, and Imagined Return*, Cambridge MA/London: Harvard University Press, 2011, page 246.

4   William Klein, 'Un livre d'auteur', in *Cahiers du Cinéma*, issue 497, December 1995, page 73.

5   Eikoh Hosoe, 'Photographer's Note by Eikoh Hosoe', in *Ba-ra-kei/ Ordeal by Roses*, New York: Aperture Foundation, 2002, unpaginated.

6   Shuzo Takiguchi, 'Kamaitachi: Towards a Vacuum's Nest', in Eikoh Hosoe and Tatsumi Hijikata, *Kamaitachi*, Tokyo: Gendaishichosha, 1969, unpaginated.

7   Eikoh Hosoe, 'Afterword', in Eikoh Hosoe and Tatsumi Hijikata, *Kamaitachi*, New York: Aperture Foundation, 2009, unpaginated.

8   Eikoh Hosoe, 'Afterword', in Eikoh Hosoe, *Simmon: A Private Landscape*, Tokyo: Akio Nagasawa Gallery, 2012, unpaginated.

9   Ibid.

10 Daido Moriyama, 'memories of a dog – conclusion: Osaka', in Sandra S. Phillips and Alexandra Munroe (eds.), *Daido Moriyama: stray dog*, San Francisco: San Francisco Museum of Modern Art, 1999, unpaginated.

PART THREE

Tokyo's Transmutation, Hijikata's Dance

Hijikata's films counterpoint and reveal the deep historical upheavals experienced in the riot-lacerated urban fabric of Tokyo across the 1960s, ending with the monumental event of Expo '70 to which around half of the population of Japan travelled and which itself provided visions of a new, technologically adept but pacified, non-confrontational urban life. Across the 1960s, filmmakers and artists such as Takahiko Iimura and Hiroshi Nakamura filmed Hijikata's performances, not to document, preserve or represent them, but to interrogate the ways in which film interconnected with Hijikata's distinctive corporeal gestures, emphasising the status of film as an autonomous medium absorbing unique activations from Hijikata's Ankoku Butoh project. Film itself is a performance. Alongside the 1960s turmoil of Tokyo's dance culture, set into upheaval by Hijikata's choreographic experiments and his reconfigurations of dance into corporeal amalgams with art, architecture and other media, film itself shifted in form as a medium in Tokyo across the 1960s, primarily through the innovative work of Toshio Matsumoto, which responded to the distorted immediacy of the new 'actuality' media environment of Tokyo and investigated the sensitised terrain between film and art, especially installation art. As with Hijikata's work of that era, Matsumoto's projects of 1968–70 were extraordinarily dense with experimentation and contestation, focused largely on the cityscape and subterraneas of Tokyo, notably through his intimate probing of Tokyo's transsexual cultures in his full-length film FUNERAL PARADE OF ROSES. That tumultuous era of work ended, as Hijikata's did, with Matsumoto's participation in Expo '70.

The city itself is a performance, as with film, and dance, when it undergoes momentous transmutation in a concentrated span of time, as Tokyo did in the 1960s. That exceptionally volatile, tense urban time then readily resonates into the petrified dynamics of the contemporary moment, in Tokyo, as well as into other international cities, in the same way that Hijikata's Ankoku Butoh project of the 1960s also does. The timescale of Hijikata's 1960s performances was erratic; often, lengthy spans elapsed between the moments when he had the opportunity to present his work to larger-scale audiences, as at the Nihon Seinenkan in 1968, with smaller-scale performances for a hundred or less spectators undertaken more frequently at the Asbestos Studio or in small gallery and art spaces. Apart from the *Kamaitachi* journeys with Hosoe of 1965–68, Hijikata rarely travelled outside Tokyo during most of the 1960s, forming a sustained witness – albeit one with aberrant, askew vision – of the city's overhauling.

Tokyo's own reconfiguration accelerated in the years between Hijikata's work on WARGAMES with Richie in 1962 and his first *Kamaitachi* journey to Akita in 1965; among the most prominent manifestations of that transformation in Tokyo was the generation of the new networks of inner-city overhead highways, visible as a negligible element behind Simmon Yotsuya's face in one of the Sumida riverscapes of *Simmon: A Private Landscape*, with the highway following the river's eastern side, as well as subterranean highways that infiltrated the city's compacted, ghost-history embedded strata.

That highway oscillation between elevation and subterranea in relation to Tokyo's urban space is especially pronounced in the sequence that Andrei Tarkovsky shot for his film SOLARIS, having wanted to film a disjunctive future-city for a scene in which the disgraced astronaut Burton is traversing an endless megalopolis in his car, accompanied by his young son. In intense melancholic solitude, Burton appears not to be driving at all, but is either collapsed in despair over his steering-wheel, or gazing at the city beyond his car. Tarkovsky's future city is never named in SOLARIS, but the elevated gantries over the highway hold signs indicating the names of the Tokyo districts into which vehicles can now exit. When the sequence retracts from the car's interior to the highway itself, it shifts to capturing the exhilarating or annulling sense of travelling under and above – and again under – the city's tower-carapaced skin. Those new highways bypassed Tokyo's previously traffic-snarled and riot-blocked streets and avenues, but generated new proliferations of collisions, with their accentuated dimension of speed and complex cross-highway intersections. At the end of Burton's sequence, his perspective, and that of the spectator, is propelled by Tarkovsky upwards, to gaze omnisciently on the multiple crossings of highways, angled so that they appear as 'X'-negations over the city, annulled from sight only by the sequence's sudden end, as with Hosoe's 'X' over the child's navel in NAVEL AND A-BOMB, torn-off by Hijikata's hand: an expansive city inside the hand. That sensation accorded to the spectator of looking down at the abruptly nocturnal traffic-striated city is above all a filmic one, the city negated in itself but liberated in its transportation into filmic zones.

Those highways formed part of the new urban landscape of Tokyo prepared for the Olympics, to highlight the status of the reconstructed megalopolis, and of Japan itself; numerous immense stadia for the Olympics were built for that spectacular reconceptualisation of Tokyo as an enticing, no longer scarred city, by Kenzo Tange and other architects. Many districts, such as Shinjuku, were extensively amended, especially with groupings of multi-storey concrete corporate towers facaded with neon and other signage. Even films of that era which appear to have no vested interest in vaunting the new corporate architecture of Tokyo or its Olympic stadia, such as Seijun Suzuki's gangster film TOKYO DRIFTER, 1966, perversely highlight it; TOKYO DRIFTER announces its location (following a bleached, black-and-white opening sequence set in a bayside wasteland of abandoned railway freight wagons), with a colour title sequence moving between Tokyo's new cityscapes of rapid-transit railway stations, elevated highways and Tange's Olympic arena in Shibuya with its distinctive sweeping roof, along with the Tokyo Tower, opened in 1958, which also appears in Matsumoto's

FUNERAL PARADE OF ROSES as an elevated ocular aperture on the expanding new Tokyo, with its correspondingly expansive new wastelands, that had been installed at the expense of multiple vanished or evanescing Tokyos. Filming the new Tokyo served to generate spectral cityscapes of those surpassed Tokyos, such as the rapidly erected constructions of the immediate postwar period within which figures such as Hosoe had grown up, all the more present now as film's ghosts for their demolition and razing, or in the few raw fragments remaining of them.

Intimate corporeal life in Tokyo mutated correspondingly in that era of architectural, speed-inflected upheaval, with the city's inhabitants increasingly living in small apartments in new concrete multi-storey blocks on the city's peripheries, in its accumulating suburbs along train routes extending far to the west of districts such as Shinjuku, Ikebukuro and Shibuya, or in areas which had not previously ever been built on, such as bay-reclaimed land, riverside wastelands prone to flooding before the recent concretisation of the rivers' channels, and other areas; Hijikata's own Tokyo district of Meguro developed rapidly in that era. The interiors of apartments now more frequently had bathrooms, installed as mass-produced, uniform plastic panels for the inter-attached sink and bathtub, though for many apartments that development would still be decades in the future, eventually annulling for millions the regular trip to neighbourhood bathhouses.

Many of Tokyo's thousands of local cinemas began to close in the 1960s with the rise of television, though televisions were still rare in low-income areas and often shared among neighbours for such regular events as *sumo* tournaments; factory production focused increasingly on the supply of electronic components for television sets and for other visual and sonic media. Urban inhabitants rapidly became adhered to television broadcasts from the Olympics, alongside the pervasive new media-environment 'actuality' of abrasive news broadcasts, with viewers especially following the decade's violent manifestations of street protests, and murder. More and more impoverished people poured into Tokyo from the north, especially from Hok-kaido, Aomori and Akita prefectures, arriving at Ueno station (as Hijikata had, in the previous decade) to attempt the often harsh transit from rural life to factory life or other roles, especially construction work, including the building of business towers and sports stadia, or crime (Hijikata's own first Tokyo occupation, alongside dock work), in the ascendently but selectively wealthy 1960s megalopolis.

Policing, security-guard culture and surveillance media all became escalating urban presences in Tokyo across the first half of the 1960s, responding to the insurgence of strange corporeal presences into the city as its population changed, as well as to baffling new spatial forms such as entrances into towers and buildings whose enhanced aura of real-estate valuation ensured they now needed to be protected. Crowds attending the Olympics events (including international visitors unfamiliar with the city's dense, address-less topography) in 1964 needed to be controlled, anticipating the intricate manoeuvring of the tens of millions populating the 1970 Expo future-city. The electronic mass production that generated television sets also increasingly encompassed components for surveillance screens. Yuriko Furuhata, in her book *Cinema of Actuality: Japanese Avant-Garde Filmmaking in the Season of Image Politics*, emphasises that the security industry's growth was linked to the influx of the rural population into Tokyo and the mass expansion of electronic media production: 'The birth of the Japanese security-guard business in 1962 was, in fact, a direct result of the intense immigration of the uprooted rural population into the Tokyo metropolitan areas. Two massive construction projects led by the state – the Tokyo Olympics in 1964 and Expo '70 in 1970 – further accelerated the growth of the security guard industry in Japan ... The introduction of closed-circuit television (CCTV) for crowd-control purposes during the Tokyo Olympics also marks an increasing confluence of the burgeoning security and electronics industries.'[1] At the far end of the decade, that security industry, along with Tokyo's riot police forces, had to exact the extinguishment of the street-riot culture which accumulated across the 1960s to its 1968–69 maximal furore, as a corporeal face-to-face confrontation, with the simultaneous burning and damaging of the infrastructure of the avenues (such as police boxes and ostentatious storefronts), especially those of Shinjuku, through which the riots passed. Once that riot culture expired, Tokyo was left, even in its relative calm, with the security industry; it persisted, and even strengthened in numbers. Tokyo became the pacified, street surveillance-oriented but architecturally spectacular, engulfing mega-city which endures to the contemporary moment, and for whose effective control Expo '70 formed a densely crowded, sometimes-unruly experimental testing zone.

The mass availability of 8mm, super-8mm and 16mm cameras, as well as professional news cinematography and surveillance footage, ensured that Tokyo was extensively filmed across the 1960s, for the immediate transmission of 'actuality' events and for personal or amateur filmmaking that recorded individual memories, as well as by experimental filmmakers, especially those attempting to locate a distinctive corporeality within the city via the filming of street-located performance or activist acts, and occasionally through the infiltration of Tokyo's performance-imbued interiors, such as its subterranean nightclubs and art-galleries. Along with Toshio Matsumoto's experimental filming of Tokyo for FUNERAL PARADE OF ROSES, Nagisa Oshima also filmed its bodies, streets and riots for his 1969 film DIARY OF A SHINJUKU THIEF, in which Simmon Yotsuya appeared, and Masao Adachi filmed Tokyo's void, seemingly depopulated and spectral streets, which for him pre-eminently emanated state power, for his 1969 film A.K.A. SERIAL KILLER. The 1960s city of Tokyo is an endlessly filmed city.

The image-rendered 1960s Tokyo possesses a concentrated urban history of constellations of uproar which is marked most enduringly in film; that uproar is transmitted, obliquely or directly, also in films of Hijikata's performances, exacerbated by the volatility, provocation and exploratory velocity of his own corporeal acts, through filmic fragments in Takahiko Iimura's anti-documentational films of Hijikata's 1963 and 1965 performances *The Masseur* and *Rose Coloured Dance: To Mr Shibusawa's House*, then in Hiroshi Nakamura's film of Hijikata's 1968 performance *Tatsumi Hijikata and the Japanese People: Revolt of the Body*.

Hijikata's work was always far more hidden in its filmed street manifestations than that of other prominent performers and artists of that era, such as Juro Kara; if Hijikata's work was ever directly concerned with revolution, it was to position his work as a corporeal revolution, of the form also envisioned by Artaud at the end of his work in the 1940s. As a result of that habitual hiddenness of Hijikata's figure, it appears more startling still when he is occasionally filmed or photographed in Tokyo's urban space, in moving and still images that demonstrate a city at the heart of its turmoil, and in which Hijikata's body is directly juxtaposed, for example, in a 1969 Tokyo street photograph by Masahisa Fukase (a photographer himself only intermittently visible in Tokyo's external space, his work more pervasively associated with darkened images of the north, of Hokkaido ravens and crows, or with the photographing of sexual acts and furores in the enclosed subterraneas and bars of Shinjuku) with a long line of black-clad riot police, protective masks poised to shield their faces, on their way to dispel urban insurrection, while Hijikata walks determinedly in the inverse direction, dressed in a kimono, carrying a watermelon in a bag.

The films of Hijikata's 1960s performances demonstrate that to film or to photograph a performance is not necessarily to record it or to document it: especially in film, sequences combatively engaged with performance's corporeality can also intentionally form anti-documents, anti-records, even archive-annulling irreconcilable filmic gestures, often undertaken with the aim of elevating the status of film as an experimental medium, and to cast dance aside at the same time, even if the film itself is intent on its own future disintegration or dissolution, and even if dance, with its tangible hold on corporeal time, and in its manifestations in urban space or in its performance's darkened hiddenness – always a gesture away from vanishing – will perpetually have the last adroit word on the matter, above or under film.

The young experimental artist who filmed Hijikata's mid-1960s performances, following on from Hijikata's film collaborations with Hosoe and Richie of that decade's beginning – Takahiko Iimura – began his film work in 1962, at the age of 25, having previously experimented with painting and poetry. He oscillated across the first four years of his filmmaking practice between shooting his work in exterior Tokyo locations, such as wastelands and contaminated bayside sites, as with JUNK, 1962, and in constricted corporeal space, such as that of sex acts, for LOVE, 1962, with a soundtrack of cacophony by Yoko Ono, and within art or performance venues, in which he filmed two of Hijikata's performances, *The Masseur* and *Rose Coloured Dance: To Mr Shibusawa's House*, exactly two years apart, in November 1963 and November 1965. Iimura associated closely with Richie during those years, in part because Richie was technically a marginally more adept 8mm filmmaker and Iimura wanted to learn from him, but also because Richie had seen all of the European and US experimental films which Iimura desperately wanted to see (such as Genet's UN CHANT D'AMOUR, works by Stan Brakhage, and the French Surrealist films that would not be projected in Tokyo until the mid-1960s). In that era of cumbersome celluloid prints, Richie had nothing to project to Iimura beyond his own 8mm films, including his two films with Hijikata, but he had amassed many film stills and *Life*-magazine film-focused cuttings on his travels in Europe and during his years as a student in New York, and he could readily evoke the immense, interconnected corpus of European and US experimental filmmaking.

Iimura and Richie submitted their films together to emergent experimental film festivals, together with a manifesto (written by Iimura) of their jointly independent, autonomous approach to filmmaking, and won prizes together, as at the Knokke-le-Zoute festival in 1964, which neither of them could afford to travel to Belgium to attend. They also presented their films together, along with films by Stan Brakhage, at the Sogetsu Art Center in 1966. Since, in my meeting with Iimura in 1998, he had told me how precious his association with Richie had been, and that he was eager to meet him again after not seeing him for perhaps 30 years, I was struck by Richie's irascible dismissal of Iimura when I mentioned him at our next meeting (this time we travelled to the north of Kujukurihama, to walk to the Kashima shrine, where a great stone embedded in the shrine's grounds helps to hold down the head of an immense subterranean catfish whose contortions, if released, would bring down a destructive seismic calamity upon Tokyo; the shrine itself was extensively damaged in the 2011 Tohoku earthquake): Iimura was always hanging round in the early 1960s, wasting Richie's time and that of younger filmmakers such as Adachi. He was an upstart. Richie had no interest in seeing him again; it was a mystery to me exactly what had riled him, though he was easily riled. In an essay commemorating Richie's work after his death in 2013, 'Donald Richie: Life Life Life', the film scholar Julian Ross recounted witnessing the accidental encounter between Iimura and Richie at the opening of an exhibition devoted to 1950s experimental art in Japan, at the Museum of Modern Art in Tokyo, that finally brought them together in 2012, for a moment, in the awry conjunction of their respective filmings of Hijikata's body, when Richie was already fading towards death.

By the time Iimura met Hijikata in 1963, with a request to film his next performance, *The Masseur*, he had conceived of an approach to experimental filmmaking which he called 'Cine-Dance', in which the filmmaker films a live performance at very close proximity, even standing directly within the performance space to jostle and impede the performers during the act of filming, dancing with his camera in a contrary dance to the performance itself, in order to accentuate or elevate film's autonomy as a medium alongside performance. Hijikata's two performances, *The Masseur* and *Rose Coloured Dance: To Mr Shibusawa's House* formed Iimura's optimal experimentation site for that Cine-Dance project as it was carried through in the interiors of performance venues; Iimura also made several Cine-Dance films in the external space of Tokyo, on apartment-building rooftops and through wastelands, such as A DANCE PARTY IN THE KINGDOM OF LILLIPUT, 1964 (resonant in its improvised urban-journey form of the trilogy of films that Kazuo Ohno made with Chiaki Nagano later in that decade), in which Iimura tracks and filmically haunts the figure of the artist Sho Kazakura, occasionally colliding with him whilst filming. Iimura summarised his cross-media approach: 'One example of "expanded cinema" is the experimental combining of film and performance to arrive at a "film performance"... I was creating "Cine-Dance", a rare combination of media and dance.'[2]

Iimura's conception of Cine-Dance – as the filming of dance performance in such a way as to prioritise the film camera's fluid movements and to make the filmmaker's own insurgent, insistent corporeality a pivotal element of the performance, whether shot in urban space or in venues that intimate the cities around them – contrarily resonates with the work of the Hollywood-musical directors Gene Kelly and Stanley Donen, in their own innovative development of a form of urban 'Cine-Dance', especially in their film ON THE TOWN, 1949 (shot at Kelly's insistence in part at striking New York locations, such as its docksides, which give immediacy to the action). In ON THE TOWN, choreography exists solely in order to be filmed, through the deploying of agile camera movement and screen effects in direct rapport with the film's dancing figures in their explicitly urban locations. Kelly commented: 'Call it "cine-dancing", or whatever, but I tried to invent the dance to fit the camera and its movements.'[3] ON THE TOWN's outlandish Cine-Dance narrative of concertinaed urban sexual compulsion possesses elements prescient of the preoccupations of experimental-film culture of the subsequent two decades, with elements of looped repetition in the arrival of a new set of sailors at 6am at the New York dockside to perform again the accelerated urban actions just urgently completed (or abandoned) by the previous figures, along with the cross-dressing that is pervasive in Japan's urban-located experimental culture of the 1960s (such as Matsumoto's film FUNERAL PARADE OF ROSES, and Klein's Tokyo street-photography of Kazuo Ohno); the abrupt vertical elevation of ON THE TOWN's final shot, positioned to survey New York with glacial, disabused omniscience, as a now exhausted corporeal site about to vanish, also prefigures many such shots in Tokyo's 1960s experimental-film culture.

In Gene Kelly's variant of Cine-Dance, choreography's bodies work solely to be absorbed into film's domain. In order to embody Iimura's desire for a direct confrontation of the film-maker and film-camera against the performer's figure, Cine-Dance films ideally also need to be works made entirely for the camera, in an internal space of isolation, or within delineated urban space, as with Kurt Kren's experimental films of that same era in Vienna, such as ANA, 1964, and SELF-MUTILATION, 1965, made with the performance artist Günter Brus and others, shot in cellars and wastelands (Brus's figure in Kren's films, as with that of Hijikata and his dancers in Iimura's two films, is carapaced in rough semi-liquid plaster that painfully sets around the body across the performance's duration). However, both of Iimura's films with Hijikata were made at public venues, into which the audience is seen entering with enthusiastic speed at the two films' openings; THE MASSEUR's final shot is of the spectators still absorbed, mid-spectacle. Live performance and the corporeal presence of the audience sharpen the acute abrasive intimacy of Iimura's own filmmaking body in conjunction with Hijikata's body in movement, evoking 8mm footage shot at the heart of Tokyo's street riots in subsequent years, with figures of activists and riot police colliding, film cameras often dashed to the ground by batons or fists.

I met Takahiko Iimura in 1998 in Tokyo to speak of his work with Hijikata; he had left Tokyo for New York in 1966, soon after his Sogetsu Art Center screening with Richie, as part of an exchange programme, and had been primarily based there for over twenty years, though he was now living again in Tokyo. He wanted to travel while speaking, so we took a nocturnal Chuo-line train west to east across the city, from Koenji to Tokyo terminus and back, fragments of the illuminated cityscape seizing our eyes as we talked; at one point the train stopped dead at the abandoned Manseibashi station, its 1920s platforms frozen on its closure in 1943, our eyes now directly facing the illuminated Akihabara digital-technology towers. The disparate decades jarred and converged. Iimura remembered visiting Hijikata at the Asbestos Studio; Hijikata responded to his request to film *The Masseur* with indifference, simply acceding, in a dismissive, offhand way. Iimura's combative presence in the performance appeared not to disrupt Hijikata's concentration at all; his rapports with his dancers (Kazuo Ohno, Yoshito Ohno, Akira Kasai and others) were already saturated with acute tension and volatility, as they frequently obstructed one another in the course of the performance, so Iimura's body only marginally edged that corporeal tension. After each fifteen seconds' filming, he had to rewind his malfunctioning camera's spring, so each sequence of his film, already fragmentary, is further splintered.

Two years later, Hijikata – recently returned from his first *Kamaitachi* journey with Hosoe – again assented with disengagement to Iimura's request to film *Rose Coloured Dance: To Mr Shibusawa's House*; this time the layout of the venue (the Sennichidani Kokaido hall) and the tight positioning of the audience against the performers impeded Iimura's attempts to film in combative proximity to Hijikata's figure, and he was again preoccupied with technical issues with his 8mm film camera. The filmic war on dance misfired, though the resulting film's subsequent editing served to resuscitate it. After that performance, Iimura rarely met Hijikata, apart from giving copies of both films to him; the films then appear to have formed part of the Asbestos Studio film programme spectacles of the end of the 1960s at which Hijikata danced with the Studio's film projector in his arms, so that those erratic dance move-

Ill. 7 – *The Masseur*, 1963, filmed by Takahiko Iimura.

ments finally outmanoeuvred Iimura's attempt to give to film the pre-eminent status in the obstinate dance/film collision. Iimura emphasised that they were never friends, distanced in their personal rapport by a far greater margin than that of their performance-space intimate face-on combativity. By the time of Hijikata's next major performance work, *Tatsumi Hijikata and the Japanese People: Revolt of the Body*, in 1968, Iimura had already left Tokyo for New York, to shift ground and focus on film-installation works. Then that engulfing city overrode his immediate past, overrode his memories, and for many years he forgot Hijikata utterly.

The Masseur opens with the dancers' preparations for the performance, their bodies assiduously coated by assistants with raw plaster. Hijikata is absent in the first sequences of the film, as the all-male dancers, naked apart from underpants, undertake acts on a large *tatami*-mat plain, chasing, upending and flinging one another, their gestures interconnected but also emanating derangement. Hijikata arrives on a bicycle, veering across the mats, and is enmeshed in the figures' obsessive, looped acts, which veer far more towards performance art than to dance. Hijikata wears a military cap, saluting, a grotesque bag of fluid hanging beneath his penis. The dancers interact with several elderly women, who appear to be blind and confused, simultaneously *samisen*-playing musicians and counterfeit masseurs. The dancers' cracked-plaster heads are overlayered still further by papier-mâché masks. Iimura's filming reveals those acts within the rare cogent instants between camera-wielded blurs and between camera movements tilting so close to the figures of Hijikata and his dancers that only whirls of skin and flesh are discernible; whatever sense the film carries of a collision and violence inflicted by Iimura's filming against dance is diffused in the aberrant, hallucinatory aura and acts of Hijikata's figure.

Two years later, in *Rose Coloured Dance: To Mr Shibusawa's House*, Iimura is filming from far less of a position of intimate corporeal abrasion; often, he films from an elevated location above the performance space, and even retreats to the rear of the auditorium, so that the heads of the audience are interposed between his camera's lens and Hijikata's figure, annulling his own Cine-Dance. At one point, he films two photographers approaching the performers at speed with camera flashes, as though his own filming has been relegated to a subsidiary position in the performance's 'actuality' environment. Almost throughout, Iimura's film is severely over-exposed through light-setting problems (though Iimura told me that the resultant erasure and vanishing of bodies exacted by that camera-malfunction only enhanced his film), generating an irradiated white-light performance space that is the exact contrary to Richie's under-exposed, darkened filming of Hijikata and his dancers in the Shinagawa factory yard for HUMAN SACRIFICE, prior to that film's digital correction. Iimura's film was not corrected; it refuses the regime of documentation, or even of recording and representation, attuned to the malfunction of media, and to corporeal light-searing and obstruction. At the opening of the film, the dancers' heads are being shaved, and Hijikata himself performs with an ineptly half-shaven head. His dancers, again rawly plaster-skinned, race and collide in the performance space's confines; Hijikata and Kazuo Ohno then perform an intricate dance of sexual subjugation, before the film abruptly cuts into darkness.

The most extraordinary of all of Hijikata's films, in its approach, survival and fragmentary form, is REVOLT OF THE BODY, shot by the artist Hiroshi Nakamura, an inexperienced filmmaker who only ever made that one performance film, in October 1968. REVOLT OF THE BODY gives the sensory impression of filming an entity that is barely filmable, holding a volatility and immediacy that is transmitted directly to the film and to its spectatorial experience. Never projected in its era in a cinematic environment or even within an experimental-cinema context, Nakamura's film remained vitally attached corporeally to Hijikata's work, and appears to be the film which Hijikata himself preferred to project to visitors to the Asbestos Studio, both during the period of his dancing-projector performances of around 1969–70, and to the end of his life. REVOLT OF THE BODY is a film situated at the extreme limit of filming, only realizable at all because of the total absence of documentational intent in Nakamura's approach (more advanced, in its contrary disassembly of Hijikata's performance and in its annulling of its own status as a 'record', than that of Iimura). In filming, Nakamura does his semi-improvisional, alert best to maintain the operation of his camera, but is evidently immersed simultaneously in the performance, watching it as he films it. His film camera was new, and a primary intention in Nakamura's filming of Hijikata's work was to experiment with the camera itself. He used 8mm film cartridges and had to rely on the erratic illumination of the hall.

Although Hijikata appears to have been deeply attached to Nakamura's film, his widow Akiko Motofuji was not, and told me that it was one of those she liked the least. She occasionally invited Nakamura to introduce his work in the film programmes she arranged at the Asbestos Studio around 1997–99, a decade or so after Hijikata's death, but still berated him for what she perceived as his lack of serious intent (even Iimura's films, which she viewed simply as inept, had been done with serious purpose). She altered Nakamura's intended soundtrack on several occasions, alternating Artaud's voice and passages of Wagner, among other variants. Since it had been Hijikata's final solo performance in Tokyo, she retrospectively wanted a coherent document of it. That one-sided dispute recalled the quarrel (more violent, in that it ended in a fist fight) in the filming of Vienna's Action Group performance art when Kurt Kren's 8mm filming of Otto Muehl's 1964 *Mama and Papa* cellar performance (undertaken solely to be filmed) resulted in a film of multiple cuts and deliriously fragmented space, dissolving the intended corporeal outrage of Muehl's performance with a film that, at first sight, appeared useless for Muehl's documentational aspirations; Muehl eventually grew to appreciate Kren's filmmaking approach, but Akiko Motofuji remained dismissive of Nakamura's film, with its fragments' resolute incapacity to render a transparent, formal record of Hijikata's performance, which took place in the year of her marriage to Hijikata and his legal assumption of her family name.

Hijikata's intensively prepared performance, *Tatsumi Hijikata and the Japanese People: Revolt of the Body* (Nakamura attached only the second part of Hijikata's full title to his film), was presented on two successive evenings in October 1968 at the Nihon Seinenkan, a large hall built collectively in 1925 by Japan's youth organisations; its main auditorium, where Hijikata performed, had been renovated in 1964 in advance of the influx into Tokyo of visitors to the Olympics and its accompanying cultural programmes, and the venue's space was inflected with associations with Japan's history. To enter it, from the streets of eastern Shinjuku, entailed a corporeal separation from that district's urban-riot unrest (which only intensified over the following year), and an entry into Hijikata's internal domain; the choreographer Ko Murobushi, who attended the performance (and told me that it determined the course of his own dance work) but had not yet met Hijikata, remembered a black horse tethered at one side of the venue's grand entryway, surrounded by arrays of white chrysanthemums. Hijikata's allies, Mishima, Shibusawa and Hosoe, all attended the second of the two nights. Although Hijikata had undertaken several small-scale performances, and had choreographed works by his dancers, in the three years since *Rose Coloured Dance: To Mr Shibusawa's House*, it was his first major performance since Iimura had filmed his work in 1965; elements and obsessions of *Tatsumi Hijikata and the Japanese People: Revolt of the Body* endured in his work of the following two years, such as the suspended panels which also appeared in his misfired solo performance for the Pepsi pavilion at Expo '70, as well as in his commercial horror-film appearances of 1969–70.

Nakamura's film begins with that seminal urban transition from the Shinjuku streets into the Nihon Seinenkan's entrance hall and illuminated corridors, moving on until he enters the venue itself. The film holds no credits or title, indicating Nakamura's lack of intention to project it in public environments. Between those first moments of the film and its last moments, it possesses a mysterious approach to the manoeuvring of time. It appears initially to have been edited as an accumulation of chronological sequences, as though corresponding to the components of Hijikata's performance; at the same time, it presents no guidance or even indication that it holds that authentic temporal correspondence, and could just as easily be presenting the sequences in reverse order, or at random, with voids between its fragments. The film undermines all certainty that it records the actual events of performance as they unfolded over each of its two nights; instead the performance is integrally in non-linear, resistant and irresoluble sequences whose multiple times exist in disintegrative disconnection. Accentuating that sense of temporal fragility, the film has an air of elated ludicrous hilarity, emphasising moments of Hijikata's evident joy and exhilarated pleasure in his own performance, as well as a tightrope-walking, end-of-world precarity; Nakamura is nowhere intent on conjuring the engulfing darkness of Hijikata's Ankoku Butoh project.

In the first sequence of Nakamura's film, Hijikata arrives in the hall on a makeshift chariot – evoking the peasant-carried litter in *Kamaitachi*, inspired by Shibusawa's evocations to Hijikata of Heliogabalus's imperial excesses – with bicycle wheels at either side, accompanied by a further chariot transporting a pig in a cradle, with a rabbit on a bowl or pan, balanced on a long vertical pole. This outlandish ceremonial entrance takes up a disproportionately extended part of Nakamura's film.

The second sequence emphasises Hijikata's dance with the golden phallus (whose exhibited reconstruction was studied by Richie with Akiko Motofuji in 1994), and focuses on his corporeal intersections with six vast brass-surfaced panels, suspended from the ceiling with piano wire and with several of them also attached to one another. Hijikata's figure collides sharply with the panels, which twist and jar wildly in space. The panels simultaneously form projection screens for flash-reflected momentary projections of Hijikata's rapidly moving body within the hall's lighting; the lighting technicians also deploy the panels' surfaces as screens returning intense beams of light, aimed directly at them, so that those screens oscillate between the projection of Hijikata's body and its illuminated absence, as his figure plunges away into darkened space.

Hijikata next undertakes a flamenco-costumed dance which, in Nakamura's filming of it, transmutates into a sequence of infantile dancing, again with an emphasis on collisions with the performance space's hanging panels; the momentary appearance of a pianist at an upright piano indicates the actual sonic environment of the performance, which Nakamura himself supplanted with Ravel's *Bolero* and tango music for his film's soundtrack.

In Nakamura's subsequent sequence, shot with rapidly moving and fluid cinematography, Hijikata's arms and legs are roped and he is propelled in suspension in the space above the audience, from one end to the other of the space and back again, with the audience's heads moving wildly to follow that transit, high at one point and in acute proximity to those heads

Ill. 8 – Nakamura's film camera.

at another. The corporeal suspension is overseen by concerned-looking stage managers who give the impression that they are participating in a dangerous or exacting event, running rapidly to the point at which Hijikata's body is returned to the ground; Hijikata himself appears exhausted at the end of this sequence.

Hijikata is returned to his chariot by the stage managers, but is not transported from the venue; instead, he responds to applause and adulation from the spectators, inciting more of it by waving his arms from his precarious elevation on the chariot, and trying to catch flowers; in fragments at the film's end, Hijikata holds a large flat fish in his mouth. The performance, at its last instant, coincides exactly with the film, as though that film's relentless veerings and disjunctions across time are aberrantly reconciled finally, Hijikata moves backwards under the hall's stage curtain, while the film begins to burn out at its reel's end, with terminal damage and scratching to the celluloid.

Archived plans and spectators' memories of Hijikata's performance indicate that it held sequences which Nakamura did not film, either because he was changing film cartridges or was otherwise distracted, or did film but chose not to incorporate into the surviving version of his film. In one performed sequence, Hijikata appears as a ghost figure: a sequence ghosted by its filming's loss into invisibility or into moving-image non-existence. Every spectator present at the performance, on one or other of its two nights, gave conflicting accounts, perceived it in disparate sequences, or remembered nothing of it, noting that it had been too arduous or intensively experienced for coherent seizure by memory's capacities. In many ways, the performance had proved a memory-scrambling or even memory-erasing event, whose residual sensations were of contradiction, corporeal insurgency and oblivion, propelled beyond memory. Many spectators who experienced both the performance and then projections of Nakamura's film saw no correspondence at all between those dual, interlocked events, and perceived them even as contrary entities (as with Akiko Motofuji's response to the film) fragmenting against one another.

In 2018, in the tea lounge of the Agnes Hotel in Tokyo, I met with the philosopher and translator Kuniichi Uno, who had known Hijikata only at the end of his life, after Uno had returned to Tokyo from undertaking his PhD work in Paris under the supervision of Gilles Deleuze. Uno had brought back a cassette of Artaud's censored 1947–48 radio-recording *To have done with the judgement of god*, holding Artaud's screams alongside his vocal, cacophonic and percussive experiments, and gave a copy to Hijikata. Since that recording had once been attached to Nakamura's film for its Asbestos Studio projections, Uno began to speak of his intermittent, snatched talks with Nakamura during their occasional meetings over several decades. Since Nakamura formed no part of Ankoku Butoh events, other than on that one night in 1968, Uno had encountered him in other contexts, in meetings on Tokyo's streets or in bars. Uno (who had not attended Hijikata's performance at the Nihon Seinen-kan) remembered that Nakamura emphasised that he was working with an unfamiliar camera, whose dual-lens system was still mysterious to him as he filmed Hijikata's figure. Uno recalled that Nakamura said he had added tango music and what he viewed as 'light' music (not Artaud, nor Wagner) to his film because he saw Hijikata not as a 'serious' character in a 'heavy' sense, so his dance required a corresponding soundtrack; Nakamura had evoked to Uno the 1960s rapport and informal vocal dialogues between Hijikata and Kazuo Ohno as resembling those of a comedy duo, with the wild and outlandish Hijikata pitched against the quiet and introspective Ohno. Uno told me that Nakamura had said he had shot far more of Hijikata's performance than the surviving film carried of it, potentially all or most of it (allowing for breaks between film cartridge changes), but then gave away numerous sequences of the film, razoring them out of his original developed film reels before he had a chance to copy them, gifting them to friends or acquaintances who had requested pieces of film that held Hijikata's figure, for their own interest, and who had never returned them (or had never been expected to return them), and ultimately lost or discarded them, since they were never located or rediscovered and integrated back into the film.

I commented to Uno that, if that were the case, then the surviving REVOLT OF THE BODY film existed through subtraction, via an editing strategy motivated by a generosity of gifting that irreparably wounded the film. Those cut-out fragments or absences (potentially including Hijikata's ghost sequence) accentuated the incoherence of the surviving film, perhaps the vital incoherence of Hijikata's performance too, and left behind only those parts of the film which Nakamura would not give away, or which nobody wanted, thereby rendering the final, surviving film into one of detrital elements: a film doubled by a spectral film of absent, irretrievable and never-seen-again ghost fragments. But on listening to Uno's narrative assembled from snatched conversations with Nakamura, I felt unconvinced about it; from watching the film in the form in which Nakamura had given it to Hijikata, it appeared as though he had simply filmed a certain amount of each part of the entire performance, focusing disproportionately – perhaps in his initial enthusiasm with the act of filming – on Hijikata's entrance into the hall, before editing the material to create the performance's pivotal filmic transmutation. Uno had been 20 years old in 1968, and was aware that the only way to have seen the film in that era would have been if Nakamura or Hijikata had projected it publicly, and that most likely happened only rarely, so Nakamura's friends may well have requested parts of it, to project themselves (in an era when 8mm projectors were widely owned), simply to see it. What was certain, at least – whether that arbitrary gifting of razored-out film fragments had taken place or not – was that Nakamura had finally gifted the entirety of his remaining 14-minute film to Hijikata for the Asbestos Studio, along with the camera with which he shot it.

Uno returned to his translations of Beckett, and I left the Agnes Hotel and crossed Tokyo to the Hijikata Archive in Mita district to examine the film reel of REVOLT OF THE BODY which Nakamura had given to Hijikata, still held in its original case with Nakamura's ticket for the performance pasted to it, showing a photograph of the facade of the Nihon Seinenkan. After projecting the film, I then picked up the small Bell & Howell Director Series/Electric Eye 8mm film camera, with its distinctive dual-lens arrangement, with which Nakamura had shot his film. Even with the tangible experience of the original film reel and the camera with which Nakamura had materialised Hijikata's performance, I still needed to look further into the aberrant transformation of Hijikata's corporeality into film.

A few days later, through the artist Yoshiko Shimada, I arranged to meet Hiroshi Nakamura, who planned to visit the opening of a retrospective exhibition by the artist Tatsuo Ikeda in the western Tokyo district of Nerima, and could meet me there. As I arrived, Ikeda was being brought into the museum in a wheelchair; born in 1928, he was Hijikata's exact contemporary (he too gifted his works to Hijikata, and attended his performances throughout the 1960s), and the exhibition marked his 90th birthday. After Ikeda had given a talk, invoking his first works of the 1940s, when, to survive, he made paintings of women's faces from photographs for US occupying soldiers, I walked through the galleries and stopped in one room, surrounded by Ikeda's 1960s menacing ink drawings of masked, multiple-eyed heads, often in ocular confrontation with one another, and of decrepit, emptied Tokyo back streets. I felt it was the last-gasp moment to be encountering Hijikata's filmic collaborators. But when Nakamura appeared, dressed casually and wearing a soft hat, he struck me as disgorging animated life, far younger in appearance than 86, irrepressibly ready to speak about his film of five decades earlier, appreciative of interest in it, with still-vivid memories of its filming.

As we stood in front of Ikeda's drawings, Nakamura told me that he shot almost the entire performance of *Tatsumi Hijikata and the Japanese People: Revolt of the Body*, around an hour in all, on the first of the two nights; he wasn't an invited guest and had to pay for his own ticket. The only exceptions were the moments when he was changing his film camera's cartridges. He had started filming at the moment that he left the street and entered the venue's entrance, initially moving at speed through its corridors. During the performance, he had constantly rushed around the auditorium from shooting location to location, to get what he saw as the best shots, feeling as though he were a spy or peeping tom, though in full view of the audience. He approached the edge of the performance space and filmed in as immediate a proximity to Hijikata's body as he could, while (in an opposing strategy to that of Iimura) being sure not to intervene or intrude in the performance or to get in the audience's way. He used 100 ASA double-sided 8mm film, the camera lenses both fully open, and switched between them whenever he needed to film up close, or else from a distance, as with the sequence in which Hijikata is suspended in the auditorium above the spectators' heads; he had been experimenting with his camera, which he had not used before, but at the same time, he was captivated by the performance, and the immediacy and hilarity of Hijikata's movements. He was not a filmmaker and had never subsequently filmed another performance.

Soon afterwards, he had edited his footage down to around fifteen minutes, to what he saw as the essentials of the performance; he simply discarded the footage he didn't use (he didn't give any of it away, as in Uno's narrative), because, at that time, he thought it was of no importance and there was no reason to keep it. With his filming and editing, he had tried to do the best work he could, bearing in mind he had little film-shooting or film-editing experience; he had been hapless, inexperienced, even inept, but even so, he had been determined to film Hijikata's performance. Long ago, probably around 1969–70, he had given away his Bell & Howell camera to Hijikata, and didn't regret that gift, along with the original reel of the film; he had added his own soundtrack to the copy he kept for himself, deciding to use what he saw as light tango and popular music (this time confirming Uno's account). This was because he viewed Hijikata himself as light and as being full of life and movement, and that extended to his work, which required music that didn't crush his film. He perceived and remembered Hijikata in his own distinctive way, which he saw as being contrary to a more 'official' perception of Hijikata in Japan as a serious, profound artist with weighty ideas; he viewed that perception as totally wrong. He remembered Hijikata laughing or joking through many sequences of the performance at the Nihon Seinenkan, and emphasised that this is clear in his film, as at the moment at which Hijikata, in celebration of his performance's end, holds a fish in his mouth. He always experienced his meetings in Tokyo bars and unexpected street encounters with Hijikata as light and humorous; his dialogues with Hijikata were inevitably full of great laughter and enjoyment, with Hijikata always saying outrageous, imaginative and outlandish things. He had been friendly with Hijikata but didn't know him as a close friend, and had not directly asked his permission to film his performance; when he gifted his film and camera to Hijikata for the Asbestos Studio, Hijikata was happy.

I mentioned to Nakamura that I would soon be meeting the filmmaker Masao Adachi, and Nakamura said he had known him well in Tokyo's activist art culture of the early 1960s, then fifty or more years had suddenly passed; he would like to see him again. Before Nakamura left to view the rest of the exhibition, he was keen to ask how his film's title, as the second part of the performance's original title in Japanese, *Hijikata Tatsumi to nihonjin: Nikutai no hanran*, was translated into English. I told him that it was usually approximated as 'Revolt of the Body', or 'Rebellion of the Flesh', but the term *nikutai*, especially in the 1960s, held far deeper dimensions of carnally focused experimental corporeality than either of the words 'body' or 'flesh' can catch: the sense of a raw physical entity. Nakamura listened closely, then told me that it could be better if his film were known by its Japanese title when shown in Europe, or in the US, and asked me to write, in this book, this one time, now: Nikutai no hanran. Finally, Nakamura expressed laughing delight when I told him that, at occasional projections of his film in Europe, young artists and filmmakers had told me that Nakamura's film – simultaneously Hijikata's film, in its acute intimacy with his body, and in Hijikata's corporeal projections of it – was inspirational for them, in its uniquely inventive and unconstrained movement; he took off his hat, shook my hand, and thanked me for telling him that.

Once he had left, I thought about the history of Nakamura's own body, simultaneously aged and young, and about that elusiveness of the strata, contradictions and dynamics of corporeality which *nikutai* holds in its rendering into English. Nakamura was born in the coastal city of Hamamatsu in 1932 and, as a child, witnessed its destruction through firebombing in June 1945; as he told me, he expected to die, to be incinerated. In the second half of the 1950s, he had been preoccupied with activism and the US forces' continuing presence in Japan, making 'reportage' paintings and drawings, especially of incidents around the US airbases to the west of Tokyo. From 1960, his paintings were engulfed with crimson or blood-red clouds connected to his memories of witnessing Hamamatsu's firebombing and the residues of other cities' destructions. Later, he began to paint the figures of strange schoolgirls, unsettling presences in surreal urban space. And on one night in October 1968, in Tokyo's Shinjuku district, he entered the Nihon Seinenkan with a new and unfamiliar 8mm camera and made a one-off, unprecedented film of corporeal revolt that is the most precious source for envisioning Hijikata's work.

The Tokyo cityscape surrounding Hijikata's body, in his performance within the Nihon Seinenkan's auditorium in Shinjuku, is most exhaustively anatomised in Toshio Matsumoto's film FUNERAL PARADE OF ROSES, shot in the spring of 1969 and released in September of that year, eleven months after Hijikata's final solo Ankoku Butoh performance in Tokyo. While the film REVOLT OF THE BODY infiltrates the Nihon Seinenkan's doorway from the Shinjuku street outside – Nakamura already filming as he enters its chrysanthemum-marked entrance to encounter Hijikata's figure in his Heliogabalus chariot-ride opening to the performance – an imagined film in reverse could well take the inverse direction, leaving behind Hijikata with the celebratory fish in his mouth at his performance's reel-end closure, and go back out into the tumultuous Shinjuku streets. Matsumoto's film holds many sequences of its transvestite figures reeling out of buildings, from nightclub interiors into alleyways, or from department-store foyers into plazas, or, in its final sequence, staggering from an apartment building, blinded, to be scrutinised in bewilderment by passers-by on the pavement outside. FUNERAL PARADE OF ROSES and Oshima's DIARY OF A SHINJUKU THIEF also extensively incorporate sequences of street performance-art interventions in urban space. Shinjuku's distinctive auditoria, in which Hijikata performed around the end of the 1960s, such as the Nihon

Seinenkan, with its resonances of Japan's history and the Shin-juku Art Theatre, with its direct conduit into the ongoing furore of the district's art and riot protests, formed part of a volatile topography in which interior could always readily mutate into exterior, via channels, mappings and lenses such as corporeal acts and mobile film cameras.

Matsumoto's film was co-produced by the Art Theatre Guild organisation, which specialised in supporting and distribut-ing feature-films by innovative directors, such as DIARY OF A SHINJUKU THIEF, released in February of that same year, and also produced films in which Hijikata appeared as an actor in that era, such as EVIL SPIRITS OF JAPAN, 1970; in tension with Japan's dominant film studios such as Nikkatsu and Toei, the independent Art Theatre Guild accorded filmmakers excep-tional autonomy to develop their own projects, to shoot at will in Tokyo's urban space (in filming Shinjuku, Matsumoto drew on his enthusiasm for European urban filmmakers such as Godard) or in cramped, constrained locations, as in the film's apartment and nightclub sequences. Matsumoto's film was screened in the US in 1970 and also programmed at festivals in Europe, generating for viewers a rare international sight-ing of contemporary film's sexual and activist experimenta-tion in Tokyo that paralleled the then-low international profile of Hijikata's Ankoku Butoh project, promoted by Richie in his *Japan Times* art columns but otherwise largely unknown.

FUNERAL PARADE OF ROSES is a feature-length film experi-menting in a sustained way with many of the concerns of shorter films of the 1960s, such as those of Richie and Iimura with Hijikata: isolation and subjugation, artifice and its unscreen-ing, performance and its confrontational filming. Matsumoto incessantly arrests and fragments his film's loosely oedipal nar-rative, pulling back from scenes to reveal his film crew's work (as also frequently occurred in the films of Shuji Terayama, such as PASTORAL HIDE AND SEEK), halting the action to interview his cast along with street-encountered transvestite 'gayboys' in nocturnal Shinjuku's avenues – filmed in darkness with illuminated hoardings behind them – and also to probe, in animated and stop-motion sequences, the commitment and aims of political activists and activist filmmakers, whom Matsumoto often presents with abrasive irony.

Matsumoto films primarily in the streets of Shinjuku, around both the west and east entrances to the immense Shinjuku train station, which was wildly overrun by thousands of rioters (on that occasion, factory workers as well as students) during one of the district's protests in October 1968, the month of Hijikata's *Tatsumi Hijikata and the Japanese People: Revolt of the Body* performances; Matsumoto focuses upon the East Plaza, which was often the site of open-air performance actions. In Matsumoto's film, no riots occur, and the only trace of that unrest is when the film's transvestite character Eddie finds a wounded protester hiding in the foyer of her building after being beaten by the police. Matsumoto films the Shinjuku streets as crammed with bodies but bleak, enlivened solely by their walls' saturation with posters, against which Eddie leans exhausted after one of her relentless bouts of street harassment, only to be harassed yet again and to flee, in the process colliding with a delivery bicyclist whose fall cascades to the pavement the many boxes of *soba*-noodles he is transporting. Matsumoto's camera follows Eddie through the streets, always alert to the stares and hostility which her figure provokes. Occasionally, the camera ascends to a position of elevation to film Shinjuku's neon-illuminated advertising screens, or positions the film's characters in building-top cafes whose windows look out on the city below them.

To escape street harassment, Eddie descends a dark stairway into a subterranean art gallery, which appears barely lit and intensively shadowed. On the gallery's walls is an exhibition of the 1960s ink drawings of masked faces by Tatsuo Ikeda which, fifty years later, surrounded Nakamura and me in the Nerima art-museum while we spoke of his Hijikata film, REVOLT OF THE BODY: solitary masks and twin masks in gaping-mouthed confrontation with one another. From the floor of the gallery, a voice (presented as being that of Ikeda) transmitted from a reel-to-reel tape machine speaks of those masks, which, if removed, only hide further masks, so the face is never revealed. The corporeal appears to be bleeding out, in the near darkness of that subterranean gallery, the artworks barely emerging from the darkness in which they are sunk. Eddie's principal subterranean location is the Bar Genet where she works as a hostess, dancing wildly and enticing the elderly customers, though they appear distracted, lost in nostalgia and memories of another transvestite bar culture, in the pre-war Asakusa-district whose emptied-out 1971 variant Simmon Yotsuya's transvestite figure traverses in Hosoe's *Simmon: A Private Landscape*. When the proprietor of the Bar Genet commits suicide, Eddie attends her funeral, but the immense cemetery is waterlogged, the ancient graves collapsing into contaminated floodlands or already submerged, and Eddie comments that she wishes all of Tokyo would now sink below ground.

Eddie ascends to the summit of the Tokyo Tower in the company of one of her activist filmmaker friends, Matsumoto's camera filming Tokyo through the gantried aperture of the tower's elevator during its ascent, so that it appears as though the city is being slowly propelled through a projector's gate, alternately visible and barred from sight. At one moment, that prominent perspective over the city's elevated highway intersections possesses the cold omniscience that Tarkovsky accords to that viewpoint in his filming of Tokyo in Solaris, but, as the ascent continues the city's clear delineation gradually vanishes so that it resembles the future-city which Marker's doomed time-traveller glimpses, part spider-web and part digital network, in La Jetée: 'ten thousand incomprehensible avenues'.[4] The heated corporeal confrontations and street harassment are erased at that level, and the city appears irradiated; Eddie's urban commentary emphasises Tokyo's strangeness and its capacity to impede its own envisioning: 'I see nothing ... Is it gone?'; on entering the viewing-platform at the tower's summit, she pushes away the telescopes that facilitate intimate urban inspection, and instead closes her eyes as she gazes down at the city.

By the film's final sequence, Eddie's urban vision is entirely extinguished after she stabs herself in both eyes and goes to stand on the pavement outside her building, the knife still in her hand. An expectant crowd has already gathered there, as though anticipating the spectacle of that ocular cut. But after the relentless vocal harassment she endured in previous scenes, the figures now surrounding Eddie are silent, the only exclamations those emitted from urban hoardings and street signage. Matsumoto's camera itself now harasses those spectators, intent on colliding with them, as though deploying Iimura's Cine-Dance approach, and they rapidly move aside, cover their faces or turn their backs. Matsumoto finally erases Tokyo by intentionally over-exposing his camera's filming of it, the sequence's figures fading out, as with Iimura's accidental over-exposing of Hijikata's figure in Rose Coloured Dance: To Mr Shibusawa's House (or, contrarily, Hijikata's figure consigned to near darkness by Richie's accidental under-exposing of it in Human Sacrifice), and the sequence ends in void white light.

Matsumoto's film is conceptually engaged with responses to 'actuality' media environments whose rapid expansion and prominence proved contentious in that era, especially in their relationship to emerging manifestations of art, revolution, film projection and performance. The film's activist filmmakers concentrate on shooting a television-set's malfunctioning screen with its distorted news-broadcast imageries of the street riots going on in the Tokyo streets outside their confined, windowless apartment, rather than filming the riots themselves, in their immediacy. In his own filming of Funeral Parade of Roses, Matsumoto himself was directly immersed in the process of transitioning from his earlier experimental short films to larger-scale film-installation spectacles. In evoking his participation of 1970 in the Osaka Expo, for an interview accompanying the DVD release of Funeral Parade of Roses in 2003, Matsumoto (who died in 2017) focuses not on what the Expo's opponents saw as the momentous event's corporate, revolution-annulling dimensions, but instead on the unprecedented opportunity it gave him and other film artists to develop intermedial multi-screen projection experiments, for vast audiences, and on his own ocular captivation by the proliferations of imageries he encountered at Expo '70.

In her book *Cinema and Actuality*, Yuriko Furuhata evokes a 1968 dialogue between Oshima and Mishima, conducted for the film magazine *Eiga Geijutsu* (*Film Art*), in which they probed the impact of all-consuming media environments on experiments in art and urban protest: 'Oshima and Mishima concur that the New Left generation of Japanese student protestors are the children of television whose political actions are deeply conditioned by the ubiquitous presence of the news camera. Oshima calls this media-conscious form of student protest an "expressive act" akin to an artistic performance. Mishima criticizes this view by noting that the substitution of political action by the expressive act attests to the bleakness of the television age in which they all live. Oshima, by contrast, regards this blurring of the boundary between artistic performance and political action in a positive light, suggesting that the very meaning of politics and art should be rethought in light of this situation.'[5] That 'positive light' Oshima appeared to perceive in 1968 would be utterly darkened over the following two years of film's contrary amalgams with revolutionary violence, with the Expocity's immense corporate spectacle, and with the feature-film imageries of outlandish corporeal horror that foregrounded Hijikata's body as their primary site.

Hijikata's REVOLT OF THE BODY performance-film generates an intimate sense of his Ankoku Butoh project in its rawest, optimum state of realization, and in its multiple intersections with the transmutations of 1960s Tokyo, from whose tumultuous, riot-torn streets Nakamura entered the performance's venue with his film camera already primed and open-lensed. *Tatsumi Hijikata and the Japanese People: Revolt of the Body* was Hijikata's final solo performance in Tokyo; he also performed an unfilmed solo dance seventeen months later, at the

Osaka Expo in March 1970. But the filming of Hijikata's performances continued over the precipice edge of the 1960s and beyond the moment of the Expo (a terminal moment, in many ways, for the film and performance culture that had generated Hijikata's 1960s films in Tokyo), both in the domain of performance films shot in auditoria, and that of film sequences shot in urban space. Hijikata continued to dance in public for three further years, usually undertaking short appearances within programmes otherwise performed by his young Asbestos Studio dancers, including a large-scale programme of works choreographed by Hijikata and staged at the Shinjuku Art Theatre in 1972. In 1973, Hijikata performed several short sequences within a programme presented at Kyoto University's Westside Auditorium, SUMMER STORM, and, in October of that year, over three nights, made a guest appearance – filmed in colour, but in an incomplete form, presumably because a finite celluloid cartridge's duration expired, so the footage cuts while Hijikata is still dancing, fragmenting his last dance before an audience and propelling it into a final filmic void – in *Phallic Mythology*, drawn from writings by Hijikata's friend Tatsuhiko Shibusawa and once again (as with the first sequence of *Tatsumi Hijikata and the Japanese People: Revolt of the Body*, five years earlier) preoccupied with the acts of the Roman emperor Heliogabalus, and again – as with that 1968 performance – presented at the Nihon Seinenkan's auditorium, by the Dairakudakan dance company of Akaji Maro which, at that time, included Ko Murobushi as a performer.

SUMMER STORM was shot in colour by three Kyoto University students, each holding an 8mm camera and positioned at the rear, centre and front of the auditorium, under the supervision of the promoter and filmmaker Misao Arai, who had previously made a sex film, HOT SPRING SPA MAID PIMPS, with Hijikata's participation in 1969. The university's 1930s-built Westside Auditorium (often also used as a rock-music venue in the 1970s, especially for a legendary 1976 concert by Frank Zappa, and with wide-ranging historical associations with

Kyoto's counter-cultures, community and arts groups, activism and Red Army Faction terrorism) was a distinctive building that varied from the other, more formal auditoria – such as the Nihon Seinenkan – in which Hijikata and his dancers more usually performed, constructed largely from wood and corrugated iron, and with a vast, sloping roof. The building resembled in some ways a larger-scale version of the Asbestos Studio as it had been photographed by Hosoe in the mid-1960s for *Kamaitachi*, and was already archaic and dilapidated in appearance by the early 1970s. The auditorium possessed a unique, autonomous atmosphere (still intact in its largely-unchanged 2010s form) which worked to impart an outlandish aura to the figures filmed in SUMMER STORM.

After SUMMER STORM's filming, the 8mm footage was abandoned, and not relocated and assembled by Irai for thirty years, until 2003. The neglected celluloid's colour deterioration during those decades accentuated the already predominant darkness within the filmed auditorium. Hijikata performed two variants of a dance fragment titled *Leprosy* in the programme, which especially emphasised the work of his young dancers rather than his own work. In the film's sequences, the bodies performing in front of the auditorium's wooden rear wall, embedded with a succession of metal panels, appear exceptionally sombre, often engulfed totally by darkness, and resonating – at the end of the filming of Hijikata's performances – with Richie's under-exposed, celluloid-darkened first filming of Hijikata's Ankoku Butoh project for HUMAN SACRIFICE.

In 2003, when SUMMER STORM's 8mm footage was finally assembled, digitised and released on DVD, several sequences featuring Hijikata's appearances in it were projected via the immense digital moving-image screens surmounting the towers around Tokyo's Shibuya-district central traffic intersection, momentarily replacing the usual advertising sequences of J-Pop idols or consumer artefacts, so that the time-veering sequences holding Hijikata's corporeal presence were transmitted both to the dense, unsuspecting crowds in the streets below and

Ill. 9 – Hijikata performing *Leprosy*, part of SUMMER STORM, filmed by Kyoto University students, 1973.

also directly into Tokyo's elevated urban space. That nocturnal projection event was itself filmed from ground level – the passers-by, ocularly snared by the otherworldly moving-image sequences projected above them, appear as bewildered as the film-camera-harassed passers-by who witness the sudden apparition of Eddie's eye-pierced figure in the final sequence of FUNERAL PARADE OF ROSES – and became incorporated into the DVD as its opening element.

Hijikata made his most extensive performance-film in Tokyo's urban space long after its streets' unique uproar of the 1960s' first and final years had definitively dissipated, as though he had been biding his time and waiting to dance in the detrital urban afterburn of that voided revolutionary frenzy. Hijikata's work (and partial inactivity) of the final fifteen years of his life often give the impression of petrified, stranded time. The film-maker Keiya Ouchida, who had made a black-and-white film recording (as an act of linear documentation) of the *Story of Smallpox* performance presented as part of Hijikata's large-scale programme at the Shinjuku Art Theatre in 1972, worked again with Hijikata in 1975 on Scenery of Wind, this time filming Hijikata in fragments, at night, in darkness-imbued colour footage, tracking Hijikata's spectral movements across Tokyo's emptied-out alleyways, wastelands and slaughterhouse zones, and through the marine peripheries extending from Tokyo's dockland areas to those of Kawasaki and Yokohama. In Scenery of Wind, Hijikata's dance movements were generated solely to be filmed, but Ouchida took the opposite spatial approach to Iimura's Cine-Dance, remaining distanced from Hijikata's figure, following and never colliding with its transits.

After an initial close-up sequence which films Hijikata's dance movements in interior space, Scenery of Wind moves out into external urban space. At first, Hijikata's figure is absent from that space: a large building's roof appears, with the flags of Japan and the US visible below it, then the film camera travels through a dirt-road wasteland with abandoned vehicles at its edges. Hijikata then appears, his face appearing far more lined and weathered than in its previous filmings, dancing in opposition to strong gusts of wind at a bayside port location; an illuminated port docking-tower shows the figure zero on all of its sides. Hijikata's figure enters an industrial building that resonates with that of Richie's Human Sacrifice, shot in that same marine-edge terrain; he then climbs onto horizontally positioned wooden posts and a part-sunk boat. After those sequences, his figure moves deeper into the city, to alleyways which the Hijikata Archive's director Takashi Morishita identified as being in the Meguro-district vicinity of the Asbestos Studio. The film was evidently shot at the dead of night; the alleyways appear deserted, lights still on but the shops' metal shutters down. Hijikata covertly enters a school building (the film's soundtrack, which oscillates between howls of wind and muted cacophonies of urban noise, marks that entry with the sound of children's cries), moving from classroom to classroom, with children's drawings of faces on the walls, and an old television set on the wooden floor. Hijikata re-enters the alleyways, climbing a slope whose shopfronts are faced with vending machines, dancing in decelerated, arduous gestures, the dawn light visible overhead at the alleyway's summit. Hijikata then moves to a slaughterhouse terrain at the bayside, his figure now supported by a slaughterman's hooked pick, as though unable to stand upright without it. Outside the slaughterhouse, many cows are constrained in concrete areas, apparently waiting to be killed at dawn. Hijikata enters the decrepit slaughterhouse with its empty hooks, now barely dancing at all, his figure forming an amalgam with the corroded floors and slabs; drains run with water around his now prone body. In the final sequence, in that urban marine landscape, he holds a flag around his body (as with the battleship flag that encloses it as he runs alongside apartment buildings in *Kamaitachi*) and clambers onto a broken breakwater wall. The film's final shot, Hijikata's figure having already vanished, overlooks urban space from a position of elevation, a dawn red sun hovering directly over that space.

In both Scenery of Wind's outdoor locations and Summer Storm's darkened auditorium, Hijikata's figure, positioned far beyond his 1960s films, emanates a bleak and cancelled, spectral quality, as though his body were now deliquescing and disappearing into blackness, and can only collapse into itself in raw, hostile environments, against slaughterhouse floors and marine-edge flotsam. In Scenery of Wind, nocturnal Tokyo and its wasteland edges appear depopulated, as an interzonal cityscape pitched between Tokyo's 1960s urban transmutation and a still-unknown, already spectral urban future whose corporeal manoeuvres remain unenvisaged, seizable by film only in their stalled incapacitation. The filmic rendering of corporeal performance and its urban environments, in that era of Tokyo's disjuncture across the 1970s' first half, appears as an exhausted, burnt-out medium, resonating with Hosoe's photographing of wasteland-Tokyo in those same years, once the vibrant figure of Simmon Yotsuya had unaccountably slipped out from his project, *Simmon: A Private Landscape*, leaving it simultaneously abandoned but obsessively still pursued, in that voided urban space. The 1970s misfired filmings of Hijikata's performances only accentuate how vital and unprecedented film's experimental intersections with performance had been, in 1960s Tokyo, with its acute urban upheavals, and its moving-image imperatives of corporeal exploration, sex and revolution.

Notes

1   Yuriko Furuhata, *Cinema of Actuality: Japanese Avant-Garde Filmmaking in the Season of Image Politics*, Durham NC/London: Duke University Press, 2013, pages 145–46.

2   Takahiko Iimura, *Media and Performance*, Tokyo: Takahiko Iimura Media Art Institute, 2007, pages 1–2.

3   Gene Kelly, quoted in the obituary 'Gene Kelly, Dancer of Vigour and Grace, Dies', *New York Times*, 3 February 1996, page 5.

4   Chris Marker, LA JETÉE, New York: Zone Books, 1996, unpaginated.

5   Furuhata, (see note 1), page 1.

Horrors, Deaths, Revolutions

At instants of urban madness or extreme transformation, pre-cipitated by conflict or internal implosion, the city turns itself inside out and becomes exposed to new anatomical possibilit-ies, for its figures and its own topographical parameters. It may appear that, apart from intermittent disruptions on its surface, confined to two or three areas, the city is functioning well, becoming ascendantly wealthy, planning global events that will enhance its international prestige. But a profound malfunction is taking place, within those same surfaces but also inside its subterraneas. In that city, film irrepressibly registers imager-ies of immense spatial and corporeal upheavals, which may oscillate between obsessions with the horrific or sexual and the revolutionary. When media technologies of communica-tion and their power expand to an overwhelming form at that same instant, from image-screened urban plazas at the city's heart to its most denuded and voided peripheries, it appears that the entire city is now the medium either of state power or of an outlandish counter-force that can imminently overturn and mutate everything within it: the configuration of the human body, above all.

The years 1969–70, following his performances of *Tatsumi Hijikata and the Japanese People: Revolt of the Body*, filmed by Nakamura, were in many ways the most intensive and over-loaded of Hijikata's work, reflecting the urban excess of that era. As with all experimental artists based in Tokyo, he was working within an urban context in which the street-riot cul-ture of the preceding year was now entering an unprecedented stage, and could either precipitate fundamental change in social life in Japan, especially in the country's rapport with the military power and political influence of the US, or else move into imageries and acts of terrorism, or else exhaust itself. At the same time, those years 1969–70 offered seductive possibilities for Hijikata's work to generate income for himself and his Asbestos Studio dancers, in that work's expansion from its habitual performance (undertaken with minimal financial gain, or a loss) in small arts venues, to its mediation in studio-made films intended for mass-audience consumption, as well as in the form of nightclub spectacles, and (as an unprecedented opportunity) as part of the most immense spectacle generated in Japan's postwar decades, in a corporate and state-conceived form, at the Osaka Expo. In 1969–70, Tokyo's transmutations simultaneously opened out into preoccupations with bodies of anatomical horror and into movements towards urban terrorism.

The conjunction in 1969 in Tokyo of intensive experimentation in art, moving-image culture and performance coincided to its maximal degree with volatile currents of accelerating street-riot protests against multiple targets. Alongside the forthcoming renewal of the US–Japan Security Treaty, which was due to take place during the span of Expo '70, protests flared against the continuing dominant US military presence in Japan. Among innumerable other grievances and contestations of 1969, protesters also targeted the construction of Narita International Airport to the north-east of Tokyo and the accompanying dispossession of farmers from their land. Haneda Airport, built within Tokyo's bayside edge at the beginning of the 1930s and a major launching site for Japan's militarist expansions across East Asia of that decade, was now seen as too constrained (between the bay and the inner city) for the rise in international flights anticipated for the new, world-city Tokyo of rising wealth and global profile; it would now be confined to domestic flights, while Narita would handle international flights. The riots around the Narita site would be at their most violent in 1971, and were filmed by many activist filmmakers of that era, including Chris Marker; Narita airport's opening was delayed until 1978, and for at least two decades afterwards it retained the aura of an embattled insular zone with a pervasive security-guard presence and fortified surrounding barriers. The intensity of that era finally dissipated into a predominantly disabused disengagement from political action in Tokyo's arts culture of the 1970s, but it left its mark on the urban space of Tokyo, in its reconfiguration as a pacified city whose architecture and topographies were overhauled to deter further riot eruptions.

Japan's studio-based system of film production was itself in an emergency situation in 1969, both from its own internal fissures of fierce competition and ossified structures, as well as through exterior economic pressure caused in part by the urban captivation with television culture that Matsumoto visualised in that year in FUNERAL PARADE OF ROSES, and which was taking urban inhabitants out of cinemas; the studios also faced opposition from alternative means of production, distribution and film-screening, exemplified by the Art Theatre Guild organisation that co-produced Matsumoto's film and Oshima's DIARY OF A SHINJUKU THIEF. To survive, studios gave greater autonomy to their directors (such as Teruo Ishii, who was instrumental in Hijikata's studio-film appearances) to create films – often amalgams of existing horror, sex and gangster idioms – that, by whatever extreme means or provocation, would bring spectators back into Tokyo's many hundreds of now emptying cinemas, such as those whose ruins and vanished sites Richie showed me on our Shinjuku walk in 1998.

That urgent impetus was aimed especially at young, male spectators who were more attracted to independent films than studio-made films, or who had never habituated themselves to cinema attendance, with its financial regime and fixed ocular rituals. As well as forming the site for television consumption, domestic space (or its expansions into small-scale arts venues or dance studios, such as the Asbestos Studio) could also be used for the projection among friends of 8mm and 16mm films, self-shot, or shared and collected in an era when projectors and film cameras were widely owned. The large-scale filming by participants of their experiences during the Shinjuku riots of 1968–69 – protestors' camera-wielding hands often beaten by riot police staves, propelling the cameras to the ground, among other fragments and blurs of mid-riot action – indicates the extent of that era's 8mm-camera ownership, which became especially apparent in the 2010s through the surviving riot-participants' digitisation of their 8mm films and their transferral to historical archives.

Films intended for large-scale cinematic audiences in 1969–70 explored unprecedented preoccupations with anatomical reformulation and resulting variants of horror, along with insurgencies of revolt against corrupt, deranged powers, sometimes positioning their figures within contemporary or recent urban Tokyo, but more often reversing in time, especially to the Taisho era, 1912–26, as one in which preoccupations with experimentation in sex and horror and with the contestation or ridiculing of oppressive power could be situated with impunity. The historian of Tokyo Edward Seidensticker told me that he believed late-1960s films often shifted their focus away from that moment's Tokyo, towards Tokyo or peripheral cities in the Taisho era because that displacement evoked the sense of freedom (along with the visually distinctive Taisho advertising cultures, evoked by Hijikata's collaborator Tadanori Yokoo in his Ankoku Butoh posters) which artists experienced in that era, prior to Japan's movement into militarism from 1931. Since the Taisho era emperor had been widely perceived as mentally impaired or simply mad, then the world around him could also be imagined as laudably mad, or unconstrained; if its leaders were mad, Japan's population was free. The filmmaker and theatre director Shuji Terayama, who intermittently collaborated with Hijikata across the 1960s, also had a deep fascination with the Taisho era, within which much of his work is set. Hijikata's 1969–70 films with Teruo Ishii, located in the Taisho era, either moved from an opening in Tokyo to wild marine landscapes or else took place entirely in the north, in Hijikata's home region of Akita; simultaneously, those films remained always deeply inflected by Tokyo's dynamics of resistance to arbitrary, punitive power and its art-propelled explorations of corporeal fragmentation.

Hijikata's films of 1969–70 – in their many forms, across studio productions, Art Theatre Guild productions, independent works, and even his film work for the Osaka Expo – always held a strong concern with sexual acts or the evocation of unconstrained sexuality. Sex is the aberrant medium of madness, manifesting resistance or obliviousness towards dominant, deviant state power, and sex's urgency also embodies the tightrope-walking, last-gasp prescient moment which many young dissidents of Tokyo's 1969 megalopolis experienced, prior to their imminent engulfing into the city's all-enveloping corporate imperatives, if their riots' aims failed. Sex, at that moment, also formed a medium of emergent terrorism, propelling acts of violent insurrection and the renunciation of state-controlled, US-military dominated Tokyo, as in the *pinku eiga* ('pink film') works – such as Go, Go, Second Time Virgin, 1969, and Sex Jack, 1970, both scripted by Masao Adachi – which Koji Wakamatsu made independently in that era, beyond the studio system, prior to the decision of Adachi and Wakamatsu to shift (a geographical movement, as well as a filmic one) into activist revolutionary cinema. Wakamatsu's films of 1969–70, when not confined to the interiors and rooftop of one building, are often situated in peripheral urban locations and riverside wastelands that resonate with those of *Kamaitachi*'s final photographs, or the Tokyo edge-sites explored by Hosoe in *Simmon: A Private Landscape*: sites of urban death.

Alongside his work in studio films in 1969–70, Hijikata also appeared in several small roles in films for independent and Art Theatre Guild productions, such as Kazuo Kiroki's Evil Spirits of Japan, 1970, in which he played a marginal figure inhabiting wastelands at a city's edge, where its detritus is burned, gathering followers around him there, but occasionally entering the city – momentarily glimpsed dancing in bleak alleyways – in order to provoke or instil unease in its inhabitants, and appearing to have a determining influence on the film's pivotal characters. Hijikata's momentary appearances in such films resulted, as with his studio films, from the desire

Ill. 10 – Evil Spirits of Japan, dir. Kazuo Kiroki, 1970.

of directors such as Kiroki to position a destabilising, eye-cap-
turing figure at the periphery of their film's action, to make its
narrative veer compellingly towards its always catastrophic end.
Although Ankoku Butoh was still not prominent as an art form
in Tokyo in 1969–70, Hijikata's figure possessed a special notoriety, often recognisable by young audiences, on the wild edge
of revolution, too autonomous and idiosyncratic to be co-opted
into the multiple factional or political agendas of Tokyo's protesters, but emanating his own awry corporeal riotousness, with
a revolutionary aura in its embodiment of experimentation.

In 1969, while Tokyo's riots, contestations and fulminations
were erupting around them, Hijikata and Akiko Motofuji found
the time to run a sex-cabaret nightclub, Club Space Capsule, in
the entertainment district of Akasaka. The club was a members-
only entity, ensuring a degree of insularity for its outrages, and
had a clientele that spanned artists and the more professional
Tokyo club goers who are seen in that same era in Matsumoto's
filmed Bar Genet, hardened in nostalgia for other sex-club eras.
Akiko Motofuji, who had started her career in dance as a child

in classical ballet, undertook almost the entirety of the cabaret's disreputable operation, expanding its 'model' to other cities in Japan when she saw opportunities to do so, and even to cities in South-East Asia. She told me in 1998 that the club had operated with great success for around a year, generating considerable income for the Asbestos Studio and its dancers, though running a nightclub was potentially dangerous in many ways; alongside the unruly clientele there were always threats from the police and gangsters for her to affront, and she had to develop a sardonic, wily approach, attuned to adeptly promoting sex and outrage: 'I was a rogue, Stephen-chan, almost a criminal myself.'

At the beginning of the 1960s, Hijikata had conceived of himself as a Genet-inspired criminal whose dance experiments would duly see him incarcerated, but his work at Club Space Capsule was confined to the domain of the spectacles' choreography. As well as using his Asbestos Studio dancers, he found available bodies for the cabaret performances among other Tokyo performance groups. There existed no fixed hierarchy between the art-focused dimension of Hijikata's work as performed at the Nihon Seinenkan in 1968, his choreography at the Club Space Capsule in 1969 and his work in horror and sex films of 1969–70. Akiko Motofuji emphasised that he took his cabaret choreography seriously, incorporating elements from his dancers' performances at the Asbestos Studio into their appearances at Club Space Capsule: the female dancers naked and painted silver, the male dancers plaster-coated. She noted that many of those young dancers perceived no distinction between the two spatial dimensions, simply doing what she and Hijikata demanded, in subjugation. She herself had subjugated her dance ambitions and the spatial control of the Asbestos Studio, to Hijikata, focusing upon designing costumes for the dancers as well as undertaking the arduous business of operating the cabaret, facing off competitors and mysterious, threatening visitors: 'It was sometimes like being in a *yakuza* movie ...'. But by 1998 she was dancing again and had reconstructed the Asbestos Studio, so she felt no bitterness; Hijikata had lived and danced for such a short time, after all. Now his body was ashes, while she was still dancing: 1969 was a long time ago.

Hijikata's studio-film work unfolded in the intensive 18-month interval between his appearance in Nakamura's REVOLT OF THE BODY film in October 1968 and his unique appearance at the Pepsi pavilion at the Osaka Expo in March 1970. That period also encompassed his journey to Hokkaido for the filming of his work that would be projected at the Expo's Midori pavilion, his cabaret choreographies, appearances in other independent and Art Theatre Guild films, work on writing and the assembly of scrapbooks, as well as his ongoing training work with his dancers. Initially, on being approached by the director Teruo Ishii, Akiko Motofuji told me, Hijikata was hesitant, but more through his unfamiliarity with industrial filmmaking and its inflexible schedules, along with his resistance to spending periods of time away from the Asbestos Studio at the Kyoto studios where many of the interior sequences of his films would be shot, rather than because it would somehow impair his experimental or revolutionary standing in Tokyo's art world to be seen appearing in low-budget horror films. Ishii convinced Hijikata to appear in his next film, HORRORS OF MALFORMED MEN, as well as other grotesque horror films he was envisaging; Ishii worked rapidly on films grouped within thematic series in order to maintain the attention of loyal spectators, and HORRORS OF MALFORMED MEN, released in cinemas in Tokyo in October 1969, was only one of seven of his films released that year. HORRORS OF MALFORMED MEN intensified Ishii's habitual preoccupations with anatomical disfiguration and mutilation, and Hijikata's presence in the film in turn accentuated its outlandish aura. Although the film's studio, Toei, gave Ishii inordinate freedom to generate outrageous films that would propel Tokyo's young audiences into the studio's cinemas and away from television consumption or street-rioting, the film's

Ill. 11 – Horrors of Malformed Men, dir. Teruo Ishii, 1969.

provocations unnerved the studio, and it was withdrawn from projection after only two weeks, reappearing rarely until 2007, when it was issued on DVD soon after Ishii's death.

Most of the film was shot on location, in widescreen format, on Japan's northern coast, around the remote Noto peninsula, which provided the crashing seascapes, marine-rock outcrops and sense of remoteness required for the film's setting on an offshore island to which all outsiders' access is forbidden. Hijikata's character, an obsessed anatomist experimenting with creating a population of deformed beings from 'normal' corporeal sources, has not left the island for several decades but receives the necessary raw material for his experiments from Tokyo, in the form of young urban inhabitants who are duped, classified as insane and then shipped to his island. The choreographer Ko Murobushi travelled to the Noto peninsula with Hijikata and appears briefly as one of the anatomist's acolytes in the film; as with Akiko Motofuji's account of Hijikata's cabaret choreography, Murobushi told me that Hijikata had approached his work on Horrors of Malformed Men with extreme seriousness (the film was the only one in which he was accorded a major role with extensive dialogue, as distinct from his more peripheral appearances in other films of that era, such as Evil Spirits of Japan). That gravity appears contrary to the hilarious levity and elation that Nakamura perceived in Hijikata's art-aligned performance at the Nihon Seinenkan and which he seized in the film-fragments of REVOLT OF THE BODY.

HORRORS OF MALFORMED MEN – drawn by Ishii from the work of the legendary Poe-inspired writer of grotesque fiction, Taro Hirai, known by his pseudonym Edogawa Ranpo, especially from his 1928 novel *Strange Tale of Panorama Island* – is set in the Taisho era and opens in Tokyo, in a lunatic asylum; Hijikata's anatomist only makes his first sustained appearance mid-film, and the entirety of the film until that point is composed of hallucinatory misunderstandings, sonic mysteries, duplications of figures and inexplicable deaths. The film's principal character, first seen lost in the women's zone of an insane asylum, remains in a state of traumatised oblivion or amnesia throughout the film's first part, eventually supplanting the status of a wealthy dead man who resembled him, and only assembles his own identity as Hirosuke, the second son of the anatomist, when he travels with a group of servants to the island to meet him.

Although Hijikata's figure first appears in Hirosuke's asylum hallucinations generated by drawings he makes in his cell of a seascape that obsesses him (the entirety of the film's elaboration from that point appears projected outwards from those drawings, as an extension of that hallucination rather than a coherent narrative), the figure only speaks when he encounters his son on a clifftop plateau after undertaking dance sequences, wearing a white inside-out and back-to-front bride's *kimono* soaked in sea-water, on the cliff's strange basalt-rock formations, then with a wild seascape behind him in a sequence that emphasises the film's widescreen format, spray from that seascape's powerful waves taking up most of the screen, with Hijikata's figure at its edge. Ishii first shot that sequence of Hijikata dancing against the cliff edge as a technical test, but decided that it worked so well, that he would expand it and incorporate it into the film. At first, only Hijikata's eyes are seen, his pupils moving rapidly from side to side, then the camera pans down to his mouth. Hijikata's dance of corporeal contortion and spasming fingers is created to be filmed; it has no narrative place other than to incite Hirosuke's unease and to plunge the film into an atmosphere of derangement. Hijikata then gradually approaches the film camera's lens, ready to speak to his son and to explain his project.

Hijikata's anatomist is himself deformed, but only to the extent of white-plaster webbing attached to both of his hands. Although his son appears to have arrived at the island through his own volition, it transpires that he is a surgeon, dispatched as a child by his father to Tokyo for medical training that will now be instrumental in the work necessary for the completion of his father's vision to create his island-population of malformed beings. The anatomist's articulation of his project for his son forms a fragmentary theory of anatomical experimentation. That project is one that proposes corporeal aberration as a prerequisite for survival: bodies perceived as normal are now fraudulent, and must be transmuted into horrific, malformed amalgams with one another, or else with animals, in order to become authentic bodies, which will then dance. The vision of Hijikata's anatomist resonates strongly with Artaud's proposal, in his final work, the radio project *To have done with the judgement of god*, 1947–48, for an urgent anatomical experiment to be conducted (universally, first of all upon the population of Paris listening to that broadcast, which was banned before transmission) on an 'autopsy table', to extricate the body's organs and reconfigure it as a skeletal but now wildly dynamic body: 'Then you will make it learn once again to dance back to front/as in the delirium of dancehalls/and that inversion will be its true place.'[1]

Hijikata's anatomist has already advanced with his project, and demonstrates to his son his raw, botched corporeal amalgams, which appear intentionally misfired and inept. Through that project, all perceptions of corporeality must immediately be disintegrated and rethought from zero, in a parallel way to that in which many of Tokyo's activists of 1968–70 envisioned the future body's existence, in sexual or radical-political variants, and its inhabitation of the utopian megalopolis, once devoid of state power and its homogenising constriction of the human body. The veering, irresoluble oscillations between the malformed and the normal, the autonomous and the subjugated, the incarcerated and the liberated, formed the preoccupations of HORRORS OF MALFORMED MEN, which simultaneously permeated the urban dilemmas of 1969 Tokyo. To contrarily deform the body, and annul its social normality, through an anatomical act or in the gestural furore of 8mm-filmed street violence, was conceived as activating that body in unprecedented ways, even if the result was malfunctioned, shortlived or bloodily awry.

In HORRORS OF MALFORMED MEN, the anatomist's experimental subjects dance, in a performance that holds elements both from Hijikata's *Tatsumi Hijikata and the Japanese People: Revolt of the Body* – Hijikata is himself part of that performance of corporeal aberration, transported into it on a variant of the Heliogabalus-inspired chariot with bicycle wheels on which he made his entrance onto the Nihon Seinenkan's stage in October of the previous year – and also from the Club Space Capsule choreographies of 1969, with acrobatic male dancers and naked female dancers whose skin is painted silver, their metallic headdresses spouting fire. The rapidly revolving metal panels that featured both in Hijikata's art-aligned and cabaret work (and which also appeared again in his Osaka Expo performance of the following year) are present too in HORRORS OF MALFORMED MEN, for his dancers' collisions. A fluid corporeal and moving-image transmissibility appears vital to all of Hijikata's work of 1968–70, its volatility carried principally by film, from Nakamura's experimental fragments to Ishii's studio-product cinematography, and back.

Hijikata's anatomist expects his son to participate fully in his vision or face incarceration or death; to exercise malformation is compulsory. But the son's first anatomical act as a surgeon is to undo his father's work, separating the mutant conjoining of his half-sister from a monstrous figure, in an anatomy-labora-

Ill. 12 – Horrors of Malformed Men, dir. Teruo Ishii, 1969 – a sequence drawn from Hijikata's 1968 *Tatsumi Hijikata and the Japanese People: Revolt of the Body* performances.

tory setting with the human detrita of in-progress malformation experiments shelved in the background. Murobushi appears in that laboratory as a revolving figure spinning from the ceiling via straps around his plaster-encrusted body, while Hijikata's anatomist oversees the dissolution of his own project, watching through the lens of snake-filled glass specimen bottles that widen and distort his face. He then takes his son into a subterranean cavern to meet his mother and vocally narrates the intricate genealogy of familial betrayal that instigated his work, but is then interrupted by a private detective who has travelled from Tokyo, infiltrating the group of servants accompanying the son in his journey to the island, and who now reveals how Tokyo's unwilling inhabitants, especially abducted young women, were transported to the island to become subjects for the anatomist's experimentation. The detective then pursues the anatomist through the clifftop landscape; Hijikata's character abruptly dies, his mouth pouring blood, and his son then detonates himself with an explosion of fireworks, his dismembered head and body parts propelled calamitously into the sky over the island.

149

Ishii's other notable film with Hijikata's collaboration, BLIND WOMAN'S CURSE, was made for another studio, Nikkatsu, as an amalgam of gangster and horror film idioms that attempted to create a distinctive new format able to entice audiences to cinemas at that moment of financial desperation for Japan's studios. It was released in June 1970, during the span of the Osaka Expo. As with HORRORS OF MALFORMED MEN, the film is set in the Taisho era, and again in a location remote from Tokyo, in a town in the Yuri district of south-western Akita, to the west of the site of Hosoe's photographing of Hijikata for *Kamaitachi*, completed two years earlier. The film proved successful, in part through its first major role for the actress Meiko Kaji, who would become a 1970s film icon, and who appears in BLIND WOMAN'S CURSE as a young gangster-clan leader who has accidentally blinded a young woman during an assassination mission some years earlier, and now again faces that young woman, who in the interim has become a master swordswoman, accompanied by a black cat and a wily hunchbacked henchman. The blind swordswoman is able effortlessly to defeat the clan leader in a duel, but decides finally to spare her life.

Hijikata appeared in BLIND WOMAN'S CURSE as the grotesque, deranged henchman, assisting the blind swordswoman in her planned revenge. Initially he appears mute, or able only to laugh, but then speaks, in his Akita accent, emphasising his loyalty to the swordswoman. He has the capacity to leap backwards from the ground onto the roofs of buildings. He skins the dragon tattoos from the backs of the clan leader's women fighters, always licking the blood of his victims alongside the black cat, and attempts to provoke mayhem among the town's rival gangster factions with the aim that this will render the clan leader finally vulnerable to the blind swordswoman's planned killing of her. The swordswoman is irascible and independent, and dismisses all of her henchman's attempts to ingratiate himself with her. Still trying to incite chaos, he is suddenly killed: pursued by fighters from one of the town's clans, he leaps backwards onto a roof, but is then injured by a thrown knife, falls to

Ill. 13 – Blind Woman's Curse, dir. Teruo Ishii, 1970.

the ground alongside a sewer and is impaled with swords; Ishii accords Hijikata 20 filmic seconds for his spectacular death sequence, which Hijikata performs as an intricate contortion, moving towards the film-camera and finally twisting around so that his head is suspended upside-down in front of the lens.

The hunchback and the swordswoman inhabit the subterranea of a carnival sideshow as their hide out, and the hunchback performs as part of the sideshow's spectacle, under wary observation by fighters of the gangster clan-leader. As with Horrors of Malformed Men, Hijikata's performance is initiated with a close-up of his eyes, then a pan down to his mouth and tongue, which he incessantly protrudes throughout Blind Woman's Curse. The sideshow's wooden facade and performances aim to evoke the aura of Taisho era funfair horror attractions, distinct from the performance presented in Horrors of Malformed Men as the autonomous conception of Hijikata's anatomist, intended to introduce his project to his son; even so, Blind Woman's Curse holds performance elements again resonant of Hijikata's Nihon Seinenkan and Club Space Capsule performances, with hanging metal panels within a gold-walled environment, and other, detached and hand-held panels pressed against Hijikata's figure by the surrounding performers.

Horror is a medium of corporeal transmutation in Hijikata's appearances in his commercial studio-system films of 1969–70 which were intended to be widely consumed in the cinema auditoria of Tokyo and across Japan; horror appears as a resistant entity with the capacity aberrantly to overturn the 'normal' body conditioned by state power, and to institute instead a new, insurgent corporeality, with experimental dimensions that resonate with the demands of Tokyo's urban protesters of that era. Ishii was evidently convinced that by infiltrating Hijikata's work (rather than more conventional horror elements) into his films, that work would serve as an accelerant for horror's capacity for corporeal provocation and for the pleasurable outrage he aimed to induce in his films' spectators. Hijikata's participation in studio-made films – and his evident readiness to integrate within those films elements allied with or identical to the Ankoku Butoh performances he presented in arts culture venues in Tokyo – forms a pivotal step in his work's expansion from the small-scale audiences of his art-focused 1960s Tokyo dance experiments to the immense audiences for his participation in 1970's Osaka Expo. Film in 1960s Japan, from Nakamura's 'amateur' fragments to Ishii's studio products, possessed the fluidity to follow that unprecedented transit of Hijikata's body.

The urban culture that surrounded Hijikata's work of 1969–70 was one strongly imbued with sexual acts and sexual imagery, with media representations of sex forming a pivotal element of Tokyo's pervasive 'actuality' environments, in which news, advertising, pornography and art formed inextricable, simultaneous components; Matsumoto's FUNERAL PARADE OF ROSES extends that sexual preoccupation into transvestism and gay sex acts, and Oshima in particular, with his films of that moment, DIARY OF A SHINJUKU THIEF and THE MAN WHO LEFT HIS WILL ON FILM, interrogated the mediatisation of sex along with sex's relationships to riot culture and activism in Tokyo's urban space. Many photographers, such as Daido Moriyama and Masahisa Fukase (who also photographed Hijikata walking in the streets of Tokyo in the reverse direction to passing riot police), photographed the frenzy of that era's Shinjuku sex parties which took place in intimacy with the cacophony of rioting on the streets outside. Above all, sex also existed only a fragile hair's breadth from that era's other seminal preoccupations with death and revolution; sexual obsessions propel corporeality into death and revolution through the aperture of urban environments that are either so electrified by riot violence that they incite elated, dangerous sexual contact, or so voided and wastelanded that they provoke correspondingly excoriated, last-ditch sexual acts. Film carries that corporeal manoeuvre across the distance (again, often a hair's-breadth span in the filming of Hijikata's work) from experimental art works to rapidly made, low-budget studio sex films.

Four years before his death, Ko Murobushi spoke in an interview about his first meeting with Hijikata in 1969 and their involvement in the studio-made sex film Hot Spring Spa Maid Pimps, released in June of that year. Murobushi and another aspiring dancer, Bishop Yamada, went to the Asbestos Studio in Meguro with the aim of beginning to train with Hijikata: 'When we met him, Hijikata said: "Ok guys, I just happened to be looking for some bodies (*nikutai*) for an orgy." We replied, "We'll do anything." It happened that Hijikata was in the midst of filming for a Toei movie, and that was what the orgy scene was for ... Hot Spring Spa Maid Pimps. (Laughs.)'[2]

As with Horrors of Malformed Men, that film formed part of an ongoing series ('geisha sex'), and crossed idioms of film from sex to gangster violence, as Blind Woman's Curse had traversed horror and gangster forms, in that era's desperation of the near-collapsing studios to conjure mutant filmic amalgams that could conceivably return mass audiences to their emptying cinemas. In Hot Spring Spa Maid Pimps, set in contemporary Japan, the young, sexually driven characters are frequently threatened or beaten by gangster-faction extortionists, and the film's sexual acts are perpetually interrupted, deferred or arrested by violence. Hot Spring Spa

MAID PIMPS possessed a far lower budget and a faster shooting schedule than other studio films Hijikata was involved in,
moving between Toei's Kyoto studios and location shooting at
a hot-springs hotel resort. Hijikata's involvement was limited
to his choreographic and organisational work on the performance and orgy scenes, and he did not appear in the film. It
was directed by Misao Arai, who maintained his contact with
Hijikata and would, four years later, promote and supervise the
8mm filming of Hijikata's SUMMER STORM performance with
his dancers at Kyoto University; that transition from low-budget
sex film to darkened, fragmentary performance film highlights
the extreme malleability of the filming of Hijikata's Ankoku
Butoh work in that era. Pinioned between the numerous sim-
ulated orgy scenes in which Murobushi participated (notably
one that takes place in the hot-springs hotel's swimming pool,
during which a speedboat crashes through the pool's windows
from the ocean outside, bloodily killing several of the orgy's
participants), the film holds a performance sequence choreographed by Hijikata for his dancers that presented an outlandish ballroom entertainment spectacle at the hot-springs hotel;
as with his choreography for grotesque horror films in the following months, Hijikata adapted elements from the sequences
he was then choreographing for the Club Space Capsule cabaret
spectacles in Tokyo, though the film's performance sequence
appears far less extravagant than in Hijikata's other studio
films, abbreviated and broken up by an eruption of gangster-
faction violence.

I spoke with Murobushi, in Tokyo in 1998 and again in
2003 in London, where he presented his work *Edge 01* at the
Place Theatre as one of his numerous performances in London, arranged by his friend Marie-Gabrielle Rotie, about his
year of working with Hijikata as an assistant or fixer or emergent dancer, from HOT SPRING SPA MAID PIMPS to HORRORS
OF MALFORMED MEN in 1969 through to Murobushi's witnessing of Hijikata's solo performance in 1970 at the Osaka Expo.
Murobushi evoked Hijikata's deep seriousness in his approach

to his work on choreographing HOT SPRING SPA MAID PIMPS, as with his later work on HORRORS OF MALFORMED MEN, and his lack of interest in any perception that he was squandering his work's most productive creative moment by choreographing risible studio sex films; Hijikata was always waiting impatiently at the Toei studio foyer in Kyoto each morning in advance of the arrival of everyone else, wearing the overalls supplied by the studio, and giving the impression he had been there all night, as though he were a ghost 'haunting Toei', as Murobushi said, though after filming he would actually spend the nights drinking with equal diligence at Kyoto's Heihachi restaurant. The gravity of Hijikata's approach to his studio-film work, recalled by Murobushi, contrasts with the laughing and 'light' Hijikata performing *Tatsumi Hijikata and the Japanese People: Revolt of the Body* in Nakamura's account, though that perceived lightness was itself the intricate result of punishing corporeal preparation. Akiko Motofuji remembered Hijikata fasting intensively for several months prior to his two performances at the Nihon Seinenkan, in which no gesture was improvised, and the technical director of Hijikata's Expo '70 film, Tomohiro Akiyama, recalled that on location in Hokkaido, soon after that studio work in Kyoto, Hijikata ate nothing for the entire duration of the shoot and drank only milk.

Murobushi observed Hijikata closely during that year of their affiliation, living at the Asbestos Studio, but his own sense of entrenched autonomy made it impossible for him to become a long-term participant of Hijikata's dance company; after two periods training with mountain monks he worked independently from Hijikata, directing his own companies and performing solo works, as well as travelling to perform extensively from the 1970s onwards, especially in Europe and South America (while Hijikata never left Japan); he interrogated the corporeal dimensions of Ankoku Butoh, and its dimensions of death and revolution, for himself. That autonomy evidently led Hijikata to respect Murobushi's work in a way that appears exceptionally rare in his responses to other dancers, and in

1977 he wrote (or vocally dictated) a text published in the pamphlet marking a performance by Murobushi, *The Mummy*, at the dance studio that Murobushi then operated in a mountainous region of Fukui prefecture (not far from the marine location of HORRORS OF MALFORMED MEN). Hijikata had seen that work presented in Tokyo in the previous year, and he evokes it with a distinctively filmic inflection, asserting that the movements of Murobushi's body in the performance had been 'projected into my retinas'.[3]

A filmic or corporeal projection into the retinas can incite a sensorial disruption or illumination so extreme that it may transmutate from sex to death, or from sex to revolutionary terrorism, or from one manifestation of death to another. At moments of acute urban upheaval, as in Tokyo in the final years of the 1960s, the imageries or corporeality held within that projection's transmission may flare with such volatility that it results in an ocular burn out so all-engulfing that nothing remains beyond an urban wasteland or corporeal ashes.

The last occasion on which I saw Murobushi was at one of his final performances, 45 years on from his first meeting with Hijikata and his transformation from available body to filmic *nikutai*. He performed an outdoor work, which he announced as concerning Hijikata's death, on the exterior surfaces of Berlin's Treptower Park war monument, whose immense granite outcrops and stele friezes with texts by Stalin overlayer vast burial-sites of the young USSR war dead, killed during the assault on Berlin in April 1945. Murobushi gave his performance twice, each time for around 20 minutes, and sat in between on a bench alongside the memorial steles, calmly smoking cigarettes. A crowd of around 40 people surrounded each performance, but nobody appeared to be filming it, perhaps through the spectators' raw intimacy with Murobushi's figure, or a confrontational prohibition to film (intentional or not) which the ocular and sensory attention demanded for the performance carried. He climbed onto the edge of one of the memorial's granite surfaces, performing sequences of outlandish, feral gestures, while vocally evoking, in intermittent gasped outbursts, his perception of proximity to death: to Hijikata's death, to the deaths of the figures in the subterranean burial vaults below him or in the city surrounding him, and to the audience's deaths and to his own death, still in the future. The spectators moved still closer to catch what he was saying, and I attempted to note it down (since otherwise it would be lost forever, beyond film): 'In his own death, in dancing, he was thinking of someone who has died, Hijikata, and his dance should now project a plethora of dead bodies, or spectres, or ghosts, that are unable to move, or to manifest themselves, except through that dance, his own dance, those "presences of the dead" expelled from their usual incapacitation, into this space, into Berlin, via the medium of his body, which simultaneously resists those spectres of the dead, but also serves as a kind of opening or aperture for them, back into the world.'

Towards the two performances' abandonments, that monologue gradually decelerated and fragmented, into exhausted utterances, whisperings, silences. A year later, Murobushi died suddenly while in transit between performances, at Mexico City airport. At the Ko Murobushi Archive in Tokyo, its director Kimiko Watanabe showed me a short digital sequence of Murobushi in his coffin, soon after his death, the iPhone camera moving around his stilled body in a way that recalled for me the work of the anonymous filmer of Hijikata's funeral ceremony at the Asbestos Studio in 1986, manoeuvring around his body, filmically studying Hijikata's death. When film's ghosts slip out of vocal range and into the void, only moving-image sequences can activate the dead.

Sex films in Japan undertook an extraordinary mutant transit into the domain of terrorism in the period 1969–71, spanning the era of the Osaka Expo, the renewal of the US–Japan security treaty, and the exhaustion of the street-riot culture that had inflamed Shinjuku and other districts of Tokyo. That movement from independent sex film (*pinku eiga*) production to

Japan's particular variant of then global revolutionary cinema was primarily the work of Masao Adachi, who was known then primarily as a scenarist for Oshima (he had worked, along with other scenarists, on DIARY OF A SHINJUKU THIEF) and for his collaborations with Koji Wakamatsu. Wakamatsu's sex and serial-killer films of the second half of the 1960s always held oblique preoccupations with militant action, and this became accentuated at the decade's end; in SEX JACK, 1970, scripted by Adachi, Wakamatsu's group of young characters remain listlessly waiting in a confined room within wasteland-zones at Tokyo's edge, undertaking sex acts, before finally emerging to perform a hijacking. Wakamatsu's film characters are often strangers to Tokyo, migrants arrived from the north.

Wakamatsu, who produced his own low-budget films in autonomy from studios and other organisations, held the young male audience that ailing studios such as Toei and Nikkatsu – which produced Hijikata's sex and horror films – coveted; those spectators, including many associated with Japan's 'New Left' political and activist groups, discerned an aberrant, attractive aura of danger in Wakamatsu's films, always set in the immediate present or imminent future, that was absent even from those films of Ishii's which were viewed with distaste by studio executives and rapidly consigned to oblivion, as with HORRORS OF MALFORMED MEN. Furuhata connects Wakamatsu's films to wider currents of social defiance: 'In addition to its growing popularity among young male audiences, the pink film, with its marginalized status and its constant struggle against censorship, benefited from an aura of oppositionality in the 1960s. In order to understand the habitual association of Wakamatsu's work with the New Left, one cannot overlook the ideological positioning of the pink film as defiant and oppositional to the mainstream cinema.'[4]

In the autumn of 1969, the Red Army Faction (*Sekigun-ha*) declared war on the Japanese state, precipitating the programme of terrorist acts that would unfold especially across the coming three years (though several participants of Japan's terrorist groups eluded arrest into the 1990s and 2000s, remaining active and committed even in hiding), both in Japan itself and through the participation of Japanese terrorists, especially in conjunction with Palestinian groups, in international terror acts, especially the 1972 Lod airport massacre in Tel Aviv. The work of Adachi and Wakamatsu of 1969–71, spanning sex film and revolutionary-film works, was undertaken within the parameters of that declaration.

Wakamatsu's commitment to militant action was an intricate one, intercut with the need to distance himself from inflexible revolutionary-group entities just as he maintained his distance from Japan's studio system after initially working with the Nikkatsu studio. Nearly three decades later, he undertook a large-scale film-project, UNITED RED ARMY, 2007, partly in narrated documentary form and partly in the form of reconstructions of events, that looks back on the tumultuous acts of the 1960s' ending, the alliances of Japan's terrorist factions with international groups, and the dissolution of those factions in Japan through arrests and lethal internal combustion, focusing especially on the unravelling of the United Red Army (an alliance of *Sekigun-ha* with another faction) in 1971–72, with its murderous 'purge' of its own members at an isolated lodge in mountains to the north-west of Tokyo and a subsequent mediatised stand-off with police units; Wakamatsu's film reflects on what exactly was meant by 'terrorism' and 'revolution' in Japan in that era. Wakamatsu continued to make and plan provocative films, on Mishima's final days and on Japan's nuclear-power industry in the aftermath of the Fukushima Daiichi catastrophe of 2011; he died suddenly in the streets of Shinjuku in 2012, struck by a taxi. Adachi's work, by contrast with Wakamatsu's studio origins, emerged from Tokyo's experimental, art-oriented film-club environments of the beginning of the 1960s in which Richie was also involved. Although Adachi's commitment to revolutionary armed struggle proved more enduring than that of Wakamatsu, he remained preoccupied in 1969 with the unstable cityscape of Tokyo – the site of Hijikata's own dance-generated experiments with revolutionary corporeality in that era – and more widely that of urban Japan.

In 1969, the riot-striated city of Tokyo appeared caught between its fixed mediation of state control, especially via its pervasive riot-prohibition forces and media systems, and its vulnerability to insurgency, embodied in the violent protests of its still prominent activist groups and in several of their factions' increasing preoccupation with armed, revolutionary action. Shinjuku's riots and its concentrations of arts activity propelled the entire city's volatility and visible tension into that western district, leaving an immense, voided cityscape around it. Adachi's 1969 film A.K.A. SERIAL KILLER – now usually solely attributed to him but made as a collective film at the time – analysed the transmutations and erasures of 1960s Tokyo as part of a project of urban landscape theory (*fukeiron*) focused on that city and formulated in textual as well as filmic forms with the participation of several other filmmakers (such as Oshima and Motoharu Jonouchi) and theorists (especially Masao Matsuda). Miryam Sas delineates that landscape theory as one with a specifically filmic focus that separates itself from and annuls linear narrative construction, arguing that in its participants' conception of the urban landscape of Tokyo solely as a mediation and projection of dominant state power, 'they propose an alternative political critique involving a decentering of subjectivity and of the spectator as that around which narrative space and time would be structured. They move toward a more fragmented and conceptual mode of analysis of the workings of power in the social and architectural landscape.'[5]

A.K.A. SERIAL KILLER transits between urban locations and attempts to extract from them – via the medium of film, and against the locked resistance of those locations' urban-landscape emanation of state power – the traces of corporeality and obsessions of a young serial killer, who once inhabited them, in the recent past, but has now vanished; that process of extraction operates in a parallel way to the films of Hijikata's performances, such as those by Nakamura and Iimura, in their attempts experimentally to extricate (forcibly, in Iimura's work) traces of Hijikata's corporeality from the inflexible temporal event of performance that simultaneously occurs and expires in its own immediacy, with those traces rendered instantly voided and detrital but contrarily enduring on celluloid as a precious filmic spectrality.

The serial killer Norio Nagayama undertook four killings in four different Japanese cities, including Tokyo, in October–November 1968 (the exact era of Hijikata's *Tatsumi Hijikata and the Japanese People: Revolt of the Body* performances), and was arrested in April 1969, the same year as the making of Adachi's film. Beyond the timespan of that film, which operates almost as a news document of events which remained immediate, Nagayama then received a death sentence for his killings which was not exacted until his execution by hanging in 1997, almost 30 years later; in the intervening decades of frozen time, he wrote several books in prison on his experiences.

Adachi accompanies the static-shot relentlessness of his filming of urban-space fragments with an experimental jazz soundtrack of blaring saxophone and intermittent percussion bursts. Those filmic fragments themselves are primarily accorded the work of narrating the movement into his acts of murder of the serial killer's life, accompanied by Adachi's sparse topographically-oriented voiceover. The film begins in the north, with the sites of Nagayama's childhood in Hokkaido and Aomori, ferry transits filmed into the sea's wake resonating with the photographs of Hokkaido ferry-transits which Daido Moriyama began to make in that era. The bleak, voided streets of Hokkaido and Aomori, inhabited by the still alive, still young (he was 19 at the time of his killings) but already condemned Nagayama's ghost, transmit an aura of acute rigidity within Adachi's film, as they do in Moriyama's photographing of them in the following years. Adachi films blank, disintegrating walls. Nagayama travelled incessantly in the years before he was arrested, taking short-term menial jobs at random, in arbitrary locations, spending time in outlying areas of Tokyo but then moving on to marine cities (filmed by Adachi at dockside locations) from which he attempted to stow away, out of Japan, but was physically beaten by the container ships' crews on discovery and returned. At one point in his drifting, Nagayama transited through Osaka, and Adachi, in his subsequent filmic tracking of Nagayama's figure, shoots Osaka's streets with their prominent Expo-promoting insignia, and, at Osaka's periphery, the Expo site itself, then still being built, with an immense earth pit of shovelling workmen around its emerging media-communications tower, behind which the under-construction white dome of the Pepsi pavilion, within which Hijikata would perform in the following year, is clearly visible.

The serial killer then makes several incursions into the US military base at Yokosuka and steals a gun. Adachi notes but gives no details of Nagayama's subsequent, rapid-succession killings – in Tokyo, Kyoto, Hakodate and Nagoya – and the film then transforms itself into a lengthy urban improvisation of fragments shot around those four cities, focusing upon sites such as wastelands, cinema foyers and docklands. Adachi films numerous close-up sequences of the faces and heads of the taxi drivers who are driving him around those cities, intimating their vulnerability; Nagayama had murdered two taxi-drivers, along with two security guards, whose profession was then in ascendancy as Japan's new urban buildings and installations, especially those in the prestigious new Tokyo megalopolis, were perceived as needing to be closely protected, above all from infiltration by the proliferation of drifters internally migrating from Japan's north, such as Nagayama himself, constantly on the directionless move from city to city, their topographical exploration only cohering in crime. In one sequence, Adachi takes a taxi ride at speed out of a city in Hokkaido and his film's soundtrack fades out for its only time into silence, in the apparent exhilaration of that journey, accelerating past slower cars and narrowly avoiding collisions, moving beyond the city. After that four-city urban improvisation, which takes up close to half of the film, Adachi briefly narrates Nagayama's abandonment and retrieval of his gun, and between those statements, incorporates into the film sequences of Tokyo's pervasive inhabitation by riot police with visored helmets and staves in the Shinjuku avenues (the prospective rioters appear exhausted in those sequences, huddled or isolated in corridors of Shinjuku's railway station) and by heavier weaponry surrounding the now voided stadia of the 1964 Olympics. Tokyo appears under assault, but the corporeal agents inciting that urban warfare seem simultaneously to be vanishing into thin air.

Apart from that massing of uniformed figures holding state power and weaponry in its final sequences, A.K.A. SERIAL KILLER is almost devoid of corporeal life as it tracks Nagayama's own vanished traces, sieved by Adachi's voice and barely there as residual fragments imprinted upon the cities' surfaces and facades, but still remaining the film's core obsession even in those traces' near invisibility. Oshima, following his collaboration with Adachi on DIARY OF A SHINJUKU THIEF, worked on a film of his own which also transmits the preoccupations of landscape theory, THE MAN WHO LEFT HIS WILL ON FILM, co-produced by the Art Theatre Guild organisation and released in June 1970 during the span of the Osaka Expo. While still incessantly making films, Oshima experienced an acute impasse in his work at that moment of the Tokyo street riots' transition either into exhaustion or into preoccupations with terrorism, and became preoccupied with the idea of a 'War of Tokyo' unfolding on its banal, everyday urban-landscape surfaces; he could no longer make studio films, nor make political-activist films that would be forced to fit within the rigid parameters of particular factions. In THE MAN WHO LEFT HIS WILL ON FILM, Oshima's filmmaking became reduced and intensified, to the forms of contested urban space, film celluloid, film cameras, film projectors, and the urban human body. Furuhata probes Oshima's filmic preoccupations of that moment: 'In Oshima's view, the New Left student movement that intensified during 1968–69 and culminated in the occupation of Tokyo University and the antiwar demonstrations in Shinjuku was a failed revolution ... The visual predominance of static long shots of cityscapes often devoid of human presence characterizes A.K.A. SERIAL KILLER and the film-within-a-film of THE MAN WHO LEFT HIS WILL ON FILM. Both films are equally obsessed with the eventless space of everyday life subsequent to a systemic crackdown on the student movement.'⁶

Between his two Tokyo-focused films of 1969–70, DIARY OF A SHINJUKU THIEF and THE MAN WHO LEFT HIS WILL ON FILM, Oshima made one further film, BOY – also co-produced by the Art Theatre Guild and released in June 1969 – which appears allied to Adachi's A.K.A. SERIAL KILLER in its relentless travels from end to end of Japan (paralleling those of Nagayama, and then Adachi) and its filmings of bleak, voided urban locations, including several in northern Hokkaido; drawing on actual events, Oshima tracks – instead of those of a serial killer – the locations traversed by the restless movements of a family who trained their young son to leap into traffic and collide with cars, in order to extort money from the terrified drivers.

The overriding perception transmitted by THE MAN WHO LEFT HIS WILL ON FILM is of an immovable urban deadlock, able only to be anatomised intimately by film; film seizes that moment's deceleration and freezing of Tokyo's riot culture and of its last corporeal tearings at speed through the city's avenues. Oshima's film diverges from Adachi's style of static-shot urban filming, especially with his characters' constant movements around urban space and their mappings of perceived dangers, but the film still emanates a strong sense of petrifaction which resonates too with Hijikata's self-arresting of his solo performance work at the 1960s' end and the gradual deceleration or abandonment of his other activities into long periods of Asbestos Studio seclusion during the 1970s and early 1980s, when Hijikata's figure, omnipresent in Tokyo's arts locations across the 1960s, largely disappeared from the city's space, filmed only at night and in peripheral locations, in SCENERY OF WIND.

In THE MAN WHO LEFT HIS WILL ON FILM, two filmic obsessives, Yasuko and Motoki, pursue mysteries and mappings of Tokyo's urban space in its mediation of an invisible but pervasive and maleficent state power; Tokyo is simultaneously dangerously war-torn and pacified. They constantly have sex, but only in wastelands or in close connection with their filmic devices. Yasuko strips naked before standing in the projector beam that imprints her body with enigmatic urban imageries in front of the projection screen; later, she and Motoki have sex directly in front of the screen, still in the beam of the clacking Bell & Howell projector's urban sequences. They are castigated by their group of friends, who each possess irreconcilable activist preoccupations; when street protesters riot in the film, they form participants in a locked, mutually-dependent choreography with the riot police, each side annulling the other. Motoki pursues a police car into which a Bolex film-camera he has stolen has now been thrown, and his headlong urban transit, to the point of exhaustion, takes him through a terrain of highway overpasses and underpasses; in a further sequence, Yasuko is abducted in a car which again traverses Tokyo's post-1964 networks of aerial highways, and Oshima upends the sequence so that the highway, and Tokyo beyond it, are seen in an outlandishly upside-down, wrong-way-round form (the contrary of Tarkovsky's SOLARIS Tokyo-highway scene of the following year, in which the astronaut Burton drives with a linear relentlessness), in a manoeuvre of ocular disorientation and scrambling, impossible to rectify unless the film's projection-screen were itself inverted. Yasuko and Motoki create intricate maps of Tokyo's conflicts, but then destroy them. The city emanates its death.

In 1971, following a visit to the Cannes film festival, Adachi and Wakamatsu travelled on to Beirut to make contact with militants from the PFLP (Palestinian Front for the Liberation of Palestine) and suspended their sex film work – for Wakamatsu only temporarily and for Adachi, permanently – to travel to the PFLP's terrorist training camps and Palestinian refugee camps in Jordan. That visit led to Adachi's polemical film advocating revolution via armed-struggle terrorism, RED ARMY/PFLP: DECLARATION OF WORLD WAR, interrogating film's status in that action and the medium of film as a weapon of terrorism.

Across that era, many other films promoting contrary variants of revolution through violence, from Maoism to populism, were made worldwide, notably in South America. In Argentina, the young militant filmmakers Fernando Solanas and Octavio Getino had attempted to create an ambitious filmic embodiment of revolutionary action with their three-part film THE HOUR OF THE FURNACES, 1968, using experimental approaches especially in the opening sequences of the film's first part, with exclamatory titles (white-lettered on black) that expand in size and advance towards the spectator, and the sudden, momentary appearances of startling fragments of film – riots and protests, police firing at rioters in illuminated bursts of weaponry – within spans of darkness; Solanas and Getino also deployed music in the relentless, incitatory way that Adachi incorporates jazz cacophonies into A.K.A. SERIAL KILLER, with drum percussion and cries.

Che Guevara, in death, was the foremost global mediatised icon of revolution in that era: Matsumoto's activist filmmaker in FUNERAL PARADE OF ROSES is named 'Guevara' and Ko Murobushi recalled that HORRORS OF MALFORMED MEN's director Teruo Ishii mockingly called him 'Guevara' because of his long hair; Solanas and Getino invoked Che Guevara with a lengthy stilled moving-image sequence at the end of THE HOUR OF THE FURNACES' first part, studying Guevara's open-eyed dead face (filmed immediately after his execution in Bolivia in 1967), though their lauded revolutionary leader was Argentina's populist former president Juan Perón, then in exile in Franco's Spain, who gave the film his approval. Every city that was the focus of revolutionary cinema, from Paris to Buenos Aires to Tokyo, was subject to a different rendering in film. Solanas and Getino emphasised Buenos Aires's acute urban poverty and regime of oppression during the militarist era since Perón had lost power, emphasising the need urgently to overturn those desolate urban conditions (and those of Argentina's rural areas) via violent revolution, while Tokyo's bleak urban wastelands and edge terrains existed more as the detrital zones left behind in the wealthy megalopolis's new imperative for economic growth that generated its security-guarded tower districts and multi-layered highway infrastructure; Adachi's concern at the end of A.K.A. SERIAL KILLER was with the heart of Tokyo as its warzone.

Tokyo's distinctive urban transmutations and propulsions generated its own revolutionary cinema with its sources in the city's experimental film culture of the beginnings of the 1960s; those filmic dynamics possessed their autonomous imperatives and envisionings of revolution in its multiple but disjunctive dimensions (from Adachi's armed-struggle revolution to Hijikata's corporeal revolution), distinct from those of all other metropolitan film-cultures. The permeability and flux in film in Tokyo around 1970 – oscillating between preoccupations with sex and pornography, horror and the grotesque, street violence and terrorist acts – accentuate the pervasive aberrations of that era that are notably transmitted via the disparate filmings of Hijikata's Ankoku Butoh work. But in Adachi's RED ARMY/ PFLP: DECLARATION OF WORLD WAR, in 1971, Tokyo is now entirely absent, voided from revolution.

The film begins in another city: Beirut, seen through moving-car windscreens (as Japan's serial-killing-marked cities were scanned through taxi windscreens in A.K.A. SERIAL KILLER), while multi-lingual soundtrack voiceovers vaunt armed struggle and analyse the meanings of propaganda in oppressive and revolutionary contexts. At first, the film appears as a form of revolution-oriented news document examining the 1970–71 era, excising catastrophes such as the (unfilmed) United Red Army purge and emphasising the many hijackings of that period, including footage of a Japanese airliner with the Expo '70 insignia on its side, and the simultaneous detonation of three hijacked airliners (a sequence also incorporated by Wakamatsu into his film UNITED RED ARMY), filmed by press cinematographers, on an airstrip in the Jordanian desert. Adachi directly films the live screens of television sets, alternately transmitting consumer images and riot sequences, as the activist film-maker 'Guevara' does in FUNERAL PARADE OF ROSES. His film camera explores a PFLP militants' training-base (which Adachi reported was destroyed soon after, the militants killed) and the Jerash Palestinian refugee camp in Jordan. The film incorporates messages of revolutionary incitation addressed to the Japanese people by PFLP leaders, and by the then leader of the Red Army Faction (following the arrest of its previous leader, Tsuneo Mori, in the wake of the United Red Army purge), Fusako Shigenobu, who had left Japan for Beirut earlier that year; she was then cohabiting with the PFLP in the period of joint planning before the 1972 Lod airport massacre, undertaken by three staidly dressed Japanese terrorists reportedly carrying their guns in violin cases. The film ends with further windscreen pans, this time through mountainous areas, with the soundtrack's final accumulation of revolutionary voices that resonates with Tokyo's urban-'actuality' overloads.

After returning to Tokyo, Adachi showed his film widely in subsequent years in mobile cinema-projection vans (while it rapidly grew distant in time from the intense furore of 1970–71's events), to university audiences and activists; in 1974, he returned to Beirut, and remained there for 27 years, working with Palestinian militant groups, often in covert isolation and danger, with that span of time including the entire duration from 1975–90 of the Lebanese civil war with its faction-ridden militias and intensive urban destructions of Beirut, until his arrest in 1997, alongside the arrests of several other Lebanon-based members or associates of Japanese terrorist groups (including the one surviving perpetrator of the Lod airport massacre), and incarceration in Lebanon until 2001; he was then deported to Japan and incarcerated there too, before his release into an indefinite, locked Tokyo urban-incarceration, as a living corporeal memorial aperture into the city's era of riot protests and revolutionary preoccupations, denied a passport and the freedom to travel to show his films in other countries, but eventually able to make new films, PRISONER/TERRORIST, 2007, and ARTIST OF FASTING, 2016, and to collaborate again as a scenarist with Wakamatsu on his film of corporeal mutilation and Japan's 1930s militarism, CATERPILLAR, 2010, though not on UNITED RED ARMY. In 2018, twenty years after Richie had first encouraged me to do so at the start of our first Shinjuku walk (and five years after Richie's death in 2013), I arranged to meet Masao Adachi at a café in Shinjuku.

Adachi arrived at the café, whitehaired but lithe, laughing and friendly, especially after moving from the café to a bar on the edge of Shinjuku's Golden Gai area (which he avoided as now overrun by tourists), and told me immediately that he was still a revolutionary and still believed that a revolution (for Japan, and globally) was imminent, still believed too in all acts and provocations against state power, whether undertaken via film or in urban space. The bar was large and crowded, distinct from the minuscule bars surrounding it, and Adachi noted he was happiest in dense environments, where he could not be overheard, and had frequently met here in this bar with Wakamatsu, as they vented their disagreements over the planning of UNITED RED ARMY. Adachi's ideas disregarded, Wakamatsu determined to focus on the era's revolution-exhausted aura of lethal dissolution rather than its inspiration for contemporary activists. They had not fought physically, but for Adachi the streets of Shinjuku outside were enduringly zones of fighting, not only in the form of riots, but in extended 1960s face-to-face street fights over the course of days and nights of uproar, interspersed with police arrests, with his enemies of that era, such as the theatre director Juro Kara.

Adachi had encountered Hijikata at the very beginning of the 1960s, but he had no interest in Ankoku Butoh, nor in its filming. He evoked his involvement in Tokyo with the instigation of university film clubs around the end of the 1950s, and their focus on experimental film; he had been a student at Tokyo's Nihon University, and joined the Nihon University Film Study group, then in 1960 co-founded the VAN Film Research Center as a film collective with radical political as well as experimental-film aims. Adachi had made his first films in that era: BOWL, 1961, and CLOSED VAGINA, 1963. The Nihon University Film Study and VAN Film Research Center organised many cross-media events in those years that also attracted performance artists, writers, architects and dancers engaged with experimental film, and Adachi's encounters with Hijikata pre-eminently took place within those events' chaotic furore and elation, of explorations across art forms, at the moment when Hijikata was making films with Hosoe and Richie and remained intensively engaged in his Ankoku Butoh project's filmic collaborations. Richie had been a seminal figure for Adachi (as he had been for Iimura in that same era), inciting him to make experimental films and also sharing his technical 8mm-camera knowledge. Now, Adachi ordered more drinks to commemorate Richie's memory, piercing a half-century with immediacy, back across the multiple temporal strata of Tokyo, decade upon decade, eliding the quarter-century in which he had himself been absent from the city, to affectionately conjure Richie's ghost.

Adachi grew more provocative and intense when he began to speak about the far end of the 1960s, and his involvement in Tokyo's protests as they transmutated into revolutionary action. He had no engagement with Hijikata's work of that era, when a gaping division had appeared between the imperatives of revolutionary militancy and Hijikata's own corporeal experiments in official venues, above all his involvement with the police-cordoned Osaka Expo, its state-power-vaunting spectacle despised by all of Japan's revolutionary groups (though they had more pressing targets, and the Expo was nothing, void, soon wasteground once again as it had been when he had filmed its site under construction in 1969 while tracking Nagayama's urban restlessness).

Now he spoke of his decades in Beirut and their omnipresent danger, the houses in which he had been hidden frequently destroyed by missiles during the civil-war era, his film reels lost, incinerated. They had also been years of solitude, obliquely evoked in the scenario he had written for the film THE UGLY ONE, made by the filmmaker Eric Baudelaire in 2013 (after Adachi's return to Tokyo), with the actor and performance artist Rabih Mroué, who had himself left Beirut – where his brother was shot by a sniper, his grandfather assassinated, during the civil war – and relocated to Berlin; when I met Rabih Mroué in Berlin several months after encountering Adachi, he told me of their one meeting in Beirut, and of his friends' fearfulness at the proximity of Adachi, with his uncompromised reputation of infernality and danger. Adachi had never learned Arabic beyond the ability to swear fluently and virulently; whenever he was asked to speak before revolutionary gatherings, he would give an extended invective performance of those curses.

In the contemporary moment, in Tokyo, Adachi told me that he would still attempt to make revolutionary acts. He planned a new film, on the US occupation of the island of Okinawa and the US's enduring military dominance there. We left the bar and walked into the alleyways of Shinjuku, then entered the main avenues, dense on that Sunday night. The city appeared identical to Adachi in its state power projecting aura to the city he had filmed in A.K.A. SERIAL KILLER, in the era of landscape theory, even more intensively so, perhaps, in its inhabitants' utterly subjugated complicity – these young bodies, now, here, in Shinjuku – with state power's ever more rigid mediation. But it held fissures and cracks, here in this city and its bodies, and the work of revolutionaries had to be to tear them open. In parting, Adachi said in English: 'Now I release you.'

Only at that moment, a few seconds later, in nocturnal Shinjuku, crossing the East Exit plaza under its raw and coruscating digital illuminations, after the previous hours' rapid-fire bar drinking, I could perceive the validity of an otherwise-untenable, split-second, aberrant conjunction: Hijikata's corporeal revolution, in its volatile and unprecedented gestural acts with their experimental filmings and their surrounding urban dimensions, in an extreme, contrary alignment or amalgam with Adachi's direct-action revolution, in its uncompromised form with its own experimental urban filming and its entrenched, irresoluble Tokyo war. But an instant later, as I reached the Shinjuku railway station's entrance, ready now to travel from Tokyo to Osaka and examine the traces of Hijikata's Expo-'70 moving-image projection and performance, that momentary hallucination of revolutionary conjoinings had already annulled itself, fading out and disintegrating into Tokyo's untold, infinite archives of misfired illusions – of corporeality and urban space, of sex and terror, of violence and insurrection – with all of those archived, spectral obsessions finally finding their location in film.

Notes

1   Antonin Artaud, 'Conclusion' to *Pour en finir avec le jugement de dieu*, in *Œuvres complètes*, volume XIII, Paris: Gallimard, 1988, page 104.

2   Ko Murobushi, in 'The body at its physical edge', interview with Takashi Morishita, *Performing Arts Network Japan*, 1 November 2011, unpaginated.

3   Tatsumi Hijikata, 'The Butoh of *The Mummy* – Ko Murobushi', in the pamphlet conserved at the Ko Murobushi Archive in Tokyo from the performance *The Mummy (Hinagata)*, 1977, unpaginated.

4   Yuriko Furuhata, *Cinema of Actuality: Japanese Avant-Garde Filmmaking in the Season of Image Politics*, Durham NC/London: Duke University Press, 2013, page 94.

5   Miryam Sas, *Experimental Arts in Postwar Japan: Moments of Encounter, Engagement and Imagined Return*, Cambridge MA/London: Harvard University Press, 2011, page 244.

6   Furuhata, (see note 4), pages 119–120.

1970: Hijikata at Osaka's World Expo

Hijikata's Ankoku Butoh film work at the Osaka Expo World's Fair of 1970 remains almost unknown; in many ways, it forms the most extraordinary moment in his work, in its experimentation across film and performance within transmutational urban contexts, and also marks an acute shift in the perception of Ankoku Butoh, from a revolutionary art form that Hijikata had conceived of in 1961 as criminal, provocative and irreconcilable with social behaviour or state power, towards its overhaul across the 1970s–80s into an institutional, codified (and global) form. At the same time, the shortlived technological megalopolis of the Expo gave Hijikata's work its greatest audiences in numerical terms, with his work viewed within a moving-image pavilion constructed by a consortium of business corporations with a view to generating art-derived prestige for their operations.

At the Midori pavilion, Hijikata's corporeal experimentation in dance was allied to advanced innovations in multi-camera filming and immersive moving-image projection technologies. After habitually undertaking his projects for audiences numbered in their tens or hundreds throughout the 1960s, Hijikata's film for Expo '70, BIRTH, was seen by an audience of millions. Alongside the conjoining of his film work with imperatives of corporate culture, Hijikata had the opportunity contrarily to outrage that corporate culture with his performance work for the Expo, precipitating the abandonment in disarray of the entire programme of events for the Pepsi pavilion; displaying the contradictions that are vital to all of Hijikata's work (itself inspired so centrally by Jean Genet's love of betrayals and contradictions), he simultaneously betrayed his work and made that betrayal an epoch-ending provocation. The ephemeral intersection between Hijikata's Ankoku Butoh project, experimental moving-image technologies, and the state-approved, corporate-funded 'Future

City' constructed for Expo '70, forms a unique constellation of conflictual aims and perceptions.

The Osaka Expo, conceived as the successor to the Tokyo Olympics as Japan's two great urban spectacles of the postwar decades (nothing of that scale happened again until the 2020 Tokyo Olympics), was intended to demonstrate Japan's industrial, technological and architectural innovations and resurgence, 25 years after its engulfing, near-total urban destruction at the war's end in 1945. For Expo '70, priorities were placed on presenting the most startling contemporary architectural forms, with invitations extended worldwide to architects preoccupied with envisioning future cities; the two Japanese architects most closely associated with the Expo, Kenzo Tange and Arata Isozaki, were widely seen as among the country's most innovative architects, often working on vast scales: Tange had begun his work in the war years and had built stadia for the Olympics as part of his immense reformulation of Tokyo's public buildings that extended from the 1950s to the 2000s, and Isozaki (though his projects in Japan often remained unbuilt) had conceived plans for towering mega-cities to be constructed on the sites of former urban ruins, and for vertical cities to be built up from the ocean floor of Tokyo Bay. Expo '70 formed a city in its own right, positioned at the northern periphery of Osaka and forming a contrary double to that still riot-seething city; the Expo, circuited by a monorail, possessed its own complex transport infrastructure.

Film and experimental moving-image projection had been prominent elements of World's Fairs ever since Muybridge's projections at the Chicago World's Columbian Exposition in 1893 and his construction there of the first moving-image auditorium (that Exposition also fixed many of the preoccupations of such events for the century to come, with 'African Folk Dances' programmed for the 1893 Chicago Exposition just as they were for the Osaka Expo in 1970). Although the experimental component of the Expo was a relatively marginal element of that immense corporate spectacle, moving-image innovation (especially in its relationship to audiences' ocular and sensory perceptions) comprised a prominent preoccupation of the entire Expo; innovations in film projection had been a key element also of the preceding Expo, in Montreal in 1967, but now appeared in more advanced, pervasive forms. Furuhata notes: 'Expo '70 in Osaka was the pinnacle of extravagant technological display and the spectacular celebration of moving-image media. It inherited a propensity towards expanded cinema experiences via the gigantic multiscreen projections and immersive audiovisual environments already featured at Expo '67 in Montreal.'[1]

While the Osaka Expo was a state-sanctioned event supported by Japan's corporate and industrial conglomerates, invitations (with considerable fees attached) for the participation of many of Japan's most prominent experimental artists, including Hijikata, were made with an aim of enhancing the Expo's aura of innovation; a further aim was undoubtedly to extricate art from its intricate entanglement with the domain of state-negating riotous activism, with its revolutionary danger, that had been so prominent in urban Japan over the past two years. One of the Expo's influential creative advisors was the young designer Tadanori Yokoo, who had previously made posters for Hijikata's Ankoku Butoh performances; Isozaki also had extensive alliances with Japan's experimental artists, although he told me in an interview in 1997 that he was himself in no way involved in inviting Hijikata's participation.

An exceptionally large-scale celluloid-film format was used to shoot Hijikata's film BIRTH – in which Hijikata embodies a diabolical or shamanic figure creating an alternative, maleficent new universe – on the slopes of a remote volcano in the north-east of Hokkaido. The film was then projected in one of the Expo's many pavilions, the Midori-kan (Green pavilion) as a 360-degree immersive experience, using an experimental multi-projector technology named Astrorama. Over the six-month span of the Expo, the film was seen by an estimated 8,000,000 of its visitors, based on Astrorama ticket-sale figures that included tour groups that may have passed rapidly through the pavilion and not experienced the entire projection.

Experimental artists from beyond Japan were involved in the Expo; for example, the internal spatial environments of the Pepsi pavilion (where Hijikata performed) were designed by the renowned New York-based collective the Experiments in Art and Technology (E.A.T.) group, who were as eager to participate as were many of Japan's artists and writers with reputations for innovation, such as Toshio Matsumoto, Hiroshi Teshigahara and Kōbō Abe. However, the Expo generated fierce dissent from artists who castigated its participants for their sold-out subservience to corporate and state power Japan, the Zero Jigen performance group prominent among them; the Expo grounds formed a rigorously controlled environment overseen by security guards and by newly invented computerised surveillance systems (though the Red Army Faction still successfully infiltrated it), in close interrelation with the ways in which Japan's cities were then being abruptly transformed into riot-free, pacified corporate environments in the immediate aftermath of the 1968–69 urban uproar.

Hijikata's own involvement in Expo '70 possesses a tangential, volatile dimension. His filmic participation had been shot in the previous year, and his sole corporeal appearance at the Expo took place prior to its official opening, within the mirrored interior of the Pepsi pavilion, whose exterior environment had been designed by the architectural artist Fujiko Nakaya in order for the pavilion's white dome to spectrally vanish from time to time in a mist cloud of released water; Hijikata had planned to consolidate that initial performance with further events, but his performance was so badly received by the Pepsi corporate directors that future performances were cancelled. As such, Hijikata's participation holds a ghostly, barely-there aura, almost conjured out of existence during the remainder of his work (he certainly never subsequently drew attention to his involvement in the Expo, which became increasingly perceived across the following decades as the last-gasp exhalation of Japan's 1960s experimental art cultures). That ghostliness was enhanced by the rapidity with which the entire Expo site was dismantled and voided after its closure; additionally, the Astrorama projection technology designed at immense expense for Hijikata's film, and intended for vast future expansion in its usage, was instead abruptly abandoned for being too expensive for wide-scale adoption, and consigned to oblivion. Hijikata's film BIRTH was stored away in a warehouse and forgotten (it was only rediscovered over forty years later, in 2011).

Hijikata's decision to be involved in Expo '70 is as mysterious as his other involvements of that era in studio-made sex and horror films, or his previous readiness to allow filmmakers such as Iimura to attempt to disrupt or fracture his Ankoku Butoh dance with their interventions into its domain. The practical factors involved in running the Asbestos Studio and supporting its dancers, emphasised by Akiko Motofuji, certainly played a role, along with Hijikata's unconstrained openness to participate in whatever new projects his friends proposed to him, from Richie's HUMAN SACRIFICE filmic-collaboration proposal of 1959 to the Expo proposal of 1969–70 by Yokoo and others (though Yokoo, as with Isozaki, was evasive on his own role in Hijikata's invitation when I spoke to him in 1998). Despite that potential sense of being subject to an inveiglement to become complicit in the entity of corporate-funded state power that suggests innocence or naivety on Hijikata's part, his work at the Expo angered figures such as Adachi and Zero Jigen. Hijikata's capacity to enter that zone of complicity, but then to provocatively explode it with his calamitous Pepsi-pavilion performance (which appears to have been his lastever solo performance, following 1968's *Tatsumi Hijikata and the Japanese People: Revolt of the Body*), indicates the contradictions and mysteries at stake in his work. The Expocity itself was a profoundly mysterious urban entity, constructed at colossal expense, to exist as a dense, immense site of intensive experimentation across urban and moving-image cultures, among many other conjunctions, only to be razed almost without trace after only six months.

Ill. 14 – Construction of the Pepsi pavilion for Osaka Expo '70, 1969.

Plans for the realization of Expo '70, and ambitions for its vast attendance, emerged in 1964 at the time of the Tokyo Olympics, and were approved by the International Exhibitions Bureau (an organisation based in Paris with the power to ratify or annul Expo aspirations) in the following year. The chosen site was the Senri Hills, north of Osaka; Osaka's corporations and industries lobbied fiercely to hold the Expo in their region, rather than in the Tokyo region. From the Expo's origins, it was planned to commemorate it with a multi-volume Official Report documenting the entire event, to appear in Japanese, English and French, and to be sent to research libraries worldwide, each of the three volumes' covers printed in different colours (red, blue and green), alongside a volume of photographs; this was eventually published in 1971. Among the many pavilions, the one which would be the location of Hijikata's film was initiated in April 1967 by the proposal of the Midori-kai group of 32 companies to build a pavilion; they were allocated a 7,289-square-metre site in the Expo grounds on 24 May 1968.

The Expo's report details the 'Master Plan' conceived for the event's construction and the major dilemmas that were immediately encountered: 'There were a host of problems to be solved in the process of making the Master Plan: how to make the most of the topography of the Senri Hills, how to cope with the hot and humid summer in Japan, and how to control enormous masses of visitors whose traffic would resemble that of a metropolis.'[2] A vast ecologically destructive initiative was needed to level the Senri Hills region in order to install a city-sized site in its place; archival photographs from the early 1960s show the hills covered by bamboo groves and red-pine groves. That intensive work took three years to accomplish, before the vast flat surface could be installed with the necessary subterranean infrastructure of powerlines, notably for air-conditioning and refrigeration. All of the sponsors of the Expo's pavilions were prohibited by its organisers from placing corporate advertising on them (only the names of the corporations involved were allowed on signboards attached to the pavilions' facades). A further challenging construction project was the installation of the monorail around the site, begun in 1968 but completed only on 13 March 1970, very shortly before the Expo's opening ceremony; it circuited the Expo site over a fifteen-minute journey. Moving walkways and an aerial cable-car line were also installed, and the entire site was equipped with lighting systems to ensure that it remained illuminated for the benefit of nocturnal visitors to the Expo.

The construction workers for the Expo project came overwhelmingly from the north, forming part of the immense 1960s internal migration whose overspill included drifter serial killers such as Norio Nagayama and which helped to precipitate the pervasive security-guard industry in Japan's major cities, Tokyo above all. Most workers came from Hokkaido (where Hijikata's Expo film was also shot) and Aomori; 17 workers were killed in accidents during the Expo's construction phase – always behind schedule and under pressure of time – which was filmed almost accidentally by Adachi in one sequence of A.K.A. SERIAL

KILLER, as well as in the promotional films which the corporate sponsors of several pavilions shot during the years 1968–70. Those 17 ghosts of the Expo were commemorated in the form of a tablet, lauding their deaths' contributions to 'Progress and Harmony for Mankind', placed in front of one of the site's principal architectural features, the Tower of the Sun (an immense, corporeally evocative construction with a face and eyes at its summit, and internal exhibition spaces) conceived by the artist Tarō Okamoto.

The Expo was held under the patronage of Japan's royal family; its report's first page features a photograph of the crown prince and a message from him lauding the report's publication. Emperor Hirohito visited the Expo site on 14 March (three days after Hijikata's performance there) and on a further seven days across the Expo's span. He visited neither the Midori nor Pepsi pavilions, avoiding most corporate pavilions and focusing on those constructed by public bodies or national governments. The report emphasises that the corporations involved in constructing pavilions had had to subjugate their own business imperatives by collaborating equally with other corporations: 'With only a few exceptions, a majority of domestic pavilions were joint projects of business groups, which had been organised by their member corporations, transcending individual interests';[3] in the absence of the kind of exclamatory signage which illuminated Tokyo's Shinjuku plazas, lauding the innovations of corporations, the emphasis shifted to expanding the scale of the moving-image spectacles developed for the pavilions' interiors.

The Expo was funded by governmental bodies, including those controlling the Osaka, Kobe and Kyoto regions, as well as through investments by business corporations. It appears eventually to have made a massive profit, though that profit's extent had still not been established at the time of the report's publication (and seems not to have ever been disclosed). Some of the resulting income needed to be spent on the site's demolition at the Expo's end (though the pavilions' sponsors were responsible for dismantling them), along with the publication of the report and the formulation of vague plans to convert the post-Expo site into a park. In addition to its state and corporate funding, the Expo relied on a Japan-wide fundraising appeal which included the sale of specially designed Expo cigarette packs and medals (pressed and sold in their millions, in gold, silver and copper variants).

Alongside the moving-image experiments planned for its pavilions' interiors, the Expo also formed an experimental site in its exterior dimensions, with numerous innovations, such as immense screens transmitting digital animation sequences. The Expo's organisers intended it to be a 'model metropolis' anticipating and inspiring future cities, and demonstrating 'a technical approach for the restoration of human dignity to modern cities'[4] that indicates how then current cities had become perceived as abjectly despoiled, polluted spaces in need of rectification. As well as showing Japan's innovations in urban technology, the Expo was designed as a laboratorial city of excess, modelling the ways in which the immense 'human flow'[5] anticipated in future cities with overloaded or insurgent populations could be stratified, through technologies of surveillance as well as by being effectively channelled or stilled through the power of amassed security guards, in ways that anticipate the corporeal 'kettling' of demonstrators, as in the 2009 G-20 protests in London.

Every last visitor to the Expo was counted: the attendance was 64,218,770 across its span, from 15 March to 13 September 1970. At the time, it was globally the largest concentration of human bodies that had ever converged at one site to attend an event. Around half of the population of Japan attended, alongside worldwide visitors. That attendance was greater than the officially anticipated attendance of 50,000,000, although several film documentaries from the era of the Expo's preparation in 1968–70 suggest that an even higher attendance had been envisaged, of up to 100,000,000 visitors, which would have strained the site far beyond capacity. The exception to the Expo's perpetually dense corporeal environment was in its first weeks, when stormy weather and heavy rainfall led to low attendances. The perception quickly developed in those weeks of an already abandoned city, especially in the rented commercial concession at the Expo's south-east corner known as 'Expoland' (a successor to the 1893 Chicago Exposition's Midway Plaisance commercial zone that had included Muybridge's moving image projection auditorium and a ferris wheel, located away from the more dignified pavilions), among whose constructions, again including a funfair ferris wheel, was the Pepsi pavilion, in which Hijikata's performance took place. Low visitor numbers in those first weeks led several Expoland attractions to close prematurely – as Muybridge's pavilion had in 1893 – including the Lanterna Magika spectacle from Czechoslovakia, which combined screen-projected moving images and 60 dancers (with an emphasis on bodies being propelled directly out of the projection screen); although successful when exhibited at previous World Expositions, the Lanterna Magika had a sparse attendance at Expo '70 and also suffered from strikes by the attraction's Japanese support staff, in that era of militancy and protest. Labour disputes were frequent at Expo '70, especially in response to sudden changes to employment contracts. The report comments: 'It brought to the fore a new type of problem with regard to the management of future World Expositions.'[6]

Admission to the Expo site was 800 yen for an adult, cut to 400 yen for evening-only admission after 5pm; the site was open until late in the evening, until 10pm in the spring months and 10.30pm in the summer months, illuminated with spectacular lighting systems and projections. Once inside, visitors had to pay extra for each pavilion that they visited; they spent an average of six and a half hours at the Expo site but devoted much of that time to queuing, for an average of 40–50 minutes at each pavilion and longer at particularly successful attractions. In a documentary made in 2011 by the Hijikata Archive in Tokyo about the projection of Hijikata's film at Expo '70, the Astrorama technical director, Seiji Mochizuki (who had also supervised the on-location shooting of Hijikata's film in Hokkaido in 1969), eagerly remembered a 12-hour wait for spectators to enter, but that memory appears vastly exaggerated, as though Mochizuki were still insistently over-promoting the specialness of the Astrorama technology, over 40 years after its obsolescence and abandonment. The report asserts that the longest waits for spectators, of around two hours, were those to see the US pavilion during the Expo's final weeks, when attendances were at their highest, with especially dense crowds.

The report meticulously assesses how visitors responded to the Expo, in surveys conducted as they left the site, with a specific focus on how it functioned as embodying a 'future city'. Evidently, not everyone responded well to the engulfing urban spectacle of corporate technology and state power. Asked if the Expocity represented 'Comfortable, pleasant life', visitors' approval rate was low, though they agreed that it showed 'Harmony with technology'. Visitors assessed the Expo experience as 'good' or 'fair' (rather than 'very good'); six per cent found the Expo 'uninteresting', while seven per cent (around the same percentage of visitors that witnessed Hijikata's film at the Midori pavilion) said it 'aroused antipathy'.

Many documentary films were made before, during and after the Expo; corporate documentaries recorded particular pavilions' construction, international film crews documented the in-progress Expo for news reports that brought accelerating numbers of visitors from outside Japan to the Expo in its closing months, and retrospective official films were edited from the vast amount of footage shot during the event. Some countries, especially those that had invested in constructing 'national' pavilions on the site alongside its many corporate pavilions, wanted to emphasise their own standing in the event; the USSR had 40 film-crew members present on the site throughout the Expo's duration, and some nations, such as Australia, compiled documentaries which recorded the event from their national perspectives. The Expo's 'official film' was made by the director Senkichi Taniguchi with a film crew of between 70 and 100

people present on site throughout the Expo's span; the resulting film, *Expo '70*, released in three-hour and two-hour variants,
was designed especially for young audiences (though most
Japanese children had already attended the Expo itself, unless
they were exceptionally poor or had radical activist parents, and
so were now watching a filmic rendering of an event that they
had corporeally experienced) and was screened in cinemas and
schools from March 1971, the first anniversary of the Expo's
opening.

Every pavilion at the Expo was extensively staffed, primarily by hostesses in special costumes designed to articulate particular pavilions' preoccupations; both the Midori and Pepsi
pavilions' hostesses wore extravagant silver vinyl short-skirted
outfits evoking futuristic space travel as they guided visitors
around the pavilions' interiors. The Expo's organisers also
recruited 517 hostesses known as 'Expo Flowers' (who received
'beauty counseling') and helped lost or bewildered visitors, as
part of the Expo's immense 'Guard Corps' of security personnel.
Around a thousand male guards were on duty at all times, with
the remit to physically restrain visitors' bodies at crisis points,
such as when immense, locked-together crowds passed through
the entrance turnstiles as the Expo opened for the day, stam-
peding and scuffling as they raced towards particular attractions. Furuhata emphasises the crucial role of those security
forces and of the computerised surveillance technologies that
guided their corporeal interventions within what she calls the
'spatial monumentality' of the Expo site, rigorously screened
from the still riot-torn, restive streets of urban Osaka: 'In addition to the construction of new transport infrastructures, such
as a monorail, a moving sidewalk, and extended highways, the
preparation for Expo '70 involved the invention of new security
strategies. Hundreds of security guards, recruited from police
forces as well as private security companies, were trained specifically for this event, and a new centralized computer system
was deployed to control and monitor the smooth circulation of
visitors between and within pavilions. Importantly, the vigilant

Ill. 15 – Security guards at Expo '70, 1970.

policing of pedestrian traffic at Expo '70 depended on the strict separation of exhibition space from the space of everyday activities. In particular, the spectacles of Expo '70 were carefully cut off from the spectacles of protests and performances unfolding on the streets.[7] The guards (many of whom, fresh from the raw, unruly streets of urban Osaka, evidently were ill-suited to maintaining public order) themselves caused frequent mishaps and were involved in fracases with visitors; numerous incidents were recorded of guards stealing from the pavilions, notably pilfering a tapestry from one of the national pavilions.[8]

The major failing of the Guard Corps occurred in the second month of the Expo's span, when their inattention allowed a Red Army Faction terrorist to infiltrate the site and undertake a rare non-violent protest against the Expo. The carefully preserved membrane between the Expo experimental city and the volatile urban environment beyond it with its still-active riot culture was pierced for an extended, spectacular and sonically focused performance. The report meticulously documents the incident:

Ill. 16 – Surveillance communications technology at Expo '70, 1970.

'Around 5:05pm on 26 April, a young man intruded into the Tower of the Sun. He climbed to the Golden Mask of the Tower and entered the right "eye". He wore a red helmet bearing the inscription "Red Army". The invasion was first discovered by a guard of the Central District Unit stationed at the Theme Pavilion. The intruder stayed in one or the other of the "eyes" for 159 hours and 30 minutes, sometimes shouting "Down with Expo" until he finally allowed himself to be arrested on 3 May.'[9]

I arranged to meet two of the last surviving architects involved in the Osaka Expo, both of whom had visited the Midori pavilion in which Hijikata's film had been projected. In 1997 I spoke to Arata Isozaki in the auditorium of the Mito Art Tower (a contemporary art museum which he had designed himself, opened seven years earlier and located to the north of Tokyo), where a concert by his friend the experimental composer Toshi Ichiyanagi, would take place later in the day; Ichiyanagi had also been closely involved in the Expo's events, and among other contributions he composed electronic music for two 14-metre-tall 'entertainment robots' which appeared during the Expo's opening ceremony and accompanied all outdoor events across the Expo's span.

We took the elevator to the summit of the art centre's helix-shaped metal tower and stood on the viewing platform. Isozaki had been a friend of Hijikata from the beginning of the 1960s and, as with Adachi, that was the era of experimentation which he vocally evoked with the greatest verve. In 1962, the year in which Hijikata and Richie made WARGAMES together, Isozaki (still working as an assistant to Kenzo Tange at that moment) arranged a performance evening on the roof of his Tokyo apartment building in which Hijikata had provocatively danced naked; finally, the police had arrived and threatened to arrest Hijikata, which had evidently elated him, since he then still conceived of Ankoku Butoh as a criminal dance intended to result in his incarceration. Isozaki told me that his urban conceptions of that era, of cities emerging from ruins (and already consigned in that emergence to future ruination), or out of the marine floor of Tokyo Bay, or from the debris of wastelanded cityscapes, formed an essential part of his engagement with Hijikata's work and of his wider cross-media collaborations with musicians, artists and filmmakers at that unique moment of early 1960s experimentation; he had conceived of architecture's pre-cast disintegration, as with a body corporeally disintegrating within its own dance. In that era, he had wanted Shinjuku to be surmounted by what he called 'clusters in the air' (multiple towers with their levels expanding choreographically into space from a central, nail-like column as it ascended).

When we spoke about Expo '70, Isozaki emphasised the exhilaration of witnessing the pavilions' moving-image experiments, especially those with mobile or revolving seating which propelled their spectators through architectural space. The Midori pavilion had been more static, in his memory, with the spectators crowded into the pavilion's dome to stand leaning on barriers as their eyes and heads revolved to follow the filmic sequences' accelerations around the dome at disorientating speed; it was as though those spectators were being tested in a laboratory to assess how much disruption their vision could take. Isozaki remembered Hijikata's filmed dance on the volcano, projected in sequences around the circular auditorium, the spectators following his leaps across the dome's immersive screens; but that performance had been very different to Hijikata's early-1960s avant-garde performances, and was now simply part of the film's spectacle, his hair extremely long, not cropped or shaved as it had been at that earlier moment of urban provocation. Since he had not attended Hijikata's Pepsi pavilion performance (and had not even heard about it), Isozaki had not met Hijikata in the Expo era.

The experience of walking around the Expo's illuminated experimental city, deserted at night, had been an unforgettable one; since Isozaki's work had mainly been the co-ordination of events and concerts, often evening events, he had done this many times, after the spectators had left. He appeared to dismiss or diminish his own role in the Expo: that was all he had really done, at the Expo: co-ordination, for which he was ill-suited. It was not architecture; he had designed nothing. The report specifies Isozaki's work as that of co-designing the Festival Square open-air environment within the immense gridded structure conceived by Kenzo Tange, with its main focus in Okamoto's Tower of the Sun corporeal structure; it presents Isozaki's involvement as a specialist one: 'In December 1969, President Arata Isozaki of Kankyo Keikaku, Ltd. was assigned as Technical Producer so that the engineering systems of the plaza, which differed from those in usual theaters, would be operated efficiently and smoothly.'[10]

Among the many open-air events overseen by Isozaki were performances by the Gutai group, based in the Osaka region, led by Jiro Yoshihara but mainly composed of younger artists such as Atsuko Tanaka and Kazuo Shiraga, who had been seminal figures in Japan's art and performance from the mid-1950s (their performance-art events of that era often filmed). Gutai's 1970

Expo performances were among their last works, and appear creatively exhausted in their filmic documentation; Yoshihara died in 1972 and the group dissolved. Across the entire span of the Expo, they undertook a series of nine 'Night Event' spectacles (each starting at 9pm) with multiple overall-wearing figures in the Festival Plaza, and titles such as *Plaza of Mobile Arts and Light*, *Mad Robot* and *Constellation Event*, explicitly subordinating their own work to the Expo plaza's space; in addition, they staged a 'Gutai Fine Arts Spectacle', mainly conceived by Kazuo Shiraga, in eleven parts, filmed in colour across three days towards the end of the Expo, from 31 August to 2 September. Alongside performances of Japanese traditional dance and music, Isozaki also supervised the Expo's events by European performers, such as Marlene Dietrich, Mary Hopkin and Marcel Marceau, which took place either in the outdoor plaza or its adjacent concert hall.

Isozaki remembered the plaza as an intentionally vast, open meeting-space, necessary for the immense, often dense and surging crowds to collect within after entering the Expo site, before dispersing towards pavilions or other attractions. Furuhata contrarily disputes the plaza's role as malleable open urban space and emphasises its restrictions as part of the intensively regulated Expo metropolis, relating it to the increasingly controlled (or, by 1970, already demolished) terrains of Shinjuku's plazas, especially those at either side of its railway station, which had been intensive zones for performance art and unrest in 1968–69: 'In spite of its pretension to openness, the Festival Plaza at Expo '70 was an enclosed space, not completely open to the public in the way the West Exit Underground Square at Shinjuku Station had been before being renamed. Only the visitors who paid the entrance fee were allowed to enter the Festival Square.'[11]

In 2016, I travelled to Arezzo in Italy, to meet the Italian architect Dante Bini, best known for his large-scale air-inflated concrete domes of the 1960s and his collaboration with the filmmaker Michelangelo Antonioni on the construction of

La Cupola, a domed house built for Antonioni (though rarely used by him, and now abandoned), built between clifftop outcrops of corporeally resonant red rock formations on the spectacular north-western coast of Sardinia. Bini had participated as a young architect in Expo '70 and had none of Isozaki's reticence about his work there; he proudly took the archive of his Expo involvement – plans, designs, photographs – from an old wooden chest in which, he told me, they had been untouched for over 40 years. His acclaimed public air-inflations of his Binishell concrete domes in New York, accomplishable in a matter of hours, had caught the attention of the Fuji Group corporation and as well as overseeing the inflation of his domes at the Expo, he had successfully licensed their construction, so that they proliferated in their thousands across Japan in the following years (and still resiliently exist, for example in the form of a 1972 dome employed as a used-car dealership's office in the town of Asahikawa in Hokkaido).

Bini's seven domes were inflated alongside the main Fuji Group pavilion. After Bini had overseen their inflation, he watched while helicopters hovered overhead and then unleashed streams of paint over each dome. He showed me a colour photograph he had taken, with the red paint being poured irregularly from the helicopters over his domes' cream-coloured, raw-concrete structures, decorated with large silver discs and built on a sand base. The Expo's report details Bini's domes, though without mentioning him by name: 'On the circumference of the [Fuji Group pavilion] dome, there were seven concrete domes, each 12 meters in diameter and four meters high, which were used as offices. / These domes made of ferroconcrete were constructed with the latest construction techniques in a short period of time and were unique and durable structures.'[12]

Bini spent several days absorbing the Expo megalopolis and its pavilions' interiors before returning to Italy. He told me it had been an astonishing experience for him to inhabit that experimental urban environment; he knew nothing of urban Japan's riots of that era, nor of the Expo's urban-pacification contexts,

and perceived the Expo-city as an unprecedented art laboratory for innovations in architecture. Domes were pervasive at
the Expo, many drawing inspiration from Bini's own experiments of the early 1960s, though most (including the Midori
pavilion) used steel-frame constructions, while Bini's inflated
domes possessed no interior frames. Bini recalled the distinctive green plastic-covered domed carapace of the Midori pavilion and the vertigo-inducing, immersively projected Astrorama
film, but not the figure of Hijikata, whom he had never heard of
at that time. Almost 30 years later, in 1999, he had attended a
performance in Venice by Hijikata's closest collaborator, Kazuo
Ohno, then 93 years old, who had been awarded the Antonioni
Art Prize by Antonioni himself (Ohno was the prize's first recip-
ient); amateur film shot from the auditorium shows Ohno's
gestural performance, face to face with Antonioni, in receiving
the prize at the side of the stage. Antonioni wrote in the event's
programme that he had awarded his prize to Ohno for his 'having transformed the dance of Butoh into a universe of poetry. /
His profound study of the soul is the beginning of a journey for
going back through the body to the origin of existence.'[13] Bini
had met Antonioni himself for the first time in many years at
Ohno's performance.

Alongside the Midori pavilion in which Hijikata's film was
projected, and the Pepsi pavilion in which he performed, the
Expo site held many other pavilions that indicate both the
depth of experimentation at the Expo into moving-image projection and its performative dimensions, and also the degree
to which Japan's experimental artists subjugated themselves
to (or appeared oblivious towards) the Expo's corporate power.
Once visitors entered the Expo site and the Festival Plaza,
they encountered the main Theme pavilion, designed by Tarō
Okamoto on multiple subterranean levels as an exploratory
space intended for spectators to reflect on the Expo's future-
oriented ethos of human harmony.

Alongside its corporate pavilions, the Expo held numerous
national pavilions. The Japanese government's pavilion, on the

site's periphery, appeared in aerial photography to resemble a
set of white fuel-storage tanks supplying power for the site, but
was actually intended to replicate the five-part cherry-blossom
logo of the Expo (glimpsed on the side of a hijacked airliner
in Adachi's JAPANESE RED ARMY/PFLP film), with round halls
containing displays on Japanese culture. Many of the national
pavilions used the dome-based architecture that was omnipresent at Expo '70, including those of France (a constellation of
four domes) and West Germany (a steel-facaded dome with its
interior used principally as an auditorium for music, especially
electronic contemporary music, such as that of Stockhausen,
who was present at the Expo). Other national pavilions, such
as that of the USSR, with its soaring concave spire construction topped by a hammer-and-sickle icon and its theme of
'Harmonious Development of the Individual under Socialism',
deployed spectacular architectural styles intended to draw visitors' attention in that ocularly competitive urban environment.
Smaller pavilions often used more traditional architecture,
such as Greece's pavilion, which resonated with the classical,
pillar-fronted design that Muybridge had devised for his Zoopraxographical Hall projection auditorium at the 1893 Chicago
Exposition. The British pavilion was exceptionally undistin-
guished in its architectural form, with thematic areas devoted
to the 'British Scene' and to 'Family', focused on British royalty;
part of the pavilion was devoted to contemporary art, with large-
scale sculptural works by the Austrian artist Ernst Eisenmayer
who was then based in the UK. Many South American and post-
colonial African nations operated minuscule, one-room pavilions, lost among the Expo's furore.

Among the corporate pavilions, the Fuji Group's inflated
vinyl-structure pavilion (alongside which Bini's smaller domes
were installed by inflation) held a moving-image environment
with striking parallels to the Midori pavilion's immersive projections, though the Fuji pavilion's spectators were corporeally
transported on platforms during the projection, while the Midori
pavilion's spectators remained static and upright. The report

evokes the Fuji pavilion's environment: 'One of the features of the Pavilion was a film projected on a huge screen. Visitors entered the Pavilion and were carried on the revolving platform which circled inside the Pavilion once every 20 minutes. / As the platform revolved, visitors went from complete darkness into what the sponsors called a "total experience". The tour combined a multi-vision film and "Mandala" for a unique film projection. On the first floor, there were various objects on display and visitors could see how the projection equipment was operated. / The multi-vision movie was projected on the mammoth screen, 13 meters high and 19 meters wide. The projectors were developed by the Fuji Group in co-operation with Multi-Screen of Canada, and 210mm film was used. Since ordinary projectors could not handle such wide film, new projectors called "rolling loop" sent the film horizontally and projected clear and vivid pictures on the screen. / The 15-minute film depicted various activities and thoughts of mankind. There was neither a beginning nor an end to the movie so that visitors could start to see it from any part.'[14] Although the Midori pavilion's corporate organisers vaunted the exceptional dimensions of the celluloid format used in its projections (around 110–120mm in width, expanded from the 70mm film shot on location), the Fuji projections far exceeded that.

The sense of projection experiments competitively needing to surpass one another in technological or audience-immersing domains is apparent both in the report's descriptions and also in the various pavilions' archival materials now conserved at the Expo's Documentation Center. Many pavilions, such as the Toshiba IHI pavilion, Rainbow Tower pavilion and Electric Power pavilion, also deployed 360-degree immersive moving-image projection environments, some in conjunction with sonic installations. The Toshiba IHI pavilion's Global Vision Theatre appears to have been the most ambitious projection environment in terms of its technological capacity to propel its seated spectators around the pavilion's interior space, so that they were confronted with a succession of projection screens,

Ill. 17 – Projection screens within the Toshiba IHI pavilion, Expo '70, 1970.

each highlighted in turn within the 360-degree environment. The moving-image sequences projected onto those screens, announced in the pavilion's programme as 'dramatically depicting the wonderful life of mankind',[15] appear from archival footage to have been exceptionally outlandish and hallucinatory, with split-screen sequences showing groups of children consumed by fire; one child spectator is shown screaming in apparent terror. The pavilion's visitors (as with the Fuji pavilion) were seated together on 'rotary platforms', confined with straps so that their bodies were not propelled into freefall during the platforms' incessant aerial revolutions. The report summarises that cacophonic environment's aims, which appear incongruous aspirations in a situation of high-velocity propulsion during which no utopian dialogues with co-spectators were possible: 'The idea of the Global Vision Theater was to create a place where spectators could communicate with people of other countries through images and think mutually about the happiness of mankind in a future society with "hope".'[16] The Electric

Power pavilion's Aerial Theatre used the same five-screen format also conceived for the Astrorama projection of Hijikata's dance at the Midori pavilion: 'At the Aerial Theater, on the five-face screen on the inner wall of the conical building was shown a documentary film entitled "Hunter of the Sun" which depicted the relation between man and energy from the time when man first discovered fire to the present nuclear age'.[17]

Several pavilions distanced themselves from the competitive furore among other pavilions' designers over their moving-image projection environments' respective technological innovations and aberrant stretchings of their spectators' sensory capacities, by remaining within the domain of still-image projection, which ostensibly enabled a closer examination of the displayed images, and evokes the oscillation between moving images and still images in Hosoe's work with Hijikata, from NAVEL AND A-BOMB to *Kamaitachi*. In the Mitsui Group pavilion, spectators were propelled through space as in the Toshiba pavilion's environment, but the Mitsui's pavilion's Creative Paradise required spectators to stand upright (rather than being strapped into immobility) on one of three 'flying saucers' before being launched through the pavilion's interior space to view slide projections: 'The visitors on the "flying saucers" experienced the sensation of travelling through space watching pictures describing civilization and nature on earth as seen from outer space.'[18]

Among the many artists, performers and filmmakers whose careers as experimental figures are widely perceived to have been destroyed by their involvement in Expo '70's immense corporatised utopia, Toshio Matsumoto's affiliation was with the Textile pavilion, whose theme was 'Textiles Enrich Human Life'; the pavilion's architectural appearance was intentionally designed to look as though it were still half built and in progress, in order to convey an aura of ongoing innovation. Matsumoto's project for the pavilion was titled SPACE PROJECTION AKO, and followed on almost immediately from his previous urban filmmaking in Tokyo and the ambitious, technologically demanding open-air projection experiments onto the surfaces of large balloons that he had begun to develop. Furuhata views Matsumoto's Expo participation (and subsequent loss of creative momentum) as especially jarring because his moving-image work of the previous two years, such as FOR THE DAMAGED RIGHT EYE, 1968, as well as FUNERAL PARADE OF ROSES, had been so pivotal to unprecedented crossovers between experimental film and art environments, often amalgamated with the live performance of music or cacophonies. She emphasises that his 'interest in the structure of multiplicity and an expanded conception of cinema led Matsumoto to generate more technologically involved projection projects. *Projection for an icon* (*Ikon no tame no purojekushon*, 1969) which used twenty gigantic balloons, five film projectors, and numerous light sources, is a work he made for the "Cross-Talk Intermedia" event. As indicated by a photographic record of the event, published in [the magazine] *Bijutsu Techō*, the balloons, floating just above the ground and colliding with one another, served as a surface onto which Matsumoto projected images … Matsumoto literally multiplied, diversified, and crossbred various image-based media.'[19]

Matsumoto appears to have been compelled to adapt his work's recent preoccupations severely to the Expo's corporate imperatives in order to display it within the Textile pavilion, uneasily amalgamating his projections with the pavilion's 'fashion show' elements and its dominant theme of 'youthfulness'; he introduced an element of grotesque horror into his Expo work. The report intimates the sharp disorientation which Expo spectators experienced within Matsumoto's environment: 'The exhibition was divided into the projection dome, exhibition corridor, dolls in the lobby, aerial display and fashion shows. In the dome, an image called "Ako" was projected on the screen and there were a number of reliefs of gigantic images of females on the ceiling and between the screens. The pictures and reliefs were intermingled with sounds, music and flashes of light in various colors. Fifty-seven speakers were built into the walls, ceiling and floor, and the sounds and lights came from all directions. / The spectators in the hodgepodge of these visual and acoustic effects experienced new and queer sensations. / The projections here were designed to express youthfulness and the new living environment of a girl called "Ako". All these plans were devised by Toshio Matsumoto. The actress who played the part of Ako was selected from among 300 young women. The film show lasted 15 minutes.'[20] The pavilion's programme and the report both include photographs of the naked dolls and robotic figures of women that had formed installation elements of the pavilion's interior, along with its outlandish, grotesque figures, located in the pavilion's lobby, which possessed sonic dimensions: 'In the lobby, 20 dolls of elderly men in frock coats spoke through built-in speakers or played cat's cradle with laser lights'.[21] The report's emphasis on Matsumoto by name as the pavilion's devisor highlights the ascendancy of his work at that time and his relative public prominence as an experimental artist (Hijikata's name, by contrast, never appears in the report). Beyond the span of the Expo, Matsumoto's work declined across the 1970s into obscure preoccupations with the nature of vision; he worked primarily in arts education, and the distinctive cross-media inspiration generated for young artists by his late-1960s work vanished.

Tadanori Yokoo was also involved in an advisory role in the conception of the Textile pavilion's projections and installations, as well as in several other pavilions, but his principal involvement in the Expo was with the Takara Group's Beautillon pavilion with its theme, 'Joy of Being Beautiful', and its emphasis on the Expo's prescient capacity to envision future cities, including their domestic environments: 'Dreams of future home life were depicted with background music, illustrations and pictures. Illustrations were by Tadanori Yokoo.'[22]

The content devised for the Automobile pavilion, sponsored by the Japan Automobile Manufacturers Association, epitomises most vividly the subservience to corporate imperatives of artists and writers whose work had previously been acclaimed as innovative. The Automobile pavilion's content was overseen by Hiroshi Teshigahara, whose distinctive, narrative-based films had already gained international prominence (WOMAN IN THE DUNES, 1964, had been nominated for an Academy Award); he was also renowned for his programming in Tokyo of the Sogetsu Art Center, where Richie had projected his film with Hijikata, HUMAN SACRIFICE, in 1959. With his regular collaborator, the novelist Kōbō Abe, Teshigahara prepared a film, 240 HOURS A DAY, for projection at the Automobile pavilion; the project competed with other pavilions' concerns with generating ever more immersive projection environments, as well as with the grotesque elements that Matsumoto, for example, had also introduced into his own work for the Textile pavilion. The film's future-oriented preoccupation probed the haywire accelera- tion of urban experiences and the acute sensory and corporeal aberrations that resulted from those experiences, which were also at stake in the Midori pavilion's projections. The report summarises 240 HOURS A DAY: 'The movie, projected on four screens, three in front and one on the ceiling, was a musical depicting the future as seen by present-day eyes. The science fiction approach showed the comedies as well as tragedies that could result from extending a day from 24 hours to 240 hours through a drug accelerating the nervous system, which would speed up man's functions by ten times.'[23]

Teshigahara, evidently engaged with responding to the opportunities presented by the Expo to the maximum extent, was also involved in what appears a more dignified contri- bution, to the Suntory pavilion, preparing a 20-minute film, WATER OF LIFE, for projection within the pavilion's water- themed environment. While many films at the Expo, such as Hijikata's Astrorama film, were projected across five screens, Teshigahara's film was excessively projected on a 'six-faced screen' through the use of six film projectors. Among the corpo- rate pavilions, the Suntory pavilion's environment was among the very few visited by royalty, with a visit by the crown prince.

Once the Midori-kai group of corporations had decided in 1967 that they would commission a pavilion for the Osaka Expo, they needed a film to be projected inside it, with a spectacular, art-inflected content, filmed and projected with new or unprecedented cinematic technologies that would give their pavilion an aura of superlative innovation and thereby distinguish it from competing pavilions. The precise content of the film was evidently a matter of indifference to the Midori-kai corporate group – mainly composed of Osaka-based banking, insurance and industrial trading companies – that commissioned it, and the film was not intended in any way to represent or embody those companies' aims; as the Expo organisers had intended, the only direct connection between Midori-kai and the pavilion was that the group's name was discreetly attached to it. Midori-kai (which eventually mutated into the Sanwa Midori-kai conglomerate, and inherited the stored-away, obsolete reels of Hijikata's film after the Expo's closure) invited proposals for the pavilion's content, and a technology company specialising in astronomical telescopes and aiming to develop their activities into lucrative large-format immersive film projection, Goto Inc., proposed their new and untried Astrorama technology, which involved large-scale 360-degree projection within a domed auditorium, the entirety of whose inner surface would comprise the projection screen.

Once Goto Inc.'s proposal was accepted, they hired a technical director, Tomohiro Akiyama, who in turn hired a prominent poet, Shuntaro Tanikawa (as with many of Expo '70's artists, Tanikawa had a reputation as an innovative figure prior to his Expo participation), to write a script. Tanikawa's disjointed script of barely connected sequences, which he appears to have conceived in haste, proposed two short films to be projected successively, BIRTH and MARCH (that second film, in which Hijikata did not appear, resonates closely with then current preoccupations with excessively accelerated urban space also explored in Teshigahara's 240 HOURS A DAY film for the Automobile pavilion). For BIRTH, whose first part explored the historical origins of the world and also of imaginary worlds, Tanikawa wanted to include the figure of a demonic shaman, inhabiting a volcanic landscape and transmitting a maleficent wild energy that could form the origins of a new planet. He wrote: 'Suddenly, a monstrous and grotesque man appears. He performs a bizarre dance.'[24] Tanikawa appears to have proposed Hijikata as that figure for the film, and since many of Hijikata's friends (such as Yokoo and Isozaki) were closely involved in the Expo's planning, he was hired; Tanikawa's prior experience of Hijikata's work had certainly been in attending his live performances in major Tokyo auditoria, such as the Nihon Seinenkan or in smaller art-venues, rather than his studio-made horror and sex films, which had not been released at the time of BIRTH's shooting. Tanikawa appears to have chosen Hijikata for the same reasons – his startling and outlandish corporeal presence – as those motivating Teruo Ishii to invite Hijikata's involvement in HORRORS OF MALFORMED MEN.

Hijikata travelled to the active volcano Mount Io (also known as Mount Atosanobori) in remote north-eastern Hokkaido in June 1969, together with the large technical crew from Goto Inc. (including Seiji Mochizuki, who also oversaw the Midori pavilion's Astrorama projections); the crew had already made test shots at the volcano in the previous months. Hijikata distanced himself from the film-crew and stayed alone at an inn beside the nearby caldera lake Kussharo, maintaining the fasting regime he had pursued in the previous year prior to his *Tatsumi Hijikata and the Japanese People: Revolt of the Body* performances, though Mochizuki recalled that Hijikata eventually grew friendly and that they took sightseeing trips together to the region's lakes. The week-long shoot took place only in the evenings, at twilight, in rocky areas of the volcano's lower slopes, between its vents emitting sulphurous smoke.

The Astrorama camera's five lenses filmed Hijikata's movements from slightly different angles, in order for the five resulting films to be projected across five adjacent areas of the 360-degree cinematic environment, emphasising the propul-

Ill. 18 – Hijikata on location at Mount Io, Hokkaido, for the filming of
Birth for Expo '70, June 1969.

sions of Hijikata's multiply fragmented figure across the volcano's space. The resulting film could only be projected successfully on its vast scale within the spectacular Astrorama
environment for which it was intended, across the Expo's
duration; in its unprojectable contemporary archival existence,
Hijikata's filmed body is held in detrital celluloid sequences,
the original high-resolution colour film now reddened in its
decomposition. Despite the film's origins as a corporate commission for a technological spectacle ultimately mediating state
power, Birth contrarily forms an integral element of Hijikata's
own films, seizing his Ankoku Butoh project's pivotal preoccupations with corporeal transmutation, performed on Mount
Io with velocity and in fragmentation, with the Astrorama film
only accentuated in its vital incorporation of Hijikata's work by
the disintegrated celluloid's long-term abandonment and contaminated discolouration.

Two months earlier, in April 1969, under Hijikata's supervision, a short film-studio-shot sequence of amassed, sexually

Ill. 19 – The Astrorama crew filming Hijikata's performance at Mount Io, June 1969.

writhing bodies, performed by Hijikata's Asbestos Studio dancers, was filmed for a sequence at BIRTH's end, with the dancers' bodies subsequently overlayered in the film by images of paintings by Hieronymus Bosch and other artists. Since no film laboratory in Japan was able to process the large-format filmic materials, Goto Inc. sent them to be developed by a specialist US company based within the Paramount Pictures studio lot in Los Angeles, Film Effects of Hollywood Inc., renowned during that era for their special-effects work on the STAR TREK television series, though rapid technological changes in the film and television industries caused the company to cease its operations a decade later.

As with several other corporations that commissioned pavilions for Expo '70, Midori-kai also commissioned a 30-minute colour documentary, ASTRORAMA, about their pavilion, tracing its development from its origins in discussions in smoke-filled corporate boardrooms to its completion and opening within the Expo's experimental metropolis. Again, that corporate film is now one of Hijikata's films, with the dissolution of its surrounding corporate imperatives and the concurrent accentuation of Hijikata's immediate corporeal presence within it. The documentary – expensively shot, over a span of two years, as a promotional film emphasising the prestige of Midori-kai's Expo participation, by a separate specialist documentary film crew that sometimes worked directly alongside the Goto Inc. film crew – begins with sequences of the Midori pavilion's inauguration ceremony, with silver-costumed hostesses attending the Midori-kai corporate executives. The film then reverses back in time to 1968, with scenes of architects preparing plans for the design of the pavilion to occupy the Expo site that had been allocated for it in May of that year. The elderly, all-male company executives then vote in their boardroom on whether to take forward the Astrorama plans; the film camera tracks across the room as some executives raise their hands, while others, grim-faced, evidently decline to approve the plans. Their dissent is overruled and press announcements are made, lauding Astrorama as an unprecedented media technology. The film then returns to the Midori pavilion's inauguration, with Shinto priests blessing it, before reversing again to the construction process; at that point, in 1968, the Expo site remained a vast wasteland of black earth following the Senri Hills' deforestation and levelling, and only makeshift wooden barracks inhabited by many thousands of construction workers occupied the site. The Midori pavilion begins to take form with the installation of its metal frame.

The film then shifts to the Goto Inc. technicians' Astrorama filming, with their transportation on the roof of a van of the immense, five-lensed camera. The crew travel to many European countries, undertaking complex shooting that includes underwater sequences. The film then analyses the construction of the special screen for the Astrorama environment, with the design and testing of a special screen fabric overlayered with many small flaps and able to absorb and transmit the high-resolution sequences; the sound design for the auditorium is also developed and tested. The Astrorama film is then seen being processed, edited and assembled. At that point, a one-minute sequence is included of the documentary crew's shooting of Hijikata's appearance on Mount Io; the crew film Hijikata obliquely, alongside the Astrorama crew, starting with the sequence's preparation, in which Hijikata appears laughing and relaxed as he receives facial make-up, and then focusing on his performance of dance gestures, leaping across the volcano's rockface and then directly towards the Astrorama camera. The Astrorama crew are seen generating artificial smoke to supplement the sulphur emitted from the volcano's vents, and their vehicle is visible, parked at the foot of the slope. The positioning within the documentary of that sequence suggests that Hijikata's Astrorama sequence may have been added at a late stage in the film's preparation. After Hijikata's insurgent sequence in the documentary, it returns to the Expo site, where the Midori pavilion has now been completed. Technical tests are undertaken in the auditorium, with the 360-degree film projected and watched by technicians and Midori-kai executives; the fast-moving sequences (from the MARCH film, without Hijikata's presence) shown are those filmed on Tokyo's aerial-overpass highways, looking down on Tokyo from a vehicle travelling at speed, and resonating with the filming of those locations in THE MAN WHO LEFT HIS WILL ON FILM and SOLARIS. Another sequence is filmed from a car's windscreen within the neon-facaded avenues of central Tokyo. The Astrorama projection screen's content appears strangely washed-out and spectral, but the technicians and executives are satisfied with the test.

After a momentary blackout, the film re-starts with the momentous event of the Expo's opening ceremony, with Emperor Hirohito giving a halting speech in the Festival Plaza; huge, international crowds surge into the Expo grounds, many of them carrying 8mm-film cameras. Sequences shot from the monorail that circuited the Expo site show the Tower of the Sun and the Dream Pond artificial lake with its Noguchi sculptures emitting spouts of water. The film elides the other pavilions to focus pre-eminently on the Midori pavilion, with its facade's vast illuminated sign: 'Midori-kan ‹Astrorama›', and a smaller placard detailing the corporations that sponsored it; vast queues are gathered under the canopies protecting them from rainfall, and the queuing figures have bought tickets for the screenings being held at fixed intervals, each 20 minutes, with the audience admitted and expelled rapidly at either side of the projection's 15-minute duration.

The spectators then enter the pavilion's foyer, in which the Astrorama film camera is prominently displayed, along with exhibited artworks, neon sculptures and large-format still images from the film. The spectators advance at eager speed into the pavilion's internal projection auditorium (which had a capacity of 1,000 spectators) via five doors, leaning on metal railings while standing, since the auditorium had no seats. The documentary then shows the technicians ready to project the Astrorama film, the huge celluloid strip running horizontally through the projector gate. In the darkened, mid-projection auditorium, filmed by the documentary crew, the spectators appear startled, their heads moving rapidly, looking in all directions, tightly grouped together. One shot, positioned from behind several figures in the audience, tracks the sharply shifting focus of their heads as they move in oscillation between the five parts of the immersive screen. Hijikata's sequence in the Astrorama film is represented by the documentary through four colour still images intended to encapsulate his part of the film, rather than by a moving-image sequence; the deliriously accelerating urban movement seen previously on the auditorium's screen is abruptly halted in order to focus, in aberrant stillness, upon those few images of Hijikata's body, as though his animated presence in the documentary would now risk corroding its corporate aims. The audience then emerge from the film's projection, through doors that take them directly out into the Expo's open-air environment; they appear bewildered and jarred. Many of the Astrorama spectators are very young, brought to the Expo on school trips. The documentary's closing sequences pan over the illuminated Expocity at night, focusing first upon the Midori pavilion's facade, and then scanning the entire site.

Alongside the corporate documentary commissioned by Midori-kai to record and vaunt its investment in the Expo's technological spectacle, several of the Goto Inc. film crew's members shot their own individual films during the Astrorama shooting-schedule in Hokkaido and the Midori pavilion's construction. Those improvised films, shot in transit with 8mm cameras as personal records, resonate more closely with the performance films made in that format by Nakamura and Iimura than with the documentary's official status. One film shows the work of the film crew on location at the Hokkaido volcano, with Hijikata's dancing figure shot from a peripheral perspective, and in fragments, as the Goto Inc. crew struggle to manoeuvre and position the immense Astrorama film camera. Another film is located at the under-construction Midori-pavilion site as it emerges from the Expo wasteland; a hoarding on the pavilion's facade (removed before the official opening) gives the name of the construction company, Ohbayashi Gumi Ltd., who built the pavilion's steel framework and installed its plastic covering; that company also built several of the other pavilions, including the sole-surviving one, the Steel pavilion. The film then records the pavilion's inauguration ceremony under heavy rainfall, focusing (as with the official documentary) on the many hostesses in their short-skirted silver outfits, alongside sequences with the dense crowds gathered around the Midori pavilion and the visits to it of celebrities, including the Everest-mountaineer Edmund Hillary. Further 8mm films by the Expo technicians show the wild weather and storms of the Expo's first weeks, which discouraged initial visitors and led to several attractions' closures, or focus on the spectacle of the morning opening of the Expo's turnstiles, with security guards releasing thousands of jostling, pressed-together figures to head at careering speed towards particular pavilions.

As with all of the Expo's pavilions, the Midori pavilion had a theme: 'Multi-Dimensional World'. The pavilion's architectural space was almost entirely taken up with the projection auditorium; the only other spaces it contained were the entrance

Ill. 20 – The Midori pavilion exterior in the Expo '70 nocturnal cityscape, 1970.

Ill. 21 – The Midori pavilion exterior with amassed spectators, 1970.

foyer in which the Astrorama film camera was displayed, for inspection by spectators before they experienced the sequences which that camera had captured, and its subterranean power-regulation instruments. The pavilion also contained a small kitchen servicing a lounge area that could be entered after the projection and which extended beyond an opening in the pavilion's facade to a terrace for use in warm weather; slide-transparencies conserved at the Expo's Documentation Center archive show spectators recovering from the Astrorama projections in the lounge area's blue swivelling armchairs.

The Expo's *Official report* details the pavilion's architectural form: 'Building: The main Pavilion of the Midori-kan exhibition was a gigantic dome, 46 meters in diameter and 31 meters from the ground level to the top, presenting "Astrorama" as its main attraction. / The main building, with one floor above ground and one underground was made of steel frames except for the foundation which was made of ferroconcrete. / Multifacet triangular steel pipes were used in the upper part of the building. The covering was 640 plastic panels strengthened with glass fiber./The multi-facet building was brightened by a total of 160 color combinations.'²⁵

In summarising the Midori pavilion's cinematic experience, the report emphasises the spectators' capacity to 'participate' in that experience in an unprecedented way, though the exact status of that participation is not made explicit (the word's enclosure within inverted commas indicates its ambivalence) and appears to extend only to their ocular and corporeal captivation within the Astrorama projection, which – as the documentary sequence shot inside the auditorium demonstrates – precipitated rapid, erratic oscillations of their eyes, heads and bodies. The report describes the Astrorama auditorium, including elements of its sonic environment which are otherwise undocumented and lost: 'Exhibits: "Astrorama", the main feature of the Pavilion, a word coined by the combination of "Astro" and "Drama" presented a hemispheric-vision film projection. / The movie, aimed at having visitors "participate",

Ill. 22 – Hostesses employed to guide visitors into the Midori pavilion, 1970.

differed from mere viewing, and was the first method of this type in the world. / Visitors entered the dome from the waiting tent and first inspected the Astrorama unit camera and still photos showing scenes of the film in the entrance hall before the start of the "Astrorama". Works of modern fine arts were also displayed in the hall. / The whole inner wall of the dome was a single screen, 2,000 square meters in size, 12 times that of Cinerama. The screen was made of 190,000 special nylon tapes, each four centimeters wide. Spectators were able to enjoy clear and beautiful images on all sides. / The screen image, 360 degrees horizontally and 210 degrees vertically was called a super-visual image. The camera and projectors used were all newly invented. The camera was equipped with the world's biggest lens, with an aperture of 300mm and a wide range of 133 degrees. / Five cameras were able to shoot at one time all in view from earth to overhead. Five films could be projected simultaneously by five projectors. / As a result of adopting the equidistance projecting system, there was no fear of distortion of images even when they were projected on the huge dome, 30 meters across and 23 meters high. / The film was 1.7 times the size of ordinary 70mm film and had no sound track. The sound-reproducing device was also a new invention. Stereophonic sound filled the whole dome through 515 speakers.'[26]

The two films projected as the 15-minute Astrorama programme appear retrospectively incoherent, with wayward, disjunctive sequences that must in part have resulted from the widespread disengagement of the commissioning corporations from the pavilions' contents, beyond their capacity to encompass aspirational, fluid 'themes', such as the Midori pavilion's 'Multi-Dimensional World' and other pavilions' vaguely future-oriented mottos. The printed programme for the Midori pavilion, read by spectators as they queued for admission to its auditorium, gives an awry account of what they were about to experience, enticing them with a definitive vision of the future: 'There are fantasies, adventures, impacts, astonishments, and discoveries ... Astrorama is the image of the twenty-first century'.[27] Certainly, many experimental artists and writers commissioned to work on the Expo's films approached that lucrative activity with subversive irony, or else half-heartedly neglected it, though Hijikata appears to have undertaken his work in Hokkaido with the same intent seriousness that he devoted even to his work on HOT SPRING SPA MAID PIMPS, as evidenced by his intensive fasting during the Astrorama filming.

Almost all of the Expo films had a 15- to 20-minute duration, as though a pre-set formula had been designed for them, into which formulaic or grotesque content could be incorporated at will; similarly, many pavilions – such as these of Fuji Group, Toshiba IHI, and Midori itself – deployed almost identical large-format immersive projections in uniformly domed auditoria, while competitively emphasising the distinctive uniqueness of their own technologies. Although the Expo had an ostensible emphasis on global harmony and future peace, the contents of many of the films projected contrarily obses-

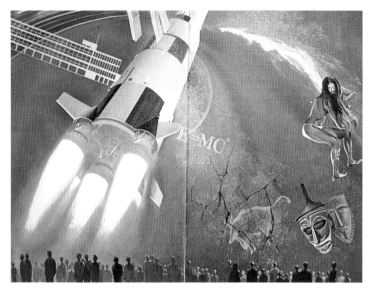

Ill. 23 – Hijikata's performance illustrated in the Midori pavilion's programme, 1970.

sions with sudden outbursts of uproar and violence, with corporeal fragmentation and precarity, and with an overwhelming aura of dystopia, as though those contents had irresistibly infiltrated themselves from the security-cordoned Expo's volatile, riot-striated urban surroundings, as well as more directly from corrosive art projects such as Hijikata's Ankoku Butoh, which were embedded within the heart of the Expo's ostensibly utopian imageries. The Astrorama films formed exceptionally anomalous, misfired entities (their preoccupations veering wildly from mountain-shamans to Hitler to space exploration), even when set alongside other pavilions' outlandish films, such as Teshigahara's work for the Automobile pavilion.

The Expo's report summarises those filmic materials projected within the Midori pavilion: 'The film was composed of two parts including "Birth" and "March". / "Birth" showed the exciting drama of history from the beginning of the universe to the distant future. Following the prologue, scenes including dances by primitive tribesmen in white robes, clay dolls, clay images, Hitler, air raids, and the launching of an Apollo spaceship were shown in a fantastic and satirical manner to raise the question in the audience's mind: what is mankind? / "March" was the world of speed and thrills. The film began with a scene of an autumn festival in which the decorated floats moved to the playing of flutes and drums. It was followed by a procession of young baton twirlers, then yachts under full sail, thundering steam locomotives, and fast-driven automobiles, enthralling the audience with impressive sights and sounds./The films symbolised man marching dynamically toward the future.'[28]

In the Midori pavilion's Astrorama projection of BIRTH, Hijikata's figure appeared on an immense scale, transmutated into film and multiplied so that his body appeared five times in variants spanning the immersive screen's five projection areas, leaping across those filmic zones in propulsions that took the spectators' eyes and bodies with him; his own sequences, as the demonic shaman, were projected directly alongside sequences of urban Tokyo's late-1960s elevated-highway accelerations, and his corporeal presence in the film resonated both with the Expo's experimental megalopolis into which the spectators were propelled immediately after the film's ending, to make way for the next audience group, and also with the figures contesting Japan's state power in the riot-convulsed raw urban environments of Osaka beyond the Expo's security guarded barriers. The projected Astrorama film, glimpsed in fragments in the corporate documentary's test sequences and also during the audience's experience of its projection, appears strangely bleached and excoriated, so Hijikata's filmic body too must have appeared spectral in its projection; many technical difficulties assailed the Astrorama crew and projectionists, and although the Midori pavilion was evidently successful in terms of visitor numbers, the Astrorama multi-lens film camera and immersive projection technologies were never adopted or used again.

Ill. 24 – The interior of the Midori pavilion with immersive projection screen, 1970.

Ill. 25 – Spectators entering the Midori pavilion projection environment, from the Astrorama corporate documentary, 1970.

By contrast, at the Pepsi pavilion in the Expoland zone, on the evening of 11 March 1970, Hijikata's own body appeared in its immediacy in performance, for the pavilion's preview event, three days before the Expo's opening ceremony and four days before the pavilion's public opening. The Japanese corporate sponsors of Expo pavilions were invariably disengaged with the specific contents of the pavilions which they commissioned, concerned only that their pavilions would be perceived as optimally innovative and leaving it to hired designers and filmmakers to generate strikingly standardised immersive moving-image environments and often grotesque, wayward and ill-conceived films that could only very loosely be encompassed within the pavilions' harmony-focused, future-oriented themes. By contrast, the joint US-Japan corporate sponsors of the Pepsi pavilion decided to scrutinise the planned contents (exemplified by Hijikata's preview-event performance) of their pavilion's events programme, according themselves the power of intervention. The abrupt collision of Hijikata's art-allied Ankoku Butoh project and the brutal imperatives of US corporate culture led to the last-minute disintegration of that programme, and the need for an entirely new six-month programme of anodyne content to be conjured for the Pepsi pavilion's spectacular interior.

The design team from the E.A.T. group were given no choice about the architectural form of the domed environment whose interior they were invited to design and programme, and arrived at the Expo site from New York to find it already constructed, to their dissatisfaction. The architectural conception of the multi-panelled white dome, very similar in form to the Midori pavilion, had been decided upon in 1968; as well as in Adachi's accidental filming of its near-completed form in 1969 in the Osaka sequence of A.K.A. SERIAL KILLER, the scaffolding-clad in-progress construction, emerging out of the painstakingly flattened Expo-site's mud wasteland, was documented photographically in images preserved at the Expo Documentation Center's archive. The Pepsi corporation and the E.A.T. group collaborated on a film-documentary, GREAT BIG MIRROR DOME, directed by the young filmmaker Eric Saarinen (whose father had been the renowned architect Eero Saarinen), but that film focused primarily on the pavilion's mirrored interior. The project of the E.A.T.-affiliated environmental artist Fujiko Nakaya to make the pavilion's dome intermittently disappear within enveloping clouds of water mist had the effect (among others) of concentrating spectators' attention more directly on their interior experience, as they entered the Pepsi pavilion's dome, greeted by hostesses in vinyl shortskirted costumes who presented them with foil-clad handsets that activated the pavilion's sonic environment, designed by the prominent sound-artist and composer David Tudor, as they transited its space.

The Expo's report highlights the Pepsi pavilion's theme: 'World without Boundaries', which (at least retrospectively) carries an incongruous aura, since the Expo itself was a fiercely guarded boundaried urban terrain, and the Pepsi pavilion itself was located within the internal boundaries of the Expo-land zone offered for hire to non-Japanese corporations or entrepreneurs who wanted to participate in the Expo's spectacle; more widely, 1970 was a year in which the global armed enforcements of urban and state boundaries, such as those contested by Palestinian and Japanese terrorist groups, were glaring and tangible. The report documents the Pepsi pavilion's appearance: 'The inner world of the dome was made of mirrors of vacuum-deposited aluminium foil which had been sandwiched between polyester and a coating. / Some 2,500 jet-spray nozzles connected with nine pumps were arranged symmetrically along the exterior ridges and constantly generated an artificial fog. / The volume of water used for the artificial fog totalled about 230 tons per day. / The artificial fog became a cloud which hung over the building and presented a fantastic feeling at night when illuminated by white beams shining from Xenon lamps. / When the visitors descended the tunnel-shaped stairway from the entrance to the interior of the Pavilion, each one received a small handset from a silver-suited hostess. / The handset was used to lead visitors to a new world of experience.'[29]

That 'new world of experience' differed sharply from most Expo pavilions' interiors in that it was intended to hold no filmic content (and Hijikata's performance there appears not to have been filmed, either officially or through individuals' 8mm-camera shots); it formed a pre-eminently sonic environment, with its grids of many hundreds of speakers installed around the space and responsive to corporeal movements through it, and its visual dimensions focused on its central area's immense mirrored environment – within which Hijikata performed – and its mirrors' capacity to disfigure spectators' corporeal reflections, so that those bodies appeared overhead in a proliferating and inverted, wrong-way-round configuration on the mirrors' foil surfacing. The pavilion's programme describes that corporeal effect as being meshed into a prismatic 'shower of light'[30] that emerged from the mirrors' multiply coloured surfaces.

The E.A.T. group's planned programme of events was assembled by informally inviting proposals from Japan's experimental artists for performances and concerts; as a result, Hijikata proposed himself for the Pepsi pavilion programme, rather than being invited. However, E.A.T.'s selection of Hijikata to perform his Ankoku Butoh project as the preview's principal attraction, shortly before the pavilion's public opening, indicates the group's evident engagement with Hijikata's work or (at least) with his status as one of Tokyo's most notorious experimental artists. When Ko Murobushi, in mid-conversation, nonchalantly evoked to me his experience of being present for Hijikata's performance at the Expo's Pepsi pavilion, it was the first I had heard of it. Akiko Motofuji subsequently told me she knew almost nothing about it, that Hijikata had disappeared so frequently from Tokyo in that 1969–70 period, for film shoots or other travels, she had lost track of it all; no, she had not attended the Expo, had no interest in it and was immersed in running her cabaret network and taking care of the Asbestos Studio. Murobushi's was the sole voice I could locate (evoking that memory in disconnected fragments, in London or Tokyo, across our subsequent meetings, until it suddenly became a vanished memory after his death in 2015) that remembered Hijikata's body at the Expo; other Expo visitors, such as the performance theorist Tadashi Uchino (then a 13-year-old child, who travelled to the Expo from Hiroshima), had entered the Pepsi pavilion and held memories of its extraordinary mirrored environment, but had not been present for Hijikata's performance, which was not public and was only witnessed by the small audience invited to attend. Murobushi had been there as Hijikata's assistant, helping to prepare the performance space over the course of a few hours (and had seen nothing of the other Expo pavilions). He had then stood at the side of the pavilion, his spine pressed against the foiled mirrors, and watched, alert for malfunctions.

Hijikata had titled his solo Pepsi-pavilion performance *Adagio*; when I discussed Hijikata's title with Richie, he guessed it could refer to the final part of Haydn's 45th (known as the 'farewell') symphony, with which he believed Hijikata was familiar, and in which, in its performance, the musicians' figures slowly disappear. But from Murobushi's account, the performance, which he remembered as lasting around 30 minutes, appears a low-key variant of Hijikata's previous 1968 solo Nihon Seinen-kan performances, *Tatsumi Hijikata and the Japanese People: Revolt of the Body*, again deploying the hanging metal panels which had been pivotal to those performances (and also to Hijikata's 1969–70 horror-film appearances), while prefiguring sonic elements of Hijikata's choreographies performed at the Shinjuku Art Theatre in 1972, such as *Story of Smallpox*, within which he would perform short dance sequences as part of wider-scale works by his Asbestos Studio dancers. It appears a lost, interzonal, stranded performance, within the engulfing Expo-city. Murobushi remembered Hijikata's intense concentration and his incessant collisions against the metal panels, which revolved in the mirrored space that also reflected dilapidated wedding robes hung from hooks from the dome's summit; the high-volume sound – funeral chants, a thunderstorm, and the cawing of crows – generated cacophonies in the pavilion's spatial environment, which had been designed by David Tudor to magnify and distort sound, causing it to ricochet and re-emerge from unexpected locations. Hijikata evidently made no attempt whatsoever to adapt his work for the Pepsi pavilion's corporate imperatives, with the result that it must have appeared uncompromising and even provocative in that context.

The Pepsi pavilion's corporate directors had anticipated a schedule of entertainment for the space that would highlight experimentation in the arts but prove especially attractive to their product's young consumers; the pavilion's printed programme pervasively features images of Japanese and American teenagers and children holding Pepsi-Cola bottles in relaxed urban environments. The president of Pepsi Japan (and a vice-president of the entire corporation), Alan Pottasch, was renowned especially for having, in the early 1960s, devised the hugely successful 'Pepsi Generation' media-advertising campaign. For GREAT BIG MIRROR DOME, he was filmed visiting the pavilion, during the E.A.T. group's installation of its mirrored environment, looking ill at ease in his corporate suit and tie,

Ill. 26 – Pepsi pavilion hostess holding visitors' sonic handset, 1970.

and made an improvised declaration to the film camera: 'Being alive and being with it and being here today and a part of things going on means paying attention to the artists, the engineers, that are trying to say something, trying to do something, trying to communicate with people all around them, today, and we feel that our contribution to what is going on, as a corporation,

219

is to see that those people have a platform from which they can express themselves and their ideas, to a great mass of the people.' Hijikata appears to have had a negative experience in being introduced to the Pepsi corporate directors and Expoland executives, later telling Murobushi that they 'looked like estate agents' (a special Hijikata insult).

After Pottasch had witnessed Hijikata's Pepsi-pavilion preview performance – which must have appeared alien to him in the extreme, and certainly antithetical to his vision of the 'Pepsi Generation' lifestyle – he evidently concluded that it exceeded the boundaries of his corporation's 'contribution'; he cancelled the entire events programme prepared by the E.A.T. group, which had been envisaged as combining experimental electronic-music concerts with performances proposed by figures such as Shuji Terayama (Hijikata had proposed larger-scale performances than his preview appearance, to take place intermittently across the Expo's six-month span, involving many of the Asbestos Studio dancers), ostensibly on financial grounds. The E.A.T. group returned to New York, and instead of their planned programme the Pepsi corporation's new organisers arranged events of 'go-go dancing' and 'rock dancing' within the pavilion's interior; photographs of those events show dancing children and adults, their figures' movements inverted in the environment's overhead mirrors, with a mixing-desk or synthesiser, cordoned by ropes at one side of the space, generating the sound.

Three days after Hijikata's performance, the Pepsi pavilion had its 'grand opening', again filmed for GREAT BIG MIRROR DOME, with a speech by the president of the global Pepsi corporation, Donald Kendall (a close ally of the US president of that era, Richard Nixon), who declared: 'We believe that the Pepsi-Cola pavilion will set a precedent in new corporate participation in the arts.' While film seized the Pepsi executives' voiced ambitions for corporate art, Hijikata's body finally eluded that agenda, and slipped through film itself, in his unfilmed Pepsi pavilion performance, so that his presence there holds only the barest, ghostliest traces, as in Murobushi's now vanished voice.

Kendall's corporate vision for the Pepsi pavilion duly went awry. Even after Hijikata's expulsion from its programme, and the censorship or negation of his planned future performances, the pavilion continued to experience severe problems, especially in its absence of visitors. Vitriolic correspondence from the first half of May 1970 (two months after Hijikata's performance), preserved in the Expo's Documentation Center archive, highlights disputes about ways of channelling prospective visitors from the main Expo site to its peripheral Expoland annex, which was now conceived as being badly located. Sebastian T. Hiraga, the deputy commissioner of Expoland, wrote to Mitsui Hayashi, the operations director for the Expo as a whole, on 9 May 1970, lamenting the poor visitor channels to the Pepsi pavilion and to Expoland in general, 'because of [the] total failure of your design of visitors' flow', and requesting approval for new proposals to expand the pavilion's nightly dance events from the Pepsi pavilion's interior to its exterior terraces. The pavilion's new theme, replacing 'World Without Boundaries', would be: 'Theme: Out-door rock dancing'.[31]

The Pepsi pavilion, despite the spectacular sensory and sonic experiences generated by visitors' transits through its interior, required a new performative input in order to achieve any profile within the Expo city's attraction-saturated environment; a film programme was also now proposed. The outdoor dancing events were duly approved by Hayashi; the Expo's Documentation Center archive holds slide transparencies of small groups of teenagers in jeans wildly dancing at night on the pavilion's ferroconcrete terrace. The Expo's report summarises those events and the other initiatives which failed significantly to increase visitor numbers to the neglected Pepsi pavilion: 'Entertainment: During the period of the World Exposition, evening go-go dances were held on the outdoor terrace. Held also were meetings for exchange of greetings by boys' sports organizations and world youths, performances by Boy Scouts and Girl Scouts, and the showing of films of young people of various countries at play.'[32]

Ill. 27 – 'Pepsi Dance' entertainment replacing Hijikata's planned Pepsi pavilion performances, 1970.

On the night of 13 September 1970, Expo '70 closed; its final weeks had been increasingly dense with crowds, but at its closure, the entire Expo city with its many pavilions' moving-image projection environments and sound-art installations became suddenly obsolete, along with its immense security-guard and surveillance network that had sealed away that experimental metropolis from the riot-seared city of Osaka. For the following decade, the Expo site reverted to the voided wasteland that had been generated three years earlier from the Senri Hills' deforestation and flattening. Only aspirational plans had been made at that stage for the site, and its obsolescence generated multiple dilemmas, as the report notes: 'How to make use of the site after the Exposition was a big problem from the very beginning as the disposition thereof was bound to be an important project from the standpoint of commemorating the World Exposition and bequeathing its legacy to future generations.'[33]

The Midori and Pepsi pavilions were completely razed. An archival aerial photograph from 1971 shows the Expo site when all but one of the pavilions had vanished: the aerial monorail and turnstiles had already been removed, and all that remained of the Expo's infrastructure were the avenues connecting the pavilions' sites (now blackened areas in the photograph, as though they had been incinerated rather than dismantled or bulldozed) and leading into its now emptied-out Expoland annex. Only the Steel pavilion remained as a potential museum site, along with the Tower of the Sun (as though that had been preserved as an urban monument devoted to resistance towards the Expo, notably in the form of its Red Army Faction non-violent infiltration); the intention at that time was eventually to demolish the Tower of the Sun too, though it remained standing and eventually formed part of the semi-wild park developed over the expanse of the Expo-city site. Almost all artworks created for the Expo were either consigned to storage in its administration building's upper levels or destroyed; the report lists the few artefacts that had ostensibly been donated by the pavilions' sponsors for preservation at a possible future Expo museum, including a sculptural work by George Rickey and the Astrorama film. However, that film was not in the end donated and instead was transported to the Midori-kai's Osaka storage facilities, unpreserved and forgotten.

The dismantling and demolition of the pavilions had been undertaken urgently, as though to generate a contrary speed to the three slow years of arduous and often dangerous (for its construction labourers from Japan's north) work that it had taken to assemble the site. Every pavilion's sponsors were compelled to empty their pavilions within a month and to raze or relocate them within six months, with the aim, as the report emphasised, of 'turning the once spectacular Exposition site into a flat piece of land'[34] whose precise future was yet to be determined. Several national pavilions were re-used across Japan, as libraries, old-people's homes or schools, but almost all of the corporate pavilions were simply destroyed without trace, the

Ill. 28 – The razed post-Expo '70 site, 1971.

imperatives of their competing technological innovations now redundant. Alongside the decision to leave the Steel pavilion in place (the Dream Pond lake with its Noguchi water sculptures also remained intact), the Telecommunications pavilion was dismantled for re-use as an auditorium, and the Sanyo pavilion became a library in Canada. It took until the early 1980s before the main part of the Expo site was re-opened as a vast, enclosed park, with an entrance fee; the Expoland zone (now separated from the main site by a busy highway) was excluded from the park's terrain and eventually became a shopping centre with a multi-storey department store overlayering the Pepsi pavilion's location.

I visited the Expo-park grounds in 2018. I had been there before, in 2009, when it was still possible to climb to the summit of the Tower of the Sun, to the eyes in its once golden face from which the Red Army terrorist had incessantly shouted 'Down with Expo', for a duration of six days, to the visitors below; the Tower of the Sun was now cordoned off for restoration of its interior spaces. Beyond the semi-wild park areas, the Expo's traces appeared lost in time and dilapidated, the Dream Pond exuding an aura of abandonment and disintegration with its disused fountains and corroded signboards. One ferrocon-crete facade of the once futuristic Steel pavilion was engulfed in vivid green foliage as though displaced from a J.G. Ballard novel; I entered the building and walked through its first-floor museum's narrow spaces, those corridors displaying Expo resi-dues such as the pavilion hostesses' costumes. The corridors circuited a large auditorium, the pavilion's 'Space Theater', its seating surrounding a central area used for electronic music concerts during the Expo; it had been left intact, its walls and ceiling now striated and damp-stained, but still transmitting the obsession with sonic experimentation that had worked to generate it.

Two films were playing in the Steel pavilion's corridors, pro-jected haphazardly on an end wall and a stairwell surface. One was shot from the windows of the monorail circuiting the Expo megalopolis in its moment of glory, immense crowds moving between its zones and forming canopied queues beside the Midori pavilion's green dome and other multi-coloured domes, the Dream Pond's sculptures at maximum operation expel-ling spectacular water cascades with children swimming in the lake under those cascades (several Expo visitors who had been small children at the time told me that they remembered this thrilling experience above all other Expo memories). The other film was a fragment from the corporate documentary made of the Toshiba IHI pavilion's interior, showing its auditorium's spectators propelled through space on seating rows affixed to 'rotary platforms' and confronted with strangely apocalyptic, horror-inflected filmic sequences of planetary and corporeal combustion. I left the Steel pavilion and walked across the Expo site to the location of the Midori pavilion in which Hijikata's Astrorama film had been projected 30 or 40 times each day to its packed spectators, eventually to millions of Expo visitors across the pavilion's six-month span, with each projection forming an intensive sensory and corporeal experience. That location, between the former sites of the Hitachi Group pavilion and the Electric Power pavilion on the park's west side, was now a deserted, tree-surrounded grass-grown area. After exiting the park, I visited the 'Expo City' shopping centre that now occupied the Pepsi pavilion's site, inscribed with a large map of the Expo's topography on its main cafeteria area's floor, crossed by the feet of oblivious shoppers.

I then returned to Tokyo to examine the original reels of the Astrorama film projected in the Midori pavilion, rediscovered in 2011 by the Hijikata Archive's staff after being long forgotten in the Midori-kai's storage warehouses. The film was now unprojectable, at least in the form and spatial environment in which it was originally shown; to project it again would necessitate the reconstruction from zero of the Midori pavilion and its specially designed immersive screen, as well as the five now lost Astrorama projectors, immediately obsolete from the moment of the pavilion's closure. After the film's rediscovery, its celluloid had been carefully unspooled from its reels in a digital laboratory to isolate the sequences showing Hijikata's body – diminished by the film's decay and crinkling to a uniformly red-hued corporeal figure, the volcanic rocks behind him now darkened – in order to digitise those sequences, spectral and disintegrated in appearance when set alongside the still vivid movement of Hijikata's body in the corporate documentary's own colour sequences. The relocated Astrorama reels were only one of the five sets needed at the Expo for the simultaneous projection of five reels by five separate projectors, each projector located in separate projection booths, in order to generate the pavilion's immersive moving-image environment; the other four sets – each shot by different Astrorama film-camera lenses, seizing Hijikata's figure from slightly different perspectives – remained lost in the Midori-kai storage facility or had been discarded.

The film was conserved at the Hijikata Archive within two enormous black rubber containers – at extreme variance in

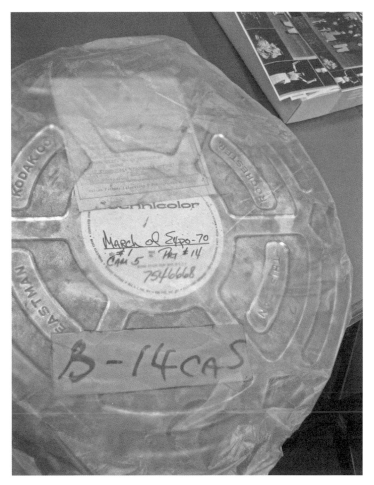

Ill. 29 – Original Astrorama film reels in their current state of archival preservation, Tokyo, 2018.

scale from the minuscule 8mm film-can containing Naka-mura's REVOLT OF THE BODY reel – and once the lid of the first container was removed, the film-reels' disintegrating cellulose acetate disgorged a strong, immediately enveloping and pungent smell, as of ammonia and vinegar. The sets of film cans, each holding two reels and stored one on top of the other, were labelled in English, from having been developed in Los Angeles.

When I opened the first can, the excessively wide-format cel-luloid inside seemed in pristine condition, tightly looped, its exterior appearance not betraying the decomposition of the images it held. Holding Hijikata's Astrorama film in my hands appeared, at that instant, with its enveloping olfactory as well as tangible dimensions, an immediate projection via film from Hijikata's corporeality.

I returned the reels to their container, left the Hijikata Archive, and returned to Osaka to visit the Expo's Documen-tation Center, its former administration building, located beyond the park area, adjacent to the site of the media-commu-nications tower whose construction Adachi had filmed in 1969, and beyond which the Pepsi pavilion's dome was then emerg-ing. No restoration work had been done on the administra-tion building since its space's re-allocation as an archive, and the upper storeys' halls still held the immense, uncatalogued detrita of the Expo pavilions' artefacts (those that had not been immediately destroyed), stored there in the final months of 1970. The building appeared entirely deserted, as though time had frozen into petrifaction at that last moment of its activity, immediately after the Expo's closure. Finally, I located the door of a first-floor lounge, its vast windows overlooking the Expo site and its Tower of the Sun, and the elderly, now-retired cur-ator of the archival collection from its origins in 1970, Toshi-hiku Okaue, emerged and invited me inside, where he and the current curator had piled up everything they had been able to find – documents, photographs, slide transparencies, film stills – over days of searching through the masses of material on the upper levels, relating to the Midori and Pepsi pavilions and to Hijikata's filmic and corporeal appearances within them.

I remained in Osaka for the time it took to examine those artefacts, returning to the seemingly uninhabited Document-ation Center each morning. On the last day, the building's aged elevator malfunctioned and, after stopping dead between floors, eventually took me to the spectral uppermost storey, and I opened door after door along the corridor, looking in at the vast, amassed and obsolete detrita of Expo '70: sculptures, screens, projectors, mirrors, loudspeakers: indistinguishable, unidentifiable and inextricable traces of memory. Finally, I opened a door and found the interior full of faces gazing back at me: the office of the maintenance staff who supervised the Expo park in its rigorously semi-wild condition.

Hijikata's near-lost Midori-pavilion film, and his near-lost Pepsi-pavilion performance at Expo '70, now held only in reels of disintegrated celluloid and in the memory of Ko Murobushi's voice – deeply precarious and spectral – carry illuminations for the performance and urban cultures of the contemporary and future city of Tokyo, and for all of the cities of Japan, in their ecological endangerment. Hijikata's Astrorama film also reveals an enduring, aberrant obsession with the unprecedented sensory and ocular innovations to be generated from moving-image projection experiments, as envisionings of the body's trans-mutations and those of the urban space around it, which also interconnects Expo '70 and the contemporary moment. Hijikata's work at Expo '70 – along with that of other experimental artists of that era, such as Matsumoto – also provides compelling insights into the amalgamation of corporate imperatives and the contrary imperatives of experimental art, and the engulfing calamities which that amalgam invariably engenders, in the contemporary moment as at the Pepsi pavilion in 1970. Although Hijikata's work intermittently continued until his death in 1986, it simultaneously transmits an exhaustion and a determined movement towards death in that era, as well as a distancing from film's provocative, abrasive intimacy with his work across the course of the 1960s, from Richie's HUMAN SACRIFICE to the Astrorama film BIRTH.

Mishima's spectacular death took place in November 1970, two months after the Expo's closure, in an attitude of revolt towards what he perceived as the erasure of an authentic Japan at the hands, among other entities, of its corporate power. From his last meetings with Mishima, during the Summer of 1970, in Tokyo and the resort town of Shimoda, Richie recalled that Mishima summarily dismissed the Expo as only one, negligible manifestation of the terminal dissolution that had already negated Japan and its cultures, leaving behind crass corporate spectacles and ludicrous media industries. At the same time, Richie was aware (as all of Mishima's friends were aware) that Mishima was primarily preoccupied with other matters in those last months; he had his long-announced death to attend to. Since Mishima had been such an immense urban presence in Tokyo for the previous two decades (his transits of the city ranging topographically from his many visits from 1959 onwards to Hijikata's Asbestos Studio in Meguro district, to his attempted coup at the military Self-Defence Forces headquarters in Ichigaya district, on the day of his death in 1970), including his prominent status in the 'actuality' media-culture of debates such as those around Tokyo's violent protests, his abrupt disappearance from the city proved seminal in the 1970s dissolution of the intensity of the previous decade's urban, experimental art, with all of its contradictions, betrayals and elations; Hijikata, in particular, lost Mishima's vital support.

Richie was mainly based in New York during the Expo's span; he was the curator of film at the New York Museum of Modern Art from May 1969 to April 1972, making lengthy stays back in Tokyo each year during that period, including the summer and autumn of 1970, before finally deciding to return permanently to Tokyo. He remembered, smilingly, that he had sided on the matter of the Expo with his friends in the Zero Jigen performance-group, whose work he had filmed in the Yanaka cemetery in Tokyo for his final film, Cybele, in 1968 (their urban performance work was also filmed by Matsumoto in Tokyo's Shinjuku avenues in 1969 for Funeral Parade of Roses, watched over by the film's transvestite character Eddie); Zero Jigen had undertaken anti-Expo street performances in 1969. Richie, in abandoning his filmmaking in 1968, appears to have presciently anticipated that the commodification and defusing of experimental culture, which he saw as a central state power project of the Expo, would exact an end to the previous decade's furore in art in Tokyo, which had brought him into contact with Hijikata, through their filmically based friendship. He saw far less of Hijikata from around 1972, and especially once Richie had a heart attack in 1978 and had to stop drinking (alcohol had always been pivotal in his encounters with Hijikata, including those in which they prepared their film projects together), though they still met occasionally, in Meguro or Shinjuku cafés. Richie noted: 'The 1960s were another world.'

After the Expo, the aura of dangerous innovation that had surrounded Hijikata's work in the 1960s diminished, while that work now became publicly more prominent, especially through the programme of performances which he choreographed at the Shinjuku Art Theatre in 1972. Miryam Sas comments on the end of the (often literally subterranean) hiddenness of experimental art and performance in Tokyo: 'In avant-garde movements, one might also note that by this point many experimental artists were seen as closer to the mainstream, no longer "underground", as many had participated in the massive, corporate-funded Osaka Expo (*banpaku*) of 1970.'[35] That post-Expo moment inaugurated an aura of intense disabusal, tangible for example in Hosoe's photographs of the wastelands of Tokyo in *Simmon: A Private Landscape*, and an absence of revolt, in Tokyo's art, though many experimental artists pursued their work in isolation, oblivious to that sense of a residual ghost city now sieved of its insurrection-focused inspirations. For Richie – who observed Tokyo's many variants of experimental art and film culture assiduously for over 60 years from 1947, but participated in it himself only during the 1950s and 1960s – that perception of disabusal and disillusionment, precipitated by what he saw as art's commodification and absorbing into state power priorities, irreparably endured over the following decades. He wrote in his journal in 1996, following a public debate with young filmmakers in Tokyo about his own 1960s films, in which he had spoken about his collaborations in film with Hijikata: 'Artists, musicians, filmmakers, writers, are all social products.

They have been subsumed into the social/financial structure of the country.'[36] That situation in Tokyo began to change urgently only at the end of the 2010s, with manifestations of revolt against Japan's state-generated ecological contamination and resultant disasters, and their accompanying corporeal scars.

Across the 1960s, Tokyo underwent profound transmutation, in its interconnections with its volatile film and art cultures, in its reconstruction for the Tokyo Olympics exemplified by its new aerial-highway networks, and also in its recasting as an immense zone of intensive surveillance, with its pervasive security-guard presence (already nascent since the early 1960s' internal migrations from Japan's north, but fully installed by 1970) and in its wide-scale redesigning for pacification and the averting of future street riots or urban terrorism. Furuhata summarises that infrastructural shift: 'The city of Tokyo also rebuilt its sidewalks to prevent demonstrators from tearing up paving stones to use as makeshift weapons during the protest. Compared to the mobilization of riot police, paving the streets with asphalt may not appear "political", yet the seemingly benign operation of governmental power must be discerned through such mundane, preventive security measures. Traffic control and urban planning clearly operate as part of the regulatory apparatuses of security.'[37]

Impelled by the enduring preoccupations driving that period of urban transmutation – which coincides and intersects intimately with Hijikata's films, into which that transmutation is deeply imprinted, from the beginning of the 1960s until the Expo era of 1970 – the contemporary city of Tokyo, in its new digital furores and oblivious consumer elations, is in many ways directly the creation of state power responses to the city's unique outburst of street-riot insurgency, and is also the creation of Expo 70's spectacularly film-projected, disintegrated urban utopias.

Notes

1   Yuriko Furuhata, *Cinema of Actuality: Japanese Avant-Garde Filmmaking in the Season of Image Politics*, Durham NC/London: Duke University Press, 2013, page 184.

2   Commemorative Association for the Japan World Exposition (1970), *Japan World Exposition, Osaka, 1970: Official Report* (in three volumes: Red, Blue, Green), Osaka: Commemorative Association for the Japan World Exposition (1970), 1971, page 158 (Green volume).

3   Ibid, page 15 (Red volume).

4   Ibid, page 11 (Red volume).

5   Ibid (Red volume).

6   Ibid, page 331 (Blue volume).

7   Furuhata, ibid, page 185.

8   *Official Report*, page 21 (Red volume).

9   Ibid, page 20 (Green volume).

10 Ibid, page 164 (Blue volume).

11 Furuhata, (see note 1), page 194.

12 *Official Report*, page 422 (Red volume).

13 Michelangelo Antonioni, programme text for the 1999 Antonioni Art Prize ceremony, Venice: Venice Biennale for Dance, 1999, unpaginated.

14 *Official Report*, page 422 (Red volume).

15 Programme for the Toshiba IHI pavilion's 'Global Vision Theater', Tokyo: Toshiba Corporation, 1970, unpaginated.

16 *Official Report*, pages 432–33 (Red volume).

17 Ibid, page 414 (Red volume).

18 Ibid, page 430 (Red volume).

19 Furuhata, (see note 1), pages 48–49.

20 *Official Report*, page 424 (Red volume).

21 Ibid (Red volume).

22 Ibid, page 418 (Red volume).

23 Ibid, page 422 (Red volume).

24 Shuntaro Tanikawa, script for Birth, in *Project Rebirth*, Tokyo: Keio University Art Center, 2011, page 8.

25 *Official Report*, page 442 (Red volume).

26 Ibid (Red volume).

27   Programme for the Midori pavilion, Osaka: Midori-kai, 1970, unpaginated.

28   *Official Report*, pages 442–43 (Red volume).

29   Ibid, pages 434–35 (Red volume).

30   Programme for the Pepsi pavilion, Tokyo: Pepsico Japan Co., Inc., 1970, unpaginated.

31   Manuscript letter conserved in the Osaka Expo Documentation Center archive, unpublished, unpaginated.

32   *Official Report*, page 435 (Red volume).

33   Ibid, page 334 (Green volume).

34   Ibid, page 464 (Red volume).

35   Miryam Sas, *Experimental Arts in Postwar Japan: Moments of Encounter, Engagement, and Imagined Return*, Cambridge MA/London: Harvard University Press, 2011, page 27.

36   Donald Richie and Leza Lowitz (ed.), *The Japan Journals: 1947–2004*, Berkeley CA: Stone Bridge Press, 2004, page 376.

37   Furuhata, (see note 1), page 146.

Film and the Dying Dance

I took a final Tokyo walk from Meguro station to the site of Hijikata's Asbestos Studio. That district had changed completely from its appearance when I first went there, in 1997, to meet Hijikata's widow, Akiko Motofuji, to watch her projections of Hijikata's films. Then, the avenue heading westward over the Meguro river had been down-at-heel and austere, lined by small manufacturing shops; now, two decades or so later, it was bustling and upwardly mobile, the shops selling vintage clothing, furniture markets improvised in parking lots attracting a fashionable young clientele for distressed wooden tables. I turned north off the avenue, through the alleyways' twists and turns, and entered the dead-end alley which appears in 1950s photographs with an industrial chimney at its end. The Asbestos Studio's facade appeared identical to when I had first seen it, reconstructed after Hijikata's death, with its domed roof and huge circular window at its upper level. But Akiko Motofuji had died many years ago, in 2003, having lost the building shortly beforehand through debts; it was now inhabited by a financier whose name was displayed at the foot of the stairs leading to its entrance, the entire interior including the basement dance-studio space now transformed. It was a house of ghosts.

Heading back to the station, I thought about Hijikata's projections at the Asbestos Studio of 1969–70, evoked already in the first part of this book, from urgent visual memories of witnesses – voiced by Hosoe, Richie and Akiko Motofuji herself – of Hijikata dancing with the hot, clacking film projector in his arms, the projector's beam ricocheting as he moved, sending the films' sequences careering wildly across the studio's walls and curved ceiling, and over and into the faces and bodies of the invited spectators. At the same time, he would play records by the Beatles on the studio's worn-out record player, at maximum

Ill. 30 – Hijikata's Asbestos Studio in its current form, Tokyo, 2018.

volume. Those projection events must have taken place several times, or at least twice, since not all of their witnesses had been there at the same time, and by that era of intensive activity in his work, Hijikata appears to have become disengaged from the contents of the films themselves (his own body, dancing) but remained determined, in his manoeuvre's immediacy, density, and searing heat – and in its refusal and overturning of film's documentational power, though most of the films he projected were contrarily intended as experimental anti-documents of his work – to corporeally perform the act of film projection.

Following his participation in the Osaka Expo '70 and his last performances in Tokyo and Kyoto in the early 1970s, such as the filmed performance SUMMER STORM, Hijikata largely withdrew to the Asbestos Studio; he still gave workshops and choreographed his dancers' work (except for several periods of a year or two in which he did nothing at all), and devoted his last decade or so primarily to drinking, writing and the compilation of scrapbooks. His engagement with scrapbooks had begun in the 1960s; he clipped out and hand annotated images (especially of artworks: Bacon, Fautrier and many others) accumulated from Japanese art magazines in a process that resonates with the tactile editing in experimental film practices of manually manipulated, affixed and spatially deployed filmic materials. His scrapbooks formed the primary source for the artist Richard Hawkins' project *Hijikata Twist*, exhibited at the Tate Liverpool art museum in 2014 and at US venues. Hijikata's page-sellotaped images in the original scrapbooks, conserved at the Hijikata Archive in Tokyo, have often now become detached and fallen away from their surfaces, their adhesive exhausted, as though forming desiccated filmic images unhinged from abandoned film reels, discoloured and crinkled, as with the celluloid images of Hijikata's own body in his Astrorama film, deadhering in their spectral autonomy and fragmentation from time's fixity and linearity.

With Hijikata's death, at the age of 57, in January 1986 (his grave is located in Usami, on the Izu peninsula, not far from Tokyo), and the vanishing of his own corporeal presence from Tokyo, 16 years after that of Mishima and more gradually, in the semi-hiddenness of his enclosed final years, that city correspondingly became imprinted – via projections of his films, alongside performances by his collaborators, such as Murobushi, until their own deaths – by the vital, enduringly provocative residues of Hijikata's Ankoku Butoh work, with that inspiration eventually extending into the arts environments of multiple worldwide contemporary cities.

The 1960s Tokyo of Hijikata's seminal films is now almost a vanished ghost city, but is still remembered vividly, in its furious contestations, experimentations and state power annullings, in the voices of its now aged witnesses and participants, such as Nakamura and Adachi, and is tangible too in topographical fragments of Tokyo that remain from that decade, from Shinjuku to Yanaka, and at Tokyo's extreme wasteland edges, too deeply abandoned or prone to inundation to be prized. It's often in those zones that film's enduring grip on Hijikata's corporeal work in that city still most strongly resonates.

By the summer of 1984, when the photographic historian Mark Holborn visited the Asbestos Studio and asked to see Hijikata's films, Hijikata's previous corporeally propulsive projection act of those films, performed a small handful of times in 1969–70, had long ended; to Holborn, Hijikata appeared entirely disinterested in the films of his work, but still prioritised Nakamura's REVOLT OF THE BODY (better known, as Nakamura emphasised to me, through its original title: NIKUTAI NO HANRAN) to show to Holborn, and stood alongside him to watch that film, only rarely projected in that era. During its projection, in silence, Holborn was aware of Tokyo's sensory and sonic environment surrounding the studio, now inhabited for what was probably the last time during Hijikata's lifetime by film: 'I had a sense not of watching a document from the Sixties, not even from Japan. It was closer to a Central Asian or Siberian ceremony, maybe even an Indian initiation rite, filmed by some explorer half a century before ... Outside it was a hot summer night and the festival of Bon Odori was beginning. The streets of Meguro were lined with lanterns. Drums were beating.'[1]

Hijikata performed a distinctive destructive volatility in those last two years or so of his life: Holborn recounts Hijikata's methodical destruction with a stabbed cigarette end of the fine grain of the antique wooden table around which they sat, and

Uno (who only knew Hijikata at his life's end) remembered him climbing onto a table during the publication party for his book of 1970s writings – obtuse, delirious, hallucinatory – around his childhood in Japan's north, *Yameru Maihime* (*Ailing Dancer*), then stamping on plates of *sashimi*. Hijikata and Uno had all-night arguments and fights over a planned performance inspired by Artaud's final sound recording which, if it had transpired, would have been Hijikata's first public performance for twelve years – though Hijikata often told his Asbestos Studio guests during that era that just because they couldn't see him dancing, it didn't mean that he wasn't dancing, in an inverted or invisible dance (as with a film of dance whose celluloid is now seen in its negative form, or is lost, or incinerated, but whose ashes still hold corporeal movement). For Uno, Hijikata appeared on those nights a man re-emerging from silence with ineradicably enduring obsessions; the recording of Artaud's screams, brought back from Paris by Uno on a cassette, formed one reactivation for those obsessions – as though Hijikata were being intolerably propelled from his withdrawal by those expelled screams, in a final riotous anger, now wrenched and wrung out after his prolonged silences and reflections – along with the finally unrealized desire to project himself corporeally, immediately live one last time.

Hijikata's final Asbestos Studio workshop took place between 24 and 30 November 1985, very shortly before his hospitalisation for terminal liver cancer. Rather than demonstrating dance movements, he stood and conjured vocal images, transcribed by one participant, Nanako Harada, in what appear as sequences of filmic flashes or fragments against darkness:

'towards the dying forest   towards the dying dance
towards light   towards death   towards "non-existence"'.

In that workshop, he evoked the work of Artaud and Nijinsky, and noted: 'Everything begins from the choice for self-destruction.'

And he visualised a final urban image, as though manually seized from film: 'an expansive city inside the hand'.[2]

Film, Hijikata's work and Hijikata's insurgent corporeality, and Tokyo across the 1960s' span, together form an impossible, crucial amalgam whose interwoven contradictions and oscillations generate its permanent inspiration for experimental creativity. At the same time, those moving images and their projections, Hijikata's work and his body's dance, and 1960s Tokyo and its urban transmutations, are now vitally all ghosts: film's ghosts.

Notes

1   Mark Holborn, *Beyond Japan*, London: Jonathan Cape, 1991, page 101.
2   Nanako Harada, workshop notes, translated by Rosa van Hensbergen, as appendix 7 of Kayo Mikami, *The Body as Vessel: Approaching the Methodology of Hijikata Tatsumi's Ankoku Buto*, Birchington UK: Ozaru, 2016, pages 189, 183 and 188.

Bibliography

This book was primarily researched at the Hijikata Archive held at the Keio University Art Center, Tokyo (and originally held at the Asbestos Studio, Tokyo), at the Library of the Tokyo Photographic Art Museum, and at the Documentation Center of the Osaka World Expo '70 Museum, as well as through interviews and discussions with the artists, filmmakers, photographers, writers, architects and performers who had collaborated with Tatsumi Hijikata or who had known him in the 1960s. This essential bibliography simply gathers the English-language (or bilingual Japanese/English) materials which were most valuable to me in preparing this book, and which I would recommend to readers wanting to explore Hijikata's work further.

Baird, Bruce, *Hijikata Tatsumi and Butoh: Dancing in a Pool of Gray Grits*, New York NY: Palgrave Macmillan, 2012

Barber, Stephen, *Hijikata: Revolt of the Body*, Chicago: University of Chicago Press (Solar series), 2010

Buruma, Ian, *A Tokyo Romance: A Memoir*, London: Atlantic Books, 2018

Centonze, Katja, *Aesthetics of Impossibility: Murobushi Kō on Hijikata Tatsumi*, Venice: Cafoscarina, 2018

Centonze, Katja (ed.), *Avant-gardes in Japan*, Venice: Cafoscarina, 2010

Chong, Doryun (ed.), *Tokyo 1955–70: A New Avant-Garde,* New York NY: New York Museum of Modern Art, 2012

Commemorative Association for the Japan World Exposition (1970), *Japan World Exposition, Osaka, 1970: Official Report* (in three volumes), Osaka: Commemorative Association for the Japan World Exposition (1970), 1971

Donald Richie Retrospective, Tokyo: Daguerreo Press, 2001

Dower, John, *Embracing Defeat: Japan in the Aftermath of World War II*, London: Penguin, 1999

Eckersall, Peter, *Performativity and Event in 1960s Japan: City, Body, Memory*, London: Palgrave Macmillan, 2013

Furuhata, Yuriko, *Cinema of Actuality: Japanese Avant-Garde Filmmaking in the Season of Image Politics*, Durham NC/London: Duke University Press, 2013

Hijikata, Tatsumi, *Costume en Face: A Primer of Darkness for Young Boys and Girls*, Brooklyn NY: Ugly Duckling Presse, 2015

Holborn, Mark, *Beyond Japan*, London: Jonathan Cape, 1991

Holborn, Mark, *Black Sun: The Eyes of Four: Roots and Innovation in Japanese Photography*, New York NY: Aperture Foundation, 1986

Homma, Yu, Kosuge, Hayato, and Morishita, Takashi (eds.), *Project Rebirth: Looking for Hijikata Tatsumi, Dancing in Astrorama*, Tokyo: Keio University Art Center, 2011

Hosoe, Eikoh, *Ba-ra-kei/Ordeal by Roses*, New York NY: Aperture Foundation, 2002

Hosoe, Eikoh, *Kamaitachi*, Tokyo: Gendaishichosha, 1969

Hosoe, Eikoh, *Kamaitachi*, New York NY: Aperture Foundation, 2009

Hosoe, Eikoh, *Simmon: A Private Landscape*, Tokyo: Akio Nagasawa Gallery, 2012

Klein, William, *Tokyo*, New York NY: Crown, 1964

Kunimoto, Namiko, *The Stakes of Exposure: Anxious Bodies in Postwar Japanese Art*, Minneapolis: University of Minnesota Press, 2017

Kurihara, Nanako, *The Most Remote Thing in the Universe: A Critical Analysis of Tatsumi Hijikata's Butoh*, PhD thesis (unpublished in English, but published in French as *La chose la plus étrangère au monde: analyse critique du Buto de Hijikata Tatsumi*, Dijon: Les Presses du réel, 2017), New York NY: Tisch School of the Arts/New York University, 1996

Kurihara, Nanako (ed.), 'Hijikata Tatsumi: The Words of Butoh', in *TDR: The Drama Review*, volume 44, number 1, Spring 2000

Marenzi, Samantha, 'Dossier: *Butoh-fu*, Dance and Words', in *Teatro e Storia*, issue 37, 2016

Marker, Chris, LA JETÉE: *ciné-roman*, New York NY: Zone Books, 1996

Marotti, William, *Money, Trains and Guillotines: Art and Revolution in 1960s Japan*, Durham NC/London: Duke University Press, 2013

Maude-Roxby, Alice, *Anti-Academy*, Southampton: John Hansard Gallery, 2014

Mikami, Kayo, *The Body as Vessel: Approaching the Methodology of Hijikata Tatsumi's Ankoku Buto*, Birchington (UK): Ozaru, 2016

Monroe, Alexandra (ed.), *Japanese Art After 1945: Scream Against the Sky*, New York NY: Abrams, 1994

Morishita, Takashi (ed.), *Hijikata Tatsumi's 'Rebellion of the Body': Imagery and Documents of Butoh 1968*, Tokyo: Keio University Art Center, 2009

Morishita, Takashi, *Hijikata Tatsumi's Notational Butoh: An Innovational Method for Butoh Creation*, Tokyo: Keio University Art Center, 2015

Moriyama, Daido, *Hokkaido*, Tokyo: Rat Hole Gallery, 2008

Phillips, Sandra S. and Munroe, Alexandra (eds.), *Daido Moriyama: stray dog*, San Francisco CA: San Francisco Museum of Modern Art, 1999

Richie, Donald, *Different People*, Tokyo: Kodansha, 1987

Richie, Donald, *Mishima*, unpublished typescript, 2003

Richie, Donald and Lowitz, Leza (ed.), *The Japan Journals: 1947–2004*, Berkeley CA: Stone Bridge Press, 2004

Ross, Julian A., *Beyond the frame: intermedia and expanded cinema in 1960–1970s Japan,* unpublished PhD thesis, Leeds: University of Leeds, 2014

Sas, Miryam, *Experimental Arts in Postwar Japan: Moments of Encounter, Engagement, and Imagined Return*, Cambridge MA/London: Harvard University Press, 2011

Taro Okamoto Museum of Art, *Tatsumi Hijikata's Butoh: Surrealism of the Flesh/Ontology of the 'Body'*, Kawasaki: Taro Okamoto Museum of Art, 2003

Uno, Kuniichi, *Hijikata Tatsumi: penser un corps épuisé*, Dijon: Les Presses du réel, 2018

Uno, Kuniichi, *The Genesis of an Unknown Body*, Helsinki: n-1 Publications, 2012

Yokogawa, Michiko, *Kazuo Ohno's final four years: Michiko Yokogawa's diary of sketches*, Tokyo: Chidosha, 2015

Yomota, Inuhiko, *Portrait of Ono Yoshito*, Tokyo: Canta, 2017